Perspectives on Women in the 1980s

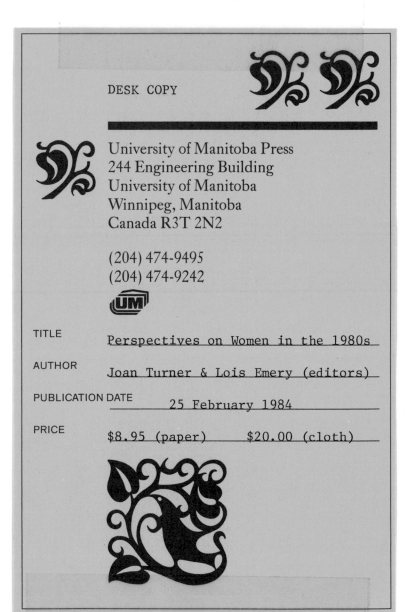

DESK COPY

University of Manitoba Press
244 Engineering Building
University of Manitoba
Winnipeg, Manitoba
Canada R3T 2N2

(204) 474-9495
(204) 474-9242

TITLE — Perspectives on Women in the 1980s

AUTHOR — Joan Turner & Lois Emery (editors)

PUBLICATION DATE — 25 February 1984

PRICE — $8.95 (paper) $20.00 (cloth)

Perspectives on Women in the 1980s

EDITED BY
JOAN TURNER AND LOIS EMERY

THE UNIVERSITY OF MANITOBA PRESS

© The University of Manitoba Press 1983

Printed in Canada

Canadian Cataloguing in Publication Data

Main entry under title:

Perspectives on women in the 1980s

Bibliography: p.
ISBN 0-88755-130-0 (bound). — ISBN
  0-88755-608-6 (pbk.)

1. Women's rights — Addresses, essays, lectures.
2. Feminism — Addresses, essays, lectures.
3. Women — Social conditions — Addresses, essays,
lectures. I. Turner, Joan, 1936-
II. Emery, Lois, 1927-
HQ1154.P47 1983   305.4   C84-091031-2

Dedicated to the memory of
Maysie Roger
1909-1978

Maysie Roger was a committed social work educator and scholar. Until her retirement in 1974, she was Professor, The University of Manitoba School of Social Work. She stimulated students to think comprehensively, to view social welfare policies and practices critically, and to work towards social justice and equality for all. She was a woman who expressed in her teaching and throughout her life all that is the best of the women's movement.

Contents

Contents

Maysie Roger:
A Memory

Dorothy Livesay

For two years of my life I knew Maysie Roger as one knows a sister. Deep in the depression of 1932-34 we had met in classes at the University of Toronto to do a post-graduate diploma course in social work. The newly established school was under the direction of two stimulating men, E.J. Urwick and Harry Cassidy. Urwick had been at Toynbee Hall in London and was devoted to the idea of better housing and community services for the disadvantaged; Cassidy was more of a socialist, interested in government and the welfare state. They were as different in their outlook as were Maysie and I: she steady, slow-moving, reticent, and I somewhat fly-by-night, impatient, outgoing. Our classroom discussions were enlivening indeed. Our friendship flourished probably because Maysie was tolerant and able to put up with my activism, my polemics, my desire to change the world immediately. Her approach to social ills was long-range and theoretical. However, our intense interest in our studies and their implications for society kept us together that first year.

On a more personal level, Maysie was a bulwark at a time when I was shattered by the end of a love affair. I was even contemplating suicide - but decided to "put it off" until after I had shared a field trip with Maysie as a partner! Her down-to-earth but detached sympathy pulled me back into reality. It followed naturally that we chose to do our second year in Montreal as apprentices in a Protestant family service agency. On a salary of $60 per month we managed to rent an attic flat on St. Denis, purposefully choosing the older part of the city where Jewish immigrants had settled next to French Canadians. I became swept up in political action on behalf of the unemployed. Maysie took up the flute. It was understood that we would not interfere in each other's social lives but in my memory now I can appreciate how tolerant

ix

Dedication

Maysie was. However, she had her fiery side, especially when her decisions as a
caseworker came up against the rules of the bureaucracy.

Once we had completed our apprenticeship by June, 1934, Maysie Roger
returned to Toronto, eventually to take up a position in Ottawa with the
Welfare Council. Her interests lay, not in casework, but in legislation and
teaching. I, on the other hand, went to New Jersey where I threw myself into
working with black families in a community centre.

After forty years, when we met again in Winnipeg, Maysie was living on
the banks of the Red River in her beautiful house, a home surrounded by fruit
trees, flower and vegetable gardens, and alive with bird-life. In spite of her
battle for health, the surroundings and the talk were always restful. We took
yoga classes together and exchanged views about aging, about religion. I felt
she was calmly happy with her life amongst close friends and devoted poodles.
Her sensitivity and empathy were perennial. For example, when I needed a
loan for a down payment on a cottage, her generosity was immediate. Throughout those last few years I appreciated Maysie Roger's intellectual gifts; but as I
look back upon them now, it is the thought of her gift of friendship that glows
and grows.

Acknowledgements

A book such as this is written because of the interest, support, encouragement and work of many individuals. First and foremost I wish to thank Lois Emery, my co-editor, who, when I was feeling very alone with the awesome responsibility of compiling this book, volunteered her services, her summer and her weekends, her precision and her ability with words and form. Lois and I have delighted in our good fortune in having engaged Betty Henry as a typist. Betty's speed, ability, and untiring enthusiasm never ceased to amaze and delight us.

The seven distinguished visitors, Margrit Eichler, Deirdre English, Judith Gregory, Helen Levine, Dorothy O'Connell, Marlene Pierre-Aggamaway and Gloria Steinem, provided the content for this book freely and without remuneration. They deserve our very special thanks. Thanks also goes to Judy Erola for her contribution to the panel, "Strategies for the Eighties," and for her suggestions and support. It was a unique experience and a privilege to work with these outstanding North American women.

Linda Block, Administrative Assistant for the School of Social Work, University of Manitoba, was responsible for keeping our finances in good order. We thank her also for her personal interest and efficient involvement in the work which pertained to the conference and to this book.

For financial contributions to the conference, we acknowledge the Secretary of State, Government of Canada; and the University of Manitoba Faculty Association, Alumni Association, Continuing Education Division, School of Social Work; and the Baird Poskanzer Memorial Fund. We also wish to express our gratitude for financial support of this publication to National Health and Welfare and the Secretary of State of the Government of Canada; to the Maysie Roger Memorial Fund, the Presidential Advisory Committee on

Acknowledgements

University Outreach, the School of Social Work, all from the University of Manitoba; and to the Canada Council.

We thank Jerry Ferenc, Instructional Media Centre, University of Manitoba, for patiently and efficiently audio-taping the proceedings of the conference, which made it possible for the lectures and panels to be transcribed into print. Thanks also to the staff of the Instructional Media Centre, to VPW Channel 13, and to Shirley Kitchen, for making the production of the video documentary, "Perspectives on Women in the 1980s," possible.

The 1982 Distinguished Visitors Committee deserves credit and recognition for the planning and organization of a very successful conference. A shared conviction that the content of the conference should be distributed as widely as possible led to the production of the video documentary and to the compilation of this text.

Thanks to the women of the Manitoba School of Social Work, including Addie Penner, Director, and to my students for their interest, ideas and support. We appreciate the skillful typing on the word processor done by Joyce McKay and Jill Winship of the general office staff and the meticulous proofreading by Jill Winship. Kim Clare deserves special mention for her painstaking work reviewing the manuscript and proofreading, assisting with endnotes, and compiling Selected Readings and Resources. Sheila Gordon worked with Kim Clare, and they were assisted by the staff of the Winnipeg office of the Secretary of State, by Lissa Donner, Sharon Corne, Marilyn Baker, Sharon Tully, and by personnel of the Liberation Book Store.

Several women assisted through the provision of statistical data. In particular, I wish to thank Carol McQuarrie, research officer of the Association of Employees Supporting Education Services (AESES), University of Manitoba, for very clearly presented data, and for negotiating on my behalf with the Board. We acknowledge the permission of AESES to use the information showing gender bias in support services, University of Manitoba. Hilda Hildebrand-Raudsepp and Linda Block assisted me with data about the School of Social Work, Thelma Lussier about the University of Manitoba, and the staff of Statistics Canada library about Canadian women.

There are many women – authors, artists and musicians – who have influenced and inspired us. We appreciate the courage they have shown as they risk expressing themselves in a world that is often critical, even belittling, of writing, art and song produced by women. The creative skill of Ellen Forrestor, formerly of Ottawa, now of Botswana, is represented in the illustration on the cover. The design of the cover is the artistry of Margot Boland. Three prairie women – Heather Bishop, Connie Kaldor, and Karen Howe – whose music inspires and uplifts my daughters and me, gave us permission to use words

Acknowledgements

from their songs in this text. We were delighted when Dorothy Livesay agreed to write the dedication to Maysie Roger. We thank all of these women sincerely.

In the process of editing this book, Lois and I have become increasingly appreciative of the women in our personal lives, and in particular of our mothers, Alice Turner of Regina, and Marguerite Emery of Winnipeg. I also wish to thank my aunt, Iona Turner, and my daughters, Joy and Cathy Zeglinski, for providing me with the incentive to speak out and to write. I thank them for their love and support, and for their critical feedback. To the men who encouraged me without fear of what I might say, understood my need for personal space and solitude, challenged my assumptions and/or expressed their need for a men's liberation movement, I express my appreciation.

Last, but not least, we wish to express our deep appreciation to Patricia Lagacé and Carol Dahlstrom, of the University of Manitoba Press, who believed in us.

Joan Turner

December, 1983

Perspectives on Women in the 1980s

1

There Comes a Time

Joan Turner

There comes a time, when you just gotta rise
You've been down so long – you can't remember why
There comes a time, when you just gotta stand
You realize inside someone will give you a helping hand

You've gotta stand up strong
Say I'm proud to be me
I've got my own sense of pride
And my dignity

There comes a time, and the time is soon
We've got to find the piper and help to change the tune
There comes a time and the time is now
You realize inside that you always knew how

You've gotta stand up strong
Say I'm proud to be me
I've got my own sense of pride
And my dignity.

(Connie Kaldor, 1979)

The concert concluding the conference, "Perspectives on Women in the 1980s" ended with Heather Bishop's moving rendition of "There Comes a Time."[1] The crowd rose, clapping in unison. There was warmth and passion, energy and excitement in the crowded room that cold winter night in Winnipeg. I stood with friends and my daughter, feeling proud of being a woman with many women (and some men), celebrating women's lives. Inspired by the four musicians who sang to us of women's pains and joys and struggles, we felt connected, woman to woman, in body, mind and spirit. In the experience of the moment we knew we held personal and collective power. Yes, we could, and we can, change the tune! Tears welled in my eyes and a lump grew in my throat. I felt as if "my cup runneth over." I was overwhelmed with the intensity of my feelings, the impact of much stirring and stimulating of thoughts, and with the growing strength of my commitment to the women's movement.

For three consecutive days and evenings, I had attended the Fifth Distinguished Visitors Conference of the School of Social Work, University of Manitoba, which included the official opening of an exhibit of Manitoba women artists, a workshop and dinner with Gloria Steinem and representatives from women's organizations, eight lectures by distinguished speakers, two stirring panels, and this grand concert of women's music. All in all, it was one of the most significant events in my life and, I think, in the history of the Manitoba School of Social Work.

It was an event, "a happening," which touched the lives of most, if not all, of the twenty-five hundred participants, in personal and political, intellectual and emotional ways. We laughed and we cried. We shared our anger, our frustration and our experiences. We celebrated. Women spoke out and were heard. Some men, including some of my academic colleagues, listened and were moved to new depths of understanding.

And now, at midnight on January 22, 1982, it was over. It was time to entice frozen automobiles back into motion or to huddle overwrapped bodies aboard a city transit bus. It was time for me to go home too, back to "normal" living as homemaker and motherworker until my work as a faculty member at the School of Social Work resumed on Monday. I, for one, would never be quite the same. I had experienced the "clicks" that Gloria Steinem talks about in chapter 2. I saw and heard and made connections in ways that I had not before.

In this first chapter, I want to share my sense of the conference as an historic event with you, the reader. I imagine you to be an adult woman, a student perhaps, or a teacher, or someone involved in one of the helping professions or in women's studies (or both). You may be a friend, or a relative, or a fellow worker, or perhaps a homemaker or a motherworker. Your interest in women's issues and in this book has probably been sparked by personal experience, likely a critical life experience. You may have attended the conference or have viewed the video documentary, "Perspectives on Women in the 1980s."[2]

We want this book to be alive, to carry with it the magic and the energy of the conference. Throughout, we write in the first person, for not only does it seem to be the best way of sharing the aliveness and colour we intend, but it also represents the personal-political style of delivery by all distinguished speakers. It is also in keeping with principles and beliefs inherent in the women's movement. "Women need first and foremost to trust themselves and their decisions and reclaim authority over their own experiences."[3] It means that each of us represented within these pages struggles with feeling exposed and vulnerable, open to personal attack. There are moments when it feels as if our whole being–mind, body, heart, spirit, soul–is open for all to see and know, and harshly judge. Robin Morgan, in *Going Too Far,* says: "I do...believe ...that the personal is political, and vice versa (the politics of sex, the politics of housework, the politics of motherhood, etc.), and that this insight into the necessary integration of exterior realities and interior imperatives is one of the themes of consciousness that makes the Women's Movement unique, less abstract, and more functionally possible than previous movements for social change.... So I must dare to begin with myself, my own experience."[4]

This first chapter reflects my perspectives and my experiences before, during and after the conference. I have been co-chair of the Distinguished Visitors Committee, applicant for grant funding, co-producer of the video documentary, and now co-editor. In many ways it is as if I have personally lived and breathed and puzzled over the conference and related readings for two significant years. I think it is important to place the conference within an historic context and that is how I shall begin. I will then provide data about the minority status of women at universities, showing that the university of the 1980s is representative of society. We need not look far for evidence of gender bias and inequality. It is within this context that plans for the conference, "Perspectives on Women in the 1980s," evolved and developed. I will describe the planning of the conference and give a brief synopsis of the chapters which follow. I conclude the chapter with a song of appreciation for the lives of women.

In setting the conference within an historical perspective, I found it interesting and relevant to look back, far back, into history. I read that powerful women were frequently depicted, feared, and hated as evil beings, inspiring lust, concerting with the devil. Feminists estimate that millions of European women were killed as witches.[5] Women were barred from the universities and professions, women's rights to property were eroded and virtually eliminated, and marriage became the only viable option. As society became more industrialized, women's work ceased to be valued as work. "Women's lives became so narrow, their options so few, that there is little wonder that a women's revolution began."[6]

In North America, the female healer was eliminated mainly by repression and slander. Only men were allowed to study medicine and hence legally to practise healing. In spite of the fact that, legally, "professional" healing-helping could be done only by men, women continued to be the family and neighbourhood nurturers and care-givers.[7] It was from the value of "woman, help thy neighbour" that social work came into being.

About the mid-nineteenth century, small groups of American women, called friendly visitors, began to organize charity groups to provide relief for distressed women and children. Jane Addams, most famous of social work pioneers, began advocating changes in society when she realized through her experiences that the poor were victims of political and economic problems. The "social feminism" advocated by Addams greatly influenced the development of social services in North America.[8]

One of the original members of the Manitoba School of Social Work's faculty writes:

> The impulses, which laid the foundation of the social welfare system in Manitoba and ultimately its school of social work, grew out of the mass immigration of the early years of this century; out of the human misery it spawned and out of the human compassion it engendered. Between 1902 and 1907 an average of thirty thousand immigrants yearly came to the Canadian west, [through Winnipeg.]... Despite the high hopes with which they started, they were inevitably fatigued, confused and frequently despairing, as they found themselves without work or money....."Here were appalling housing conditions, serious problems of health and sanitation"–and no work.
>
> Out of convictions about "the importance of a social environment adequate to the physical, mental and spiritual life of human beings," a charity organization society, a league for social service workers, night classes, a people's forum, and kindergartens grew. Manitoba was the first province to give women the vote and the first to pass a provincial law authorizing pensions for widowed mothers.[9]

The University of Manitoba was established in 1877, originally as a school of agriculture. The University's history reflects the patriarchal society we live in: presidents and all chancellors (with the exception of the incumbent), all vice-presidents and the vast majority of deans and directors have been men.

Even in 1983, there are only three female deans or directors (Nursing, Social Work and Dental Hygiene). The chair and the secretary and all but three of the twenty-four members of the University Board of Governors are men. Obviously the meeting rooms of the University are male domains.[10] By and large, University policy decisions are made almost exclusively by men.[11] Given that the University is an institution which is expected to provide leadership in society, the statistics about women's place in the University are not very encouraging.

Let us turn our attention to current information (June 1983) about those who provide support services for the University. With the help of statistics provided by the Association of Employees Supporting Education Services (AESES), the support staff bargaining unit, we can clearly show that, although AESES is composed of 68.5 percent females and 31.5 percent males, females are dispropor-tionately represented at the lowest salary levels, and males at the highest. In fact, at the highest salary level (over $22,000) males are hired on a three-to-one basis. In the administrative category, women dominate at the lowest levels, but from $25,000 and over, men are in the majority; no women are represented in the two highest salary levels. In the computer-worker category, women dominate up to the $20,000 level, then positions are fairly evenly divided up to the $26,000 level, where men become the majority. The highest clerical salary level is less than $20,000 and, as one would expect, 94.1 percent of clerical workers at the University are women. In two categories, agriculture and trades foremen, men fill *all* the positions.[12]

When we examine the University of Manitoba's *Institutional Analysis Book* for information about the teaching faculty, we find that women occupy only 14.1 percent of full-time teaching positions! At the time of the Distinguished Visitors Conference, there were 180 females, compared to 1,097 males, in full-time teaching positions at the University.[13]

It is no wonder we women find ourselves in a minority position in meetings and at the Faculty Club. The situation at the University of Manitoba is similar to that at other Canadian universities. Statistics for Canada as a whole indicate that women occupied 16 percent of university teaching positions in 1980-81. Overall, the salaries of women are lower than those paid to men within the same rank. The percentage of women in fields they have traditionally entered – education and the health professions – has declined since 1958-59.[14]

In 1981-82, there were 20,444 students at the University of Manitoba. Women represented 43.8 percent of the full-time and 61.9 percent of the part-time undergraduate population and 32.6 percent of the full-time and 38.8 percent of the part-time graduate population.[15]

When we examine the situation at the Manitoba School of Social Work we find that in November, 1982, there were 283 female students (182 full-time and 101 part-time) and 86 male students (49 full-time and 37 part-time) in the BSW (undergraduate) program. Hence, the ratio of female to males is *more* than three to one. In the MSW (graduate) program, there were 38 females and 25 males. In the continuing education program, there were 522 female participants and 252 males, a two to one ratio.[16] Obviously females represent a majority of the student population in all three program areas of the School. There seems to be no question about the ability of women to achieve academically, since the School's records show that fifteen of the seventeen gold medals awarded for highest academic achievement since 1961 have gone to women.[17]

The early history of the School of Social Work at the University of Manitoba, like that of most schools in North America, reflects the central involvement of women as administrators, professors and students. In fact, in 1943-44, when the first class of social workers graduated at the University of Manitoba, there was only one male among them. When I was an MSW student in 1962-63, I recall that all full-time faculty, with one exception, were women. A small group of women, including Helen Mann, who has written some of our history, and Maysie Roger, to whom this book is dedicated, held the senior positions and the power in the School. By the late 1960s and early 1970s, social workers were keenly working to improve their status as professionals, looking to medicine, psychiatry and law as models of successful (and, of course, male-biased) professions. Without much thought to the sexism inherent in the move, schools of social work sought to recruit more male students and more male faculty. It was anticipated that the presence of more highly educated (Ph.D.) male educators in social work would enhance the status of the schools in the eyes of the university administrations and in the communities. Connections through the informal "old boys' club" and measuring up to the expectations of the university administration became important. It became clear that job security and career advancement depended not upon one's work with students so much as upon one's academic credentials and one's research and publication.

By 1975 there was sufficient concern about the situation in Canadian schools for the Canadian Association of Schools of Social Work to support the establishment of the Task Force on the Status of Women. The Task Force Report (May, 1976) begins with the following statement: "There is a wealth of material reported in the professional and academic literature of Canada, Britain and the United States which indicates clearly that a picture of discrimination exists for women in the general labour force, women in academic life and women in the social work profession."[18]

The conclusion of the Task Force was that women in schools of social work across Canada earn less, receive fewer promotions and enjoy less job security than do their male colleagues.[19] There is no evidence to show that the situation in 1983 differs from that in 1976-77.

In fact, writing in the fall of 1982, Bonnie Jeffrey and Martha Wiebe of Saskatchewan, conclude that: "The professional schools of social work have tended to reflect the biases and various forms of discrimination of the society at large rather than being at the forefront of the struggle for equal rights and opportunities for women. Social work has only recently recognized the institutionalized sexism within our own profession. We have tended to be reactive rather than active in the growth of feminist consciousness. Courses on women are relatively new in social work curricula and little urgency or priority is accorded these courses even now. They are frequently seen as peripheral to the

8

core curriculum and are only of tertiary interest to the majority of faculty members. It is clear that most faculties of social work have resisted examining women's issues despite the fact that a majority of consumers of social services are women, the bulk of the social work student body is female, and over 50 percent of social workers working in direct practice are women."[20] In fact, the number of women in social work in Canada has increased dramatically from 6,325 in 1971 to 19,530 in 1981.[21]

In a study of two thousand employees at all organizational levels of the social services in the Atlantic provinces reported by Joan Cummings in *Atlantis* in 1981, data showed the obvious over-representation of women in the lower salary categories and under-representation in the higher ones. This was true when the educational level and total length of social service experience were held constant. Men were strikingly over-represented among those in supervisory, staff training, administrative, planning, policy analysis and research functions. In the civil service, males predominated in the administrative positions which embodied authority and control and women in positions which involved service. There is little question that this holds true also for Manitoba in the 1980s. "The virtual ghettoization of women in particular functions and even whole occupations is a strikingly persistent trend."[22]

The situation which precipitated the decision of the women of the School of Social Work, University of Manitoba, to focus their energies onto planning a conference on women's issues was set within the history and the context that I have described. The women of the School first met as a group in March, 1981. For two weeks we laboured on a carefully worded memo expressing our concern about the "absence of women and their perspectives in the MSW program at this school." We realized that there were few women eligible to teach in the graduate program: there were only six women in teaching positions (compared to twenty men). We thought it reasonable, however, for women to have some meaningful presence in the program. According to information compiled by one of the administrative assistants, there were thirty-three female and twenty-two male students in the graduate program.

When the memo was finally worded to our satisfaction, it was signed by all female staff, including the twelve "sessionals" (persons hired for eight months, usually to do field instruction). We referred to the University of Manitoba's policy statement, Female-Male Balance Among Academic Administrators, Faculty Members and Students,[23] and to the Canadian Association of Schools of Social Workers Women's caucus[24] to support our position. We soon learned that we were not being viewed as reasonable, but as troublesome.

Jean Baker Miller helped broaden my understanding beyond the personal to the political: I see it now as the power issue that it was (and is today). She says: "To the extent that subordinates [female faculty] move toward freer expression and action, they will expose the inequality and throw into question the basis for its existence. And they will make the conflict an open conflict."[25]

Miller says that early expressions of dissatisfaction will come as a surprise and be rejected as atypical. This was true in our case. Miller goes on to say: "They [the subordinates] will then have to bear the burden and take the risks that go with being defined as 'trouble-makers.' Since this role flies in the face of their conditioning, subordinates, especially women, do not come at it with ease."[26]

No, we did not "come at it with ease." We were shocked at first, then angry and frustrated. We quickly reorganized ourselves, realizing that we had liked working together and had benefited from it. Now we addressed the question of how we could direct our energy onto something constructive and potentially successful. Neil Tudiver, a member of our faculty, encouraged the idea of focusing the School's Fifth Annual Distinguished Visitors Conference on women's issues and agreed to chair with me. At the third meeting of the Women of the School, on April 14, 1981, most of the women present volunteered to work on the conference. We recruited additional women (three students and a few other women in the community) and set to work as a collective of fourteen to plan the conference. It was an especially satisfying and enjoyable experience for all of us. It challenged our awareness of contemporary feminist issues, it enhanced our connections with other women, and it gave us a sense of collective power which we had not experienced before. We voluntarily shared tasks so that no one person was burdened. We felt that we were embarking on a new adventure. Probably our most exciting moment was the bright summer day when Gloria Steinem agreed to be the keynote speaker! It amazed us that every woman we invited to speak agreed to participate. The program began to broaden and take shape to include a concert of women's music, an art exhibit, a book display, provisions for child care, and, at Gloria Steinem's request, a closed workshop for representatives from women's organizations.

On behalf of the committee, I applied for grant funds, because, as in previous conferences, we were committed to the principle that the conference be free and open to the public. In order to complete the necessary application forms, it became necessary to articulate the purposes and goals of the conference. We stated them as follows: to advance our growing interest in feminist issues; to provide an opportunity for Canadians (though originally we said Manitobans) to hear from women distinguished by their work; and to increase the consciousness of the public, including educators, administrators and students, providers and consumers of social services, about issues facing society in the 1980s.

10

Funders were interested and responsive, and the process of applying for money, though time-consuming, was not difficult. (I realize that this may seem incredible, given the controversial political nature of our topic and the current economic situation.)

We were fortunate to be able to acquire a long list of women's organizations in Manitoba and Canada from the YWCA Women's Resource Centre which, together with other lists available at the University, gave us an extensive mailing list. Bright green brochures were mailed across the country and similar bright green posters were placed about the city and the campus. The press, to say the least, was very interested. We decided to audiotape all lectures and panels and to videotape as many as possible. Shirley Kitchen suggested we produce a video documentary as a way of sharing the content of the conference with others. We agreed to work together.[27] Thus, it became clear we had not just embarked on the planning of a conference, but were on the move, as "is the nature of the Women's Movement."[28]

The chapters of this book reflect the content of the conference. Chapter 2 is the keynote presentation by Gloria Steinem, editor of *Ms. Magazine*. Gloria Steinem provides us with a history of the women's movement and defines the threat that the movement poses to patriarchal society. She addresses five themes: families, work, sexuality, culture and reproductive freedom.

Central to women's lives and to an understanding of the women's movement is the politics of motherhood. In chapter 3, Helen Levine critically analyzes motherhood in the context of patriarchy and in light of her own experiences as educator, social worker and mother. Her writing appears again in chapter 6, where she focuses on feminist counselling, an approach to working with women which is both personal and political.

In chapter 4, Dorothy O'Connell, author of *Chiclet Gomez,* writes about poverty, the feminine complaint. Recent statistics show that the poverty rate for female-headed single-parent families is rising, and is now estimated to be 44 percent.[29] Sixty percent of elderly women in Canada in 1980 were living in poverty.[30] Dorothy O'Connell uses fact, humour and song to help us understand the realities of life for mothers and children on welfare. "Welfare is a salary," she says. "It is for work that we do."

Marlene Pierre-Aggamaway speaks for women who are oppressed because of their gender and their race. In chapter 5, in her analysis of the relationship between native people and the state, she challenges us to work with native women to change the myths and the laws and rules which discriminate against native women and are destructive to them and to their culture.

The panel presentation by Helen Levine, Dorothy O'Connell and Marlene Pierre-Aggamaway "Women as Consumers and Providers" touched the hearts, minds and souls of the 250 or so people in the audience. It is a powerful chapter: in it, three women risk telling us how it is to be consumers of the health and social welfare system.

Judith Gregory, Research Director for the American working women's organization called 9 to 5, provides, in chapter 8, a comprehensive picture of the technological changes which are affecting offices and the lives of clerical workers. She warns us that we must become knowledgeable about technology or it will begin to wield too much control over the lives of women rather than be a useful tool.

Margrit Eichler addresses the social policy issues which define and limit the lives of women and families in the 1980s. She focuses on the issues of societal provision for the care of children. We learn that divorces are increasing and will likely continue to do so, and that the majority of women, many of them mothers, are working in the paid labour force. Margrit Eichler calls for changes in governmental policies in order to provide a closer match between our taxation system and social benefits.

In chapter 10, Deirdre English addresses one of the fundamental rights of woman, the right to reproductive freedom. It is the most controversial of issues, the one which threatens the basis of patriarchy, and the one which tends to divide us. We begin to understand the basis for the attack by Phyllis Schlafly and the New Right. Lest we believe that Phyllis Schlafly's attack has no relevance to Canadians, I suggest we consider that her presence as guest speaker for the Alberta Federation of Women United for Families in November, 1981, was financially supported by the Alberta government.[31]

Margrit Eichler, Deirdre English, Judith Gregory and Judy Erola propose some strategies for the 1980s in chapter 11. Margrit Eichler focuses on day care, Deirdre English on reproductive freedom and the goal of feminism itself, Judith Gregory on improving the working conditions of clerical workers, and Judy Erola on federal government provisions for women and children, including pensions. Judy Erola requests that we make our wishes known to politicians, herself included.

In "Change, Hope and Celebration," chapter 12, I outline some of the changes which have occurred since the conference, comment upon three concepts I deem to be important – language, power and expression – and close with a song of hope and celebration.

The book concludes with a section of selected Canadian reading and resource material which we hope will be useful to the reader who wishes to continue her or his study of women's issues.

The conference, "Perspectives on Women in the 1980s," was enriched by an art exhibit and a concert of women's music. In her remarks at the official

12

opening of the art exhibit, Marilyn Baker said that "the exhibition of women's art is itself a sign of the flourishing of women in the arts in Manitoba today." The expression of women's lives in the conference represented women's need to make poetry, music and art "once again relevant, passionate and accessible," something to be integrated into our daily lives.[32]

Since Heather Bishop expressed so well in song what I wish to say, I will conclude by sharing with you the last three verses of her song, "I Love Women."

I love women - women full of pride
I love seeing women - I love to see us filled with pride
That woman knows respect for who she is inside
The fighting that she's had to do has taught her not to hide
Who she really is - what she wants to say
How she's feeling now - you know she's learning how.

I love women - women full of song
I love hearing women - I love to fill us with song
Singing from our souls where a sleeping power lies
Strong enough to see us through the things we must survive
Just to carry on - we're gonna move along
You know we'll carry on - no matter how long
We're gonna move along - cause you know we're strong.

I love women - women who laugh
I love hearing women - I love to see us laugh
The laughter that's alive just behind the worried eyes
And every now and then you see it leap up to the skies
Full of energy - that's gotta be free
All that energy - is a gift of beauty.[33]

2

Perspectives on Women in the 1980s: The Baird Poskanzer Memorial Lecture

Gloria Steinem

Thank you very much for taking time out of your busy lives to come to this meeting. We have a little time together tonight in which we can, perhaps, make a psychic turf here: a place where we can come together and realize that we are not crazy, the system is crazy. We may have the time to learn from each other, and to turn this meeting into an organizing meeting. Feminist speakers say that, "if we come today, and there is no trouble tomorrow, we haven't done our jobs."

I understand very well that we outside agitators, or guest lecturers, or whatever it is that we are called, really provide an excuse for you to get together and find out, if you do not already know it, that you do not need us. All the courage and outrageousness and humour and imagination and anger that you could possibly want to make a revolution are right here. I also recognize that there is an unfortunate semi-imperialistic relationship between the United States and Canada, and I certainly do not want to duplicate that. The essence of feminism is autonomy and we do not want feminism to be seen as some kind of United States export – although it would, in fact, be one of the few healthy exports from the United States. (Please understand that I am speaking out of my own experience and in the true feminist style, hoping that when I say some outrageous thing, some other people may think, "Oh, you feel like that; I thought only I felt like that.")

Professor Baird Poskanzer of the School of Social Work, the University of Manitoba, died in 1972. He was an inspired teacher, a compassionate and generous colleague, and he held a very special place in the minds and hearts of those who were associated with him. His friends, colleagues and students present this annual lecture to perpetuate his memory and the values for which he stood.

14

I do know, however, that whatever culture or place we come from, we probably share a number of experiences. For one thing, I am sure there are people here who are new to feminism and may still believe that they should not use the word. Perhaps it means something that you will be punished for. Or you may have fallen victim to the idea of the media that feminism only concerns women. Feminism is, of course, simply the belief in the full social-political equality of human beings, which means that men can be feminists, too. Some of us here are probably in our fifth stage of burnout, have begun to realize that this is not something we are going to do for just two or three years, but for the rest of our lives, and have begun to pace ourselves.

Whatever stage we may be in, we come together tonight at a stage in history, and that stage of history is the "second wave" of feminism, or what we view in these young countries of North America as the second wave. I keep on my wall in the office a radical feminist poem from the second century A.D. to remind myself that the process of overthrowing or humanizing the caste system based on sex and race is a very long process. Nevertheless, there was a first wave within our families' memories. That was the great suffragist and abolitionist wave, which accomplished for women of all races and for black men a legal identity as human beings, an escape from the status of possession. In this second wave, we are struggling to achieve legal and social equality as human beings. The earlier wave lasted 100 to 150 years, depending on how you measure it. We are about fifteen years into this one; we probably have a long time to go. I say this because I know that, every Wednesday at tea-time, they pronounce the feminist movement "dead."

The first stage of this second wave was primarily one of consciousness raising. It was a stage that received national and international recognition, because of the courage that women had and gave each other to speak out and tell the truth about our lives. For the first time in the United States, the public opinion polls now indicate majority support for all the basic issues raised by the women's movement, whether it is the issue of equal pay for comparable work (known as "the part I agree with"), or whether it is the supposedly more controversial issue of the right to a safe and legal abortion. That is a huge job of consciousness raising, of truth-telling, and of courage on the part of many of you here who have made it happen. These are issues that were not even included in public opinion polls ten or twelve years ago; now there is majority support for them.

There are also two consequences which flow from this majority approval. The first is the necessity of a second stage to create the structural changes which will make these new possibilities real for most people. And structural change, or institutional change, takes much longer and is more difficult than

15

the consciousness raising and value change which must precede it.

The second consequence is that we now have a growing right-wing, authoritarian backlash against the movement for equality of the sexes and races. There are many who believe that their lifestyle, necessitating as it does the right to dictate to other folks, is in danger. As a result, we have a president in my country who represents the backlash. We have a president who is not a Republican as represented by the majority of Republicans, but who is a right-wing extremist. We have groups like the Moral Majority. We have the leadership of the Mormon church. We have the Bishops' Conference. This backlash, though small, is very forceful and very painful. It might help us to realize that, in some sense, it is a tribute to the seriousness of the social justice movements that we have this backlash. It is, nonetheless, dangerous, for there is nothing written that the majority shall prevail, even though the majority now has a changed set of values.

Wherever we came into this second wave, however, we probably have had a series of "clicks"; we probably have suddenly seen things that we cannot now un-see. Some of us are becoming the men we wanted to marry. We have made the revolutionary discovery that children have two parents. We have realized that, if it is logical for men to say a woman who bears a child is more responsible than the man for taking care of that child until it is out of the dependency stage, then it is equally logical for us to say, "Ah, but the child has two parents, so, if a woman spends a year bearing and nurturing a child, should the father not be responsible more than half the time after the first year?" Logic is in the eyes of the logician, we figured out.

We have new terms like sexual harassment (which ten years ago was called "life"). We have new courses like women's studies, and black studies, and Hispanic studies, and native studies. We should, perhaps, name them all "remedial studies," to put the blame where it really belongs. Some day we shall have only "human studies." We have discovered that there is nothing decreed by nature about the marriage law we inherited from England, nor about the Blackstonian principle that the couple is one person, and that person is the husband. We have redefined all kinds of things. Art, for example, had been defined as what white males did; crafts were what women and natives did. We have figured out they are actually the same thing. We have begun to integrate many exciting new craft techniques with art, and to integrate art with life again.

We have begun to look at our language and to question the politics of talking about white folks founding this country, when the relatives of some of you in this room have been here for a long time. I remember, when I lived in India, somebody finally explained to me why I should stop saying "the Far

East," "the Near East," "the Middle East." The person said, "Near or far from what, do you suppose? England?"

We have begun to think about the feeling of exclusion that women experience when only the male generic is used. If you men wonder how it feels, you might think about what would have happened if you had graduated with a Spinster of Arts degree, then had gone on to a Mistress of Science, and then had worked very hard to get a Sistership. You might feel left out, too.

We have discovered that women are the one social group that grows more radical with age. Men tend to be radical and to be activists when they are young, and then they go home to their fathers' businesses. They become less radical but more and more powerful as they become older. Women reverse the male pattern. We tend to be conservative when we are young. We become less and less powerful as we go through the four big, radicalizing experiences of a woman's life: joining the labour force and discovering how it treats women; getting married and discovering it is not usually an equal partnership; having children and finding out who takes care of them and who does not; and aging.

Those of you who are college age may find comfort in knowing that, although it is the habit of the media to look on the campuses for the most radical aspects of social movements, the media are doing that because they are accustomed to a male cultural pattern. But the women's movement is growing younger as it grows bigger and reaches younger and younger women. In the United States, so many older women have come back to campus that the average age of our female undergraduate is now twenty-seven.[1] What that means is that older women are coming back and radicalizing the younger ones. They come back and report that, "It is not exactly as Hollywood said, you know." These older women contribute to a much more real classroom atmosphere. It is a delight to see a nineteen-year-old pre-medical student arguing with a thirty-five-year-old pregnant woman about the health care delivery system.

I suppose what has happened is that we have begun to redefine politics. We have finally come to understand that the term *politics* refers not only to what happens in our electoral systems, but is any power relationship in our daily lives. Any time one group is habitually dominant over another group, or one person over another person – not because of talent or experience but because of birth group, whether of sex or race or class, or all three – that is politics, that is a power relationship. It is from those power relationships that our more conventional politics spring. So, yes, it is political that women have two jobs and men have one. If women are working outside the home, they still have to take care of children in the home. That is unfair, and that is politics.

It is political that women bear men's names and children bear men's

17

names. It certainly makes life much more difficult. I am sure there are people here who have had to explain, "This is my child by my first marriage and this is my child by my second marriage." The power of naming is a very political power. A much more logical system would be for all of us to name ourselves.

We realize, when we look at the fields of our countries and see that one kind of person works on them and another kind of person owns them, that is politics. When we look at our big corporations and see hundreds of one kind of folk typing and twelve of another in the boardroom, that is politics. When we look at who is on welfare and who is not, that is politics. And so we have begun to redefine politics and to understand that a revolution can and must be made, not because of questions many hundreds or thousands of miles away from us, but because of the power relationships in our daily lives. Indeed, true revolutions can only be built like houses – from the bottom and not from the top.

We have begun to see the connections among all of our groups and issues that might have seemed separate: the movement against racial caste and the movement against sexual caste, the peace movement and the anti-military movement. Ronald Reagan has greatly aided us in the United States because he is so wonderfully consistent: he is against everything. He makes your coalition for you. There was a nice cartoon of him wearing a western hat, just before the election; the balloon is saying, "A gun in every holster, a pregnant woman in every home. Make America a man." Does it not say why the issues are all connected? I think that it also says why the movements against sex and race caste systems are the most profoundly anti-authoritarian forces in the world today and why, without them, we will always be subject to an authoritarian threat.

The cross-cultural themes that emerged in the seventies in many countries of the world continue to be concerns in the eighties. The first concern for women of every race and group, whatever form it may take in our particular culture or lives, is clearly reproductive freedom. Ten years ago, we would have said "population control": an authoritarian phrase and a racist one. Now, at least, we have a feminist and humanist phrase to say what we mean: reproductive freedom, which is the right to decide to have or not to have children. It is logical that women's movements in every culture in the world have started with this issue. Our reproductive capacity is the only functional difference between women and men, and the "bottom line" of patriarchy is to control women's bodies as a means of production. Reproduction is the most basic means of production by which the state, or the church, or the tribe, or the family, or whatever the patriarchal unit may be, can decide how many children there will be, who owns them, and what race they are.

18

We did not come to realize that reproductive freedom was the first issue out of some intellectual process. It was not because of a lot of words that end in "tion," and it was not derived from a political theory or a book. It was a reflection of our real lives. It was because it was the biggest health concern for women. It was causing the most deaths and injuries among women, and still is. Reproductive freedom, in its different aspects, had to be the first issue. In this country, in Italy, and in many other countries, abortion has become the key issue. The issue of coerced or forced sterilization affects women within both our countries as well as women in other countries and cultures. Access to contraceptives is a primary concern in the Soviet Union where abortion is almost the only means of contraception available. The struggle of feminists in Ireland and many other countries is to gain that same access.

The struggle of women in the Middle East and Africa is to put an end to the practices of clitoridectomy and infibulation. I hope that Western feminists have learned from the example of the missionaries who condemned these procedures as primitive but excused them because of the ignorance of the people. We understand now that they are only different in degree from what we have accepted and what has been done to us. Freud performed psychic clitoridectomies on most of the women in the West. And the surgical procedure of clitoridectomy was being done in the United States and Britain, as a way of dealing with misbehaving females, up through the 1930s. We have begun, I hope, to learn to recognize all the ways in which patriarchies try to turn women into nothing but a controlled means of production. We have to reach out to each other and say, "Yes, I know there is a difference only in degree from that which has happened to us. Let us help you do what you must do within your own culture."

This has been an organic kind of process. The lack of reproductive freedom has been the cause of enormous suffering and death among women, and it seems like a reasonable idea for us to say that we would like control over our own bodies. Surely that is not too much to ask? If we do not have control over our own bodies from the skin in, how can we ever control our lives from the skin out? We have been forced by the right-wing backlash, whether the Moral Majority or the Moslem Brotherhood, to realize that we have undertaken a very radical act. We are seizing control of the means of reproduction. It even sounds radical, does it not? And it means that we are undermining authoritarian regimes. An authoritarian regime must be able to control its population, decide how many workers and how many soldiers, and of what race and class, there must be. We are also weakening nationalism which is dependent on the control of a territory and of a particular population.

It has been through this organic, simple, day-to-day process of looking at reproductive freedom for women that we have realized (as our suffragist and abolitionist sisters and brothers knew) that the connection between racial and sexual caste systems is absolutely inextricable. That is, in order to maintain the racial caste system, to maintain the racial purity of the so-called superior race, the freedom of women must be restricted. As a black feminist said to her white feminist sister in the last wave of feminism: "A pedestal is as much a prison as any other small space." And so, the women of the ruling caste are restricted in their freedom, and the women of the other groups are to be possessed by the men of their own group and the men of the ruling group. In the United States, one of the worst crimes has been the taking over of a means of production of the ruling class, that is, the body of a white woman by a black man. Of course, it was not considered to be a crime the other way around; it was quite all right for white men to have children, even by force, with black women. It only produced more cheap labour, more people who were marked by their skins to be servants of the ruling class. But the marriage of white women to black men could mean the end of the ruling caste system, and the end of white racial purity. Certainly, from looking at our own country's history, American feminists have been able to see the inextricable linkage of sexual and racial caste systems. But we could also look at male Jews and Aryan women in Nazi Germany. Or we could look at the arrival of white folks in all of North America and the degree to which their coming affected the native American nations which were not as patriarchal, which provided stronger roles for women than did the European cultures. But, as soon as the new race arrived and imposed itself, the necessity of both a racial and a sexual caste system to maintain racial purity became evident and the laws changed.

I think it is very important, as we look at the present right-wing backlash, for us to understand that the key issue is reproductive freedom as a basic human right, like freedom of speech or freedom of assembly. Otherwise, we in the United States, for instance, would not understand why abortion is the one issue on which the right-wing will vote against its own financial interest. Its members will vote against providing funds for abortions for poor women, even though they know that it will cost many dollars more to pay for pregnancy, childbirth, and child support expenses. They will vote against their own financial interests, because there is an issue of control at stake that is even more important than money, and this is the control of women's bodies as a means of production. And it is the issue on which we are most likely to be deserted by our liberal male colleagues because, through no fault of theirs, culture has failed to teach them how to talk about this issue. They are embarrassed by it; they think it is not important; they think it is a single issue.

Freedom of speech is not a single issue. Reproductive freedom is not a single issue; it affects everything.

The majority of people in the United States, however, supports the right of reproductive freedom. The majority does not want the government interfering with our decisions about having, or not having, children. Politicians will win who stand up and say, "Reproductive freedom is a basic right. Do you want the government to tell you what to do or what not to do?" We have demonstrated that. But there are all too few who are willing to do it. Even those who vote "right," hope that the issue will go away somehow. They do not talk about it; they hope no one will notice that they are voting "right."

It is important, too, that we understand that the issue of reproductive freedom is the first target of authoritarian regimes as they come to power. I had the poor judgement, just before Reagan was elected, to spend a lot of time reading about the rise of national socialism. (I was already depressed enough; I did not need that.) But I started to do it because the pro-life groups in the United States, and I suspect in Canada too, condemn pro-choice people as "Nazis." They say, "Six million babies were killed by the Supreme Court; six million Jews were killed by Hitler. Remembering somewhere in my head that Hitler had been wildly against abortion, I went back to read about that era and to read *Mein Kampf*. Hitler said in that book, "When I come to power, I will put an end to the ridiculous idea that a woman's body belongs to herself." And it becomes very clear that the rise of national socialism was a response to "uppity" women; it was a response to a breach of their racial system which was Jewish versus non-Jewish; and it was a response, of course, to the chaos of unemployment and inflation and to the national humiliation of World War I.

Now, all of these are mitigated in our circumstances. We are much older democracies than Germany was, and I certainly do not feel humiliated by the defeat in Vietnam; I just feel humiliated by ever having been there. But there are some parallels, and we must remember that Hitler was elected. And he was elected by, amongst others, the Evangelicals and the Catholic Centrist Party because they agreed with Hitler on these issues. They agreed that women's place was in the home: *Kuche, Kirche und Kinder* (kitchen, church and children). They applauded the first official act of Hitler, which was to close all family-planning clinics. There are many parallels and, though we as North Americans may not recognize fascism when we see it as quickly as do our friends in Europe and Latin America, we should think seriously about these parallels. The words that are being said now are almost indistinguishable – indeed, they are indistinguishable– from the words that were being said then.

The second big, cross-cultural theme is clearly that of sexuality, and the

21

de-politicizing of sexuality. If you want to have more and more workers and soldiers, which has been the goal of patriarchal cultures for the last five thousand years or so, or if you want, at least, to control that process, then you teach people that sexuality is only moral and good within patriarchal marriage and directed towards having children. Everything else is bad. The people who are the adversaries of contraception and abortion, therefore, are the same people who are the adversaries of lesbian rights, gay rights and extra-marital sex. They condemn sexuality that is not within the patriarchal family and directed towards having children, and in doing so, they have politicized sexuality.

I remember being with an audience, talking to people somewhere in the Midwest, tap-dancing hard, as I am now, trying to explain how we were attempting to de-politicize sexuality, and being rescued by a wonderful grey-haired woman, a true radical, with the little flowered dress and pearls (a very subversive outfit). She got up in the audience and put me out of my misery by saying, "Well, my dear, human beings have always been the only animals who could experience sexual pleasure, experience orgasm at times when they could not conceive. All other animals have periods of heat. But, for human beings, this has never been the case. Therefore, sexuality for human beings has always been not only the way we have children, that we procreate, but also a way that we communicate with each other, that we express closeness and caring, that we talk to each other, that we reach out to each other. To tell us that sexuality is only okay when it is in a patriarchal marriage, directed towards having children, and obviously heterosexual, is as crazy as trying to convince us that we have freedom of speech, but only if we say one thing."

And so, we are trying very hard to de-politicize sexuality, to release it again as a loving, intimate communication among people. And we are realizing that we have a common cause, whether we are concerned about the issue of abortion, or lesbian rights, or gay rights. My favourite resolution, made by the right-wing at a White House conference on families, was a formal resolution against masturbation. Even people who are concerned only about the right to masturbate, therefore, have a definite place in this coalition; we must not desert each other, and we must understand that our adversaries are always the same.

The second part of the process of de-politicizing sexuality is to untangle sexuality from violence. When you tell one group of people-men-that they are superior and tell another group-women-that they are inferior, it is a lie. It can only be maintained by violence, and thus the area in which we most reliably and intimately come together has become suffused by violence. Many men, through no fault of the individual man, but rather a fault of the culture, have been convinced that they are not real men unless they are dominant over women. It is like a drug. Without this sense of dominance over women, some men feel that they are nothing; they are not real men or real persons. And if they cannot dominate the women in their lives, they will rape women and believe that the women actually deserved it for having dared to think of themselves as equal, or as human beings. If that is not possible or not part of their syndrome, they may take out this need for dominance on children, perhaps their own children. If the woman is at work and is a challenge to the man, he may assert his superiority through sexual harassment on the job.

This intertwining of sexuality and violence is something we are trying very hard to disentangle through understanding that rape is not sexuality but is violence, and that pornography is the legitimizing of violence against women. Pornography is to women of all races what anti-Semitic literature is to Jews, what racist Klan literature is to blacks. We have a right to march against it, to throw it out of our homes, to penalize men in our lives who look at it, to say exactly how it endangers women.

We are also approaching cross-culturally the redefinition of a third big theme and that is families, *families* in the plural. I hope we are beginning to realize that anybody who says *family* in the singular is talking about only one kind of family, and it is usually his or hers. In fact, there have always been, throughout history, many different family forms. No one kind of family is right for everyone. We are, therefore, trying to honour single-parent families, to honour extended families, to honour people who do not wish to have children, to honour chosen families. We are trying to dispense with the authoritarian structure of the family which is the model of the authoritarian state. Once we accept it at home, we are much more likely to accept it elsewhere.

In the United States, folks like Howard Philipps, who is the head of our conservative caucus, have helped us to understand that what the right wing calls "anti-family" is any legal guarantee of rights for women and for children. This guarantee that would interfere with the patriarchal authority of the father in the home. As Howard Philipps says, "Anti-family legislation did not begin in recent times. No, it began when women were given property rights and were removed from the authority of their husbands and proceeded when they were allowed to vote, and continues with the equal rights amendment and other terrible and direct guarantees of rights, and will end in the destruction of Western civilization as we know it."

In the United States we have a piece of legislation called the Family Protection Act, which was introduced in 1979 by Paul Laxault, closest advisor to our president. This is a huge, omnibus piece of legislation in which the idea of family protection is expressed through forbidding the federal funding of battered women's centres, forbidding any federal laws against battered children, taking away veterans' benefits and other federal benefit programs from homosexuals, and, through a complicated foray into tax policy, rewarding the patriarchal family financially.

In contrast to the right wing, we have been trying to make democratic families, or to open the options. Having made the revolutionary discovery that kids have two parents, we have gone on to realize how important it is that babies and little children see loving and nurturing men, as well as loving and nurturing women. We have also realized how important it is that children see women being competent in the world outside the home. We must not continue to pattern ourselves deeply into the beliefs that, as men, we cannot be loving and nurturing towards our children in the way that women can; and that, as women, we cannot be competent and assertive in the world outside the home in the same way that men can. That is why it is so urgent for the many men who care about children and wish to make this a part of their lives to have the opportunity to do so, whether within their own families or in child-care or childhood-education centres. All children, whether they are living with a female single parent or whatever, must have the opportunity to see that men can be loving and nurturing.

I think we have, in this long decade, come to realize that there are men who know that the feminist revolution is the only path to humanism and that it is in their self-interest to support it. If there is more virtue where there is more choice, then there is more virtue among men who could have male privilege and who refuse it; who refuse to take a job that takes them away from their children, who refuse to listen to sexist remarks among their male friends, who refuse promotions above the heads of equally qualified women or minorities. We have learned to understand that there is more virtue among such men, and to reach out to them and to call them brothers.

The fourth big theme is work and the redefinition of work. This is a real problem for women in industrial countries because we suffer from a kind of semantic slavery. The work that is done at home is not work: women who work at home do not work. This is ridiculous. Women who work at home work longer hours, longer weeks, than do any workers in the country, and they do not get paid. It is more likely to be, "What did you do with the fifty dollars I gave you yesterday?" Women who work at home experience the highest rate of alcoholism, of addiction to tranquillizers and other drugs, of violence (because, in the United States the most dangerous place for a woman is not in the streets, but in her own home), and the greatest likelihood of being replaced by another worker, a younger worker. We are struggling to give a monetary and a social value to the work that women – and men – do at home.

In agricultural countries, in third world countries, women have the same problem, but it concerns the work they do in the fields. In many countries of Africa and Latin America, women are primarily food producers. They produce the food their families eat, but they are still people who do not work; they are not included in the gross national product, and they are not given technological help. They, too, are struggling to define all productive human labour as work.

In every country, it seems that women who do get into the paid labour force, though they are defined as working because they are doing something that men have done or could do, remain a caste group that devalues whatever it does. It is painful but true that when a profession becomes more than one-third female, it begins to tilt, like a neighbourhood, and suddenly it does not pay as well as it did. Secretaries used to be men; they were well paid. Then women became secretaries, and we know what happened. Bookkeepers were men; then too many women became bookkeepers, and men invented certified public accountants. Or, we can look at medical general practitioners in the Soviet Union. Ninety percent of the general practitioners are female; their profession is now equated with nursing. A specialist is the thing to be, and that is what the men are. We are all of us engaged, therefore, in various forms of the struggle to evaluate work in terms of its real value to society, and not its social value based on the sex or the race of the "doer" of the job.

Finally, there is the category that, for want of a better word, I call culture (except, in my heart, I think that culture is successful politics). Culture is what they tell you that you cannot change. It is that vast area of our daily lives – our reading, our viewing lives, our art lives – through which we have, in all of our different countries, suddenly begun to recognize the politics of the culture that we swim through every day. It is the millions of women (and, I am sure, some men too) who sit in their living rooms waiting for the woman in the "ring-around-the-collar" commercial to turn to her husband and say, "Why don't you wash your neck?" It is looking at the novels we read and suddenly recognizing the sexual and racial politics embedded there. It is trying to figure out why black families on television, if they exist at all, seem to be in comedies, while white families are rich and in high tragedies. I think they are trying to convince us that it is fun to be poor and it is a drag to be rich; they are trying to discourage us from seizing the oil wells. But, whatever form it takes, all over the world, and in every day of our lives, we experience a kind of "click" and we recognize the politics behind a particular piece of our culture.

Thanks to the extreme right-wing element, we have been greatly aided in understanding the politics of religion. All too often, religion is politics made sacred. Did you not always wonder when you were a kid why God was white and male? I was curious about that. I certainly felt ill at ease in churches, not only because I was half Jewish (I felt ill at ease in temples too), but because little girls could not participate in the way little boys did. (I am talking about institutionalized religion, I hope you understand, not about spirituality, which is quite subversive, actually, and individual.) But I really did not understand how deeply political religion was until we began to put statements from the president of the Mormon church, or the Ayatollah, or any of those folks, on a piece of paper and to say, "Guess who said this about women?" It was impossible to tell one from another. And I did not understand how deeply political religion was until this current religious backlash, with creationists trying to have their beliefs taught in schools, and with censorship groups trying to determine what children will and will not read.

When I was at the Smithsonian I came across a book by a male architect, not a feminist, who enlightened me further. He said that religious architecture in most cultures, whether of Hindu temples or Episcopalian churches, resembles the body of a woman. Why? It is because the central ceremony of patriarchal religions is one in which men give birth. Because the power of giving birth is a rather awesome power, men take it over. In tribal ceremonies or in high Episcopalian ceremonies essentially they say, "Yes, you are born of woman. You are born of this unclean creature, you are born in sin, but if you behave well, and do as you are told, you can be re-born through men. We will sprinkle imitation birth fluid over your head and give you a new name and say you have been re-born." Therefore, as the author pointed out, most religious structures literally resemble the body of a woman, with an outer entrance and an inner entrance, with a vaginal aisle, two curved ovarian structures on either side and the altar, which is the womb. This is where the miracle takes place and where men give birth. No wonder they do not want us saying mass at those altars!

I think many women and many men have begun to question any ceremony which precludes anyone from participating because of birth, and to question where we are putting our tithing money or our temple contributions. We have to make sure we are not, in fact, giving money to the adversary, that we are not saying that God exists in some people but not in others, and that those others are less valuable.

Ours is a very long, deep and profound revolution that affects everything. I know that ten years ago, I said, "Feminism is a revolution, not just a reform." That is true, except that I later realized the reason I was saying it was because my male colleagues on the Left took the word revolution seriously and I wanted them to take feminism seriously. But I finally understood that what they meant by revolution was taking over the army and the radio stations. That is nothing. We have to do much more than that. Then I started to say "anthropological revolution," which gave a good idea of the depth, but a false idea of the patience required. So now I am stuck without a word.

Whatever the word, however, the process continues. When we gather together, we discover that, although we do not have institutions reflecting our changed values yet, our values have changed, and we share them with the majority of our sisters and brothers. We are one with people who are gathering together in just this way, in groups large or small, subversively or openly, in every other country in the world that I know about, from Saudi Arabia to Sweden. We are part of the longest and deepest kind of revolution: a revolution which will humanize us and will do away with the sexual and racial caste systems that have divided us. Never again, whatever social systems we may develop, will anyone be born into a particular role because of sex or race or class. Finally, we will begin to understand the unique and human and irreplaceable individual that each of us could be.

3

The Power Politics of Motherhood

Helen Levine

This presentation derives directly from an occasional paper, "The Power Politics of Motherhood," which I wrote jointly with Alma Estable, a graduate student at the Carleton University School of Social Work. I wish to thank Alma Estable for her contribution to this presentation.[1]

I want to begin by commenting on two recent films that highlight our society's current ideas about mothers. *Kramer vs. Kramer* focuses on the remarkable loyalty and commitment of a single father who assumes day-to-day responsibility for his child, even to the extent of giving up a lucrative job (and, as we all know, making French toast).[2] The film seems to assume that the mother has appropriately yielded her name, her mobility, her paid job, financial independence, and the right to a fully adult life of her own. No heroine is she; no glory to her, no unending appreciation of such commitment. The film simply takes for granted the fact that she has naturally given up her own separate existence in order to become a wife and mother.

Ordinary People looks at how one mother's seeming materialism, selfishness and lack of feeling affect other caring members of the family, namely, the father and the son.[3] The film portrays the father and son as giving and suffering human beings, profoundly in touch with their emotions and relationships. The father, son and male psychiatrist appear to make serious efforts to include the mother in a shared family love. In reality, she is subtly excluded and is ultimately held responsible for losing that love. The mother is portrayed as a "believable, recognizable monster."[4] We are given no hint of the political and social context of women's lives as reflected in her existence.

The prescription for women in both these films is one of adjusting to the traditional institution of marriage and motherhood, or risking hatred and rejection. The films remind mothers that if they do not give what others want

28

and need, they are in danger of losing everyone and everything they possess. The men and fathers, on the other hand, are seen as heroes or victims or both. It is they, the men, who rise to fill the tragic void left by the mothers.

In real life, it is usually mothers who carry the weighty responsibility for child care after separation and divorce. In the nuclear family, it is usually women who do the domestic and emotional work and carry responsibility for interpersonal relationships. What *Kramer vs. Kramer* and *Ordinary People* do so effectively and, I think, so dangerously, is to turn these realities around 180 degrees to create sympathy, respect and warmth towards fathers, and anger, contempt and disgust for mothers.

These films are significant in that they can, if we ask the right questions, take us beyond the dominant ideology of motherhood to a critique of the traditional family. Similarly, a feminist framework applied to social work practice can help us redefine struggles within the family by taking into account the political, economic and personal context of women's lives.

Alma Estable and I developed a glossary of terms because we thought we should explain some of our assumptions.[5] One of the terms is *parents*. We think it is a misleading term. Its use obscures the fact that one sex is held primarily responsible for child care, and it masks the real work women do in the home as both domestic and child care workers. Social workers and other helping professionals generally refer to parents when, in fact, they are describing services and interventions largely directed at women.

Another term is *motherhood*. The institution of motherhood exists in diverse social and political systems. It prescribes that mothering should exist at the centre of women's lives and that all else remain secondary. It exonerates men from fathering in any authentic sense, and ensures women's containment within the home. In contrast, the experience of motherhood has to do with the joys, the sorrows and the human struggles involved in rearing children. It can be a valuable and joyful part of life. Embedded as it is within the institution, however, it has robbed most women of a full and independent adult life.

Unpaid work: When we talk about work, it is important to distinguish between paid and unpaid work. Women do the unpaid work of family and community. This includes the bearing of children, as well as the physical maintenance and emotional work in the home. There are no wages for this work. It is the only labour assumed to be undertaken for love and by one sex exclusively. Motherworkers sign on indefinitely. There are no fixed hours, there is no sick leave, no vacation, no pension, no job security, no collective bargaining and no unionization. Training is considered unnecessary, and it is assumed there are instinctive blueprints for productivity. When instinct fails or when the "plant" is in trouble, mothers do not enjoy leaves of absence, unemployment insurance or worker's compensation. Instead, we are frequently labelled inadequate or unfit.

Mothering: This term reflects our view that women are held responsible for mothering not only children, but also men, bosses, the sick, the elderly, the handicapped, and the needy in general. It is interesting to note that "to mother" is a verb related to child care, as well as to domestic and emotional work. "To father," on the other hand, is a verb related to conception and creation.

And, finally, from our feminist glossary, I present the terms *politics* and *language*. Words that imply equality, mutuality or sharing are often used as a mask for the oppression of women, as a denial of our powerlessness. For example, most professionals still refer to violence against wives and mothers as interspousal or family violence, thereby falsely implying that violence is reciprocal between women and men. Similarly, the use of the term family income sustains the myth that wives and husbands jointly own and control money in the nuclear family. It obscures the fact that most women have either restricted or no access to the husband's wage or salary.

There is a connection, past and present, between men's needs, economic conditions and specific versions of the ideology of motherhood. It is vital to get at the linkages between these elements. There are four major factors to consider:

1   Patriarchy is a male-defined system with a variety of structures and institutions which maintain power and dominance over women in family, workplace and society.

2   In all economic systems to date, women are exploited within and beyond the home and are denied full and equal participation in the public sphere. The capitalist system in particular maintains women as a reserve army of labour, to be pulled in and out of the work force as the economy requires. As "secondary workers," we are segregated into low-paying and low-status job ghettos.

3   The institution of motherhood has helped to keep women at the service of men and children. It contains women within the home, preventing us from becoming a serious threat to the power and dominance of men in the public sphere.

4   The ideology of romantic love, a powerful and political superstructure, maintains an unequal distribution of power between the sexes. Romantic love, whether of men or of children, creates a false consciousness which masks the reality of women's lives. The necessary conditions for diverting girls and women away from their own vital self-importance, individually and collectively, are created by the romanticization of family life.

The situation in North America after World War II provides an example of the use of the ideology of motherhood to coerce women to return to the domestic sphere. At that time, men returning from the war demanded their jobs and their wives back. Women were pushed off the assembly lines, out of the paid labour force and into the kitchen once more. Public child-care services, so generously provided throughout the war, were withdrawn just as the post-war baby boom began. Everyone took for granted the idea that women would trade paycheques for wedding rings, and paid work and independence for baby carriages.

As a means of reinforcing and justifying the herding of North American women back into domestic dependency, the myth of motherhood was dusted off, revised and expanded into a theory of maternal deprivation – a very powerful theory built into the practice of the helping professions. Maternal deprivation was said to occur when children did not have full-time mothers at home, mothers who exclusively cared for all the emotional and physical needs of their children, particularly during the pre-school years, but later as well. Separation of children from their mothers was considered to be harmful not only to children but also to society at large.[6]

Concerned about the needs of children, masses of women in the post-war period heeded the warnings of the new experts and went home to stay. I was one of them, and so were most of my peers. Those who could not, out of sheer economic necessity, or who did not, because they claimed their rights as adult persons, lived with public disapproval and guilt. Mothers of young children in the 1950s can attest to the fact that the question of maternal deprivaton very seriously affected major decisions about our lives.

It is my view that the current economic crisis provides an excuse for undermining, once more, the relation of women to paid employment. As unemployment rises, as the thrust of women towards liberation begins to threaten patriarchal family structures, there is once again a move to discourage, in a variety of ways, the participation of women in paid work.

A contemporary example of how the state manipulates women, particularly during periods of cutbacks and spending restraints, comes from the government of Ontario. Margaret Birch, who is a member of the Conservative cabinet, stated in a speech a few years ago to the Ontario Council for the Status of Women: "Governments, especially provincial governments, are recognizing the need for spending restraint. We are now at the stage where we may have to give back to the family some of the responsibilities that we have assumed in the past."[7] And she also said: "For those who say professional day care is the only answer, let me tell you it is no substitute for mothering; as many experts now warn us…you cannot pay someone to do what a mother will do for free."[8] "For free." Those are the key words.

Giving back to the family means, of course, giving back to women and mothers. The connection between the economy, theories of maternal deprivation, and the ideololgy of motherhood becomes clear. The term *family* is a euphemism for women and mothers who are to remain primarily within the home at the service of others, who are to do the motherwork.

What is "motherwork"? When people speak of "work" and "workers," we assume that they refer mainly to work done in exchange for money or wages outside the home, and largely by men. But there is another kind of work which was as universally unrecognized in theory (until the contemporary women's movement came along) as it was and is unrewarded in practice. It is the motherwork that women do in the family and the home, the reproductive, domestic and emotional labour of women.

Rearing children has been seen as the exclusive responsibility of females and held out as the necessary complement to men's wage labour. But most women who are mothers know that, traditionally, we do much more: cleaning, cooking, washing, budgeting, organizing, nursing, shopping, and much of it on a daily, repetitive basis. Those of you who have read Judy Syfers' classic article "I want a wife," will know what I mean.[9] Motherwork includes the socialization of children as well as the servicing of adult males in the family, sexually and/or domestically, to reinforce their ongoing attachment to the labour force. Embedded in motherwork is the emotional work that women do. We are expected, above all else, to maintain the stability of the family, to mediate conflicts within the family, and between the family and outside institutions. We defuse anger and stress, frequently by directing it onto ourselves. We are expected to be a steady source of love, needing few refills. Even when we work for pay outside the family, our motherwork does not end. Women make up the lowest echelons of the service, clerical and professional fields, and are mainly in front-line service-delivery systems, doing the housekeeping and emotional tasks of the workplace.

It is interesting to note that, although women may aspire to all kinds of occupations that men participate in, men do not usually aspire to motherwork, either its child-care or domestic component. It is a measure, I would say, of the low societal value of this kind of labour and of women. In all social systems, men do not rear children because they do not want to rear children.[10] When I use the phrase "to rear children," I am not talking about bathing the children, taking over for a couple of weeks, doing the extras, being a sport. I am talking about the ongoing, hard work involved in daily child care.

I would also say that men do not stay at home to be homemakers because they do not want to do domestic work to service others. I would suggest that arrangements between women, men and work rest primarily on a patriarchal mythology - and ideology - devised to justify exploitive social arrangements.

For many women, motherhood offers the single opportunity to meet a universal need of all human beings: to be essential, to exert influence and control in a world that has denied us other sources of achievement and decision making. Watch a mother and a young child together; for good or ill, the mother is continuously monitoring the child's behaviour. Even while performing other tasks, mothers maintain a vigilant awareness of their children's safety, behaviour and needs. Such intensity of purpose, such a single-minded focus on the job, is rewarded and recognized in most other occupations. It cannot be with mother-hood. Motherhood, like fatherhood, is no substitute for a life's work, an adult way of being in the world. It is potentially a caring, intimate and responsible relationship - no more, no less. Making motherhood the central job for women has rendered it destructive to mothers and children.

Motherwork is essential in any society. There is no question that children deserve tender, loving care, that homes and services must be maintained in some form or another. What I take issue with is the relegation of this form of work to females and not to males.

Many human ills have become entangled in the institution of motherhood. Implicit in such terms as *wife battering* is violence against mothers, since the majority of wives, world-wide, are mothers. Until the advent of the con-temporary women's movement, violence against women was seen to be primarily a matter of personal and interpersonal needs. Female victims were, and still are, often blamed for provoking male assault. So why is violence against women in particular psychologized, ignored, tolerated, condoned? What is the con-nection with motherhood?

It is my view that misogyny, that is, a hatred of and contempt for women , is deeply embedded in the patriarchal structure of this society, and in other societies as well. Mary Daly points out that "nearly everyone has been indoc-trinated in the mother-hating myths" of patriarchy.[11] Fairy tales provide us with an example. In *Snow White* and *Cinderella*, the central conflict is between good and evil, and evil is represented by older mother figures who envy or hate their young, beautiful and innocent daughters. Men, be they kings, fathers, princes, dwarves, or hunters, are portrayed as natural allies and protectors of helpless young women in distress. It is the maternal figures, thinly disguised as wicked step-mothers, who make their daughters' lives a misery. It is the men who save young women from the clutches of evil mothers.

The real-life situations of battered women are, on the other hand, telling examples of how a male-defined society condemns rather than loves and respects women, batters rather than shelters or protects them. The same is true of lesbians. In fact, lesbian mothers are so generally reviled that loss of their children is predicted in custody disputes.

Given the political reality of misogyny and of violence against mothers in the family, social workers and other professionals face a dilemma. The dilemma has to do with making a clear choice between continuing to interpret human behaviour in personal and interpersonal terms, or linking personal problems with power politics and ideology.

From a feminist perspective, the theory of maternal deprivation, which I mentioned earlier, reflects both the emphasis on psychologizing life's experiences, and on inventing slick, sophisticated and, in essence, cruel devices for holding women responsible for the outcome of personal and family life. Under the guise of sophisticated definitions of normalcy, developed primarily by men, women have been kept tied firmly to the institution of motherhood.

The concept of maternal deprivation has been built into the theory and practice of the helping professions. Freud, Bolby, Spock, Burton White, Klaus and Kennel, and many others have underscored the requirement for women to be full-time mothers, particularly in the early years of their children's lives.[12] Out of theory, devoid of everyday practice, male theoreticians have assumed that the best mothering is individualized, private, one mother to one child. According to these theoreticians, "improper" mother-child relations result in adult social deviance. In the wake of maternal deprivation theories, therefore, mothers have been held responsible by the helping professions for conditions as diverse as mental retardation, schizophrenia, delinquency, depression, incest, violent crime, slums and prostitution.[13]

It is my view that most men in the helping professions (as well as a few women)[14] have presented women, in the name of science, with sexist prescriptions for their life work as mothers. Male authors, theoreticians and philosophers abound as experts in the fields of parenting, child care and the family, despite the fact that this is the single area, according to these same experts, in which women are "naturals" and irreplaceable.

The helping professions rely heavily on the idea of maternal deprivation as cause in diagnosing personal suffering and unhappiness. Therapists, counsellors and social workers were and are intensely preoccupied with such questions as, "what his mother did to him," "what her mother didn't give to her," and "how the current mother-patient is functioning in relation to husband and children."

There are many examples. Nathan Epstein, in his 1964 family categories schema (which has since been revised, but, I would say, not fundamentally) notes eight features of the father's role in a normal family. Here are some of them: he is a successful breadwinner; in middle-class families, he makes the decisions about money; he has the ultimate responsibility for important decisions; he has the ultimate responsibility for important decisions, for example, about place of residence, major expenses, vacations. Epstein adds generously: "This does not preclude democratic discussion or taking his wife into his confidence." Epstein includes two sentences describing the wife and mother in terms of normal family functioning. (Descriptions have a way of becoming prescriptions.) He says, "She performs efficiently and happily as homemaker and mother. She enjoys marital sexual relations and functions satisfactorily in this role."[15] Joseph Rheingold says, "The syndrome of decay, the evil tendency in man, is basically rooted in the mother-child relationship."[16]

Although conventional therapy frequently makes devastating pronouncements regarding the inadequacy of mothers, it keeps the personal needs of fathers well in the forefront, with positive consideration given to the heavy pressures in their lives: "At times, he's [the father] been so helpful that he has been exploited. Too often he has been thrust into the middle of household turmoil. Too often, he has been expected to play the role of a second mother... furthermore, in recent years many households have disregarded the father's personal needs in order to make him a better father.... Might it not be preferable, for instance, for him to have a little relaxation at the end of a busy day at work, a time to read his paper and relax a little before he joins the family group and meets its demands upon him?"[17]

There would seem to be the infamous double standard at work here in terms of how mothers and fathers are different. That same double standard also applies to the concept of paternal deprivation, which is usually described as the loss of a positive influence, not deprivation (unlike the concept of maternal deprivation).

Incest is another issue that has become entangled with the institution of motherhood. When incest occurs, professional theory and practice routinely point to the mother as having been guilty in some way of deserting the family, as having withdrawn passively or actively from vital aspects, sexual or otherwise, of her role. The implication is that normal mothers should "subordinate their own needs, preferences, and wishes to those of husband and children."[18] In dealing with sexual crimes committed by men, it is common practice among helping professionals to concentrate on the inadequate performance of the wife and mother in the family. The adult men who inflict sexual violence on their daughters are frequently seen as marginal actors or just part of a "dysfunctional" family.

Social workers involved in front-line work in child and family services hear repeatedly from mothers the themes of guilt, self-blame and low self-esteem. It is my contention that such themes are structured into the very heart of women's lives and embedded within the institution of motherhood. The success of patriarchy relies on internalized guilt and self-blame in women to immobilize and then to contain us, finally and definitively, within the private sphere of life.

Adrienne Rich writes: "My children cause me the most exquisite suffering of which I have any experience. It is the suffering of ambivalence: the murderous alternation between bitter resentment and raw-edged nerves, and blissful gratification and tenderness. Sometimes I seem to myself, in my feelings towards these tiny, guiltless beings, a monster of selfishness and intolerance. Their voices wear away at my nerves, their constant needs, above all, their need for simplicity and patience, fill me with despair at my own failures...and I am weak sometimes from held-in rage."[19]

Jessie Bernard states that "...because we set impossibly high standards, our way of institutionalizing motherhood breeds guilt into every fabric of a woman's character. She blames herself for every deviation from the model."[20] In this context, I want to share some of my own experience.

I was a mother of young children during the 1950s. Prior to motherhood, I lived in an egalitarian marriage and worked as a social worker. I had two much-wanted and carefully planned children. Despite a meagre income and many interests, I became a full-time mother from the start. I did not consider being what was then termed "a working mother," or retaining a separate life of my own apart from the family. The social sciences, the media and Dr. Spock effectively persuaded most mothers that maternal deprivation might result if we were not continuously available to our children. So I became, like most of my peers, a committed mother, primarily responsible for home, children and family. At the same time, as adults, we became dependent in a fundamental sense (economically and psychologically) on our mates. Within the contained world of the family, we tried to find love and purpose by living through and for others. We tried hard to be happy, to make others happy, to live up to the prescription for normal, well-adjusted family life.

In spite of child-rearing manuals and marriage manuals and every other kind of manual, however, the prescription did not work for most of us. I was to write, many years later, "I know the deadly guilt, anxiety and stress that are frequently borne by women in the wife-and-mother role. I know the pretense that women try desperately to maintain about the joys of motherhood, the joys of nurturing others, and the joys of self-denial and service."[21] And I would now add, out of my own experience and from the wisdom of my mother, that, if we are to grasp the serious implications of the institution of motherhood, it is essential to develop a long-range perspective regarding the lives of women. The fact that things go well for one, or five, or ten years tells us relatively little about the totality of a mother's experience.

36

I am convinced that when a woman becomes a mother, she reaches a definite turning point, a "crunch" point when we become intricately enmeshed in a potentially destructive web of dependency, responsibility and isolation from the public sphere. The denial of anger and negative feelings – because "normal" women, and particularly mothers, are expected to be predominately loving, giving and nurturing – helps to create the depression, guilt and self-blame so common among women. We start to believe that "there must be something wrong with me. If I were a better, more worthy, wife and mother, all would be well. I must be the problem." The accumulated anger and guilt of mothers often emerges during the adolescent years of their children. During this period, the family frequently becomes an arena of serious conflict. The mother in a traditional family has not become more and more loved in return for her self-denial, her committed servicing of the family. She, who may have experienced some sense of power and indispensability in the early years, now begins to experience the extent of her powerlessness and the absence – very often – of reciprocal love and respect.

One of my most liberating and yet frightening experiences as mother of an adolescent occurred during a trip with my husband. Triggered by a very unhappy episode with my daughter, I screamed and cried my accumulated rage for hours within the protective walls of a moving car. Why was this experience at the same time both liberating and frightening? The fear had to do with breaking the taboo of mother love. And the liberation came from claiming my anger and from validating my own painful experience, claiming my own way of being me. My husband had no need to do likewise. The centre of his life was his work, the public sphere, and the self. He accepted separateness and difference because, as with all human beings who have their own distinct lives beyond the family, no one expected him to live through and for others.

In the name of good parenting, mothers often deny both themselves and their daughters an intimate knowledge of what life is really all about. Contemporary feminists are struggling to break through this circle of silence and alienation between mothers and daughters. We are beginning, with difficulty, to understand our own mothers and how their lives were and are circumscribed and damaged in a sexist society. Men often react with hostility to sharing and intimacy between mothers and daughters. It is said to be potentially divisive. This is true, but the fundamental question is who is to be divided from whom, and why? The traditional norm in the family is unconditional loyalty of wife to husband, and distance, if not hostility, between mother and daughter.

Feminists recognize that one way of reducing women's structural dependency on men is to strengthen bonds among women, including the bond between mothers and daughters. This bonding between women strikes at the very heart of patriarchal institutions and potentially loosens the stranglehold of men over women.

Central to the concept of motherhood as an institution is society's attitude towards its children. This society, in theory, values its children most of all. Concern for children is cheap, however, given the ways in which we stifle and stunt their mothers' lives, into whose care we deliver the children. In depriving women of economic independence and of being nurtured, we make it very difficult for mothers to nurture others authentically. I do not wish to justify the practice of judging the quality of women's lives via their children. But I do wish to expose as a myth the prevalent idea that we have designed family structures for the optimal care of children. Depriving women has meant depriving children.

Children suffer in a world where the disparity between rich and poor is increasing, and in which their economic welfare is conditional on their parents' position within society. Because of wage discrepancies between women and men, because of the fact that so many women are forced to live on inadequate public assistance, families are six times as likely to live in poverty if they are economically dependent on the mother.[22] The point I wish to make is that all mothers are entitled, at the very least, to a decent income, to recognition as primary workers both in the home and outside the home, and to free, universal day care. Without the provision of such essentials, our concern for children is shallow.

What I may be accused of, in advocating fundamental change for mothers, is indifference to the fate of children. I would like to state that I am vitally concerned with the lives of children. In our paper, Alma Estable and I developed a number of fundamental entitlements for children:

1   The right to be cherished, nurtured, protected and educated as separate individuals, regardless of who their biological parents are or the legal relationship between them;
2   The right to be nurtured and receive physical care from individuals of both sexes, rather than solely from the mother and other women;
3   The right to healthy models of human development where respectful and equal adult lives are the norm, and women are not reduced to subservience and service;
4   The right for girls and boys to grow into full adults, where girls are not being streamed into limited definitions of womanhood and where boys are not exempted from nurturant behaviour in the name of masculinity.[23]

I consider it very important that women begin to break their economic and psychological dependence on men, children and the traditional family, and begin forging primary bonds with women as important people in their lives. To create the conditions which allow for the forging of vital bonds among women, an autonomous women's movement is essential. The very existence of a women's movement helps women to support each other in fighting for their human rights and entitlements as full, adult citizens.

It is important to remember, however, that organized feminism has historically yielded the primacy of its own objectives to the greater good, and subsequently been buried and forgotten. This must not happen again. As Adrienne Rich says, "There is enormous pressure–a pressure, I think, on everybody but specifically on feminists–to yet once again shelve feminist issues, or what are seen as 'merely' women's issues rather than human issues...and save the planet from nuclear holocaust."[24]

It seems imperative that we, as social workers, develop radical new ways of working instead of helping women adjust to destructive prescriptions for motherhood. It is impossible, however, to take the first step towards a feminist redefinition of women's issues without being rooted in a well-developed feminist framework oneself. The answers to political dilemmas do not lie in therapeutic blueprints. They most often lie in a redefinition of the struggle itself.

I think that bringing women together in both personal and political ways could be a central task for social workers. It involves a major shift in our thinking, from treating women as "unmarried mothers" or "inadequate personalities," to dealing with the larger issue of consumers as an oppressed group, for example. If, as social workers, we are seriously concerned with depression, guilt, low self-esteem, fears and isolation among women, we will make "networking" our main thrust. The theory of helping people help themselves has got waylaid and needs to be re-introduced into our work, that is, if we can manage to resist the "us and them" syndrome and the categorizing and labelling that undermines consumers and makes us sound expert.

It seems to me that agencies and other social work settings could transfer some of the staff-development time and money which is now used for family therapy, for example, to a program for educating staff about the oppression of women. I think that hiring practices need to change as well. We need to employ women who bring a feminist perspective to their work and to see that perspective as a source of strength, as an important skill. Many settings still consider feminist concerns a detriment, something that will interfere with proper professional practice. We have a long way to go!

A feminist approach to practice literally requires us to respect the rights of consumers in clear and unequivocal ways, that is: the right not to be psychologized, categorized and pathologized; the right to attend all conferences concerned with our own lives and struggles, with advocates of our choice; the right to open files; the right to question workers about their values and ways of working; the right to request a specific worker of our choice; and the right to expect that providers of services practise personal self-disclosure as one means of avoiding a one-up, one-down relationship. It constantly amazes me how social workers and other people in the helping professions expect others to share endless details of their own lives, the suffering, the pain and the hurt, and somehow manage to share very little, if any, of their own.

I consider it essential for feminist social workers to organize, formally and informally, both outside and inside the workplace. We are often blocked when we first try, but there are ways around any impasse. One of the most exciting developments I have observed across the country this past year has been the gathering together of women social workers to support one another in developing new approaches to their work with women, to help ensure that feminism remains at the centre of their concerns.

In conclusion, I think that we really need to write our own prescriptions for motherhood out of our own experience. I think that it is feminism which helps us seize the experience of motherhood for ourselves. I offer no blueprints and am painfully conscious of the paradoxes, the contradictions and the ambiguities, the multiple levels of internal and external complications in all women's lives. There are no straight lines, but there are new and exciting directions to explore. I should like to end by again quoting Adrienne Rich:

What is astonishing, what can give us enormous hope and belief in a future in which the lives of women and children shall be mended and rewoven by women's hands, is all that we have managed to salvage, of ourselves, for our children, even within the destructiveness of the institution: the tenderness, the passion, the trust in our instincts, the evocation of a courage we did not know we owned....The mother's battle for her child...needs to become a common human battle, waged in love and in the passion of survival. But for this to happen, the institution of motherhood must be destroyed.

The changes required to make this possible reverberate in every part of the patriarchal system. To destroy the institution of motherhood is not to abolish motherhood itself. It is to release the creation and sustenance of life into the same realm of decision, struggle, surprise, imagination and conscious intelligence as any other difficult, but freely chosen, work.[25]

4

Poverty:
The Feminine Complaint

Dorothy O'Connell

The title of this presentation, "Poverty: The Feminine Complaint," may cause some of you to think I am going to talk about whining poor women, and perhaps others will think I am implying that women are always complaining. But I am using the word *complaint* meaning, "a statement of wrong, grievance or injury." And it is as a wrong, a grievance, and an injury to women that I wish to discuss poverty today.

The next question that may come to mind is, "Why women?" Surely poverty is a human condition which is nonsexist and nonracist. Right? Wrong. In much of the world today, it is both sexist and racist. It is noticeably so here, in North America.

Ian Adams writes of this in his book, *The Poverty Wall,* published in 1970. Since then, the numbers have grown, not shrunk: "Imagine a city, a walled city of 350,000 adults and 1.1 million children. A city larger than Winnipeg, as big as Vancouver, but different. The weird thing about this city is that it is without men: there are only women. If you can see such a city in your mind's eye, then you are looking at the real and enormous number of abandoned and forgotten people who live silently among us. Because, you see, there are that many women in this country, bringing up their children on marginal incomes and the subsistence that is welfare...because the truth is that the poor in Canada are not only the Metis, the Indians and the blacks, but women, and in the most overwhelming numbers."[1]

The next questions are obvious: Why are women poor? Why so many? Are they lazier? Weaker? Less ambitious? Sicker? What are some of the causes of poverty? Who are the women who are poor?

Is it the women who only have a grade four education? Is it the ones who quit school to become hairdressers? Some of them are. Others are women with

41

university degrees who married someone who left them or inconveniently died, leaving them with young children. Others were business women who worked until they had a nervous breakdown, or they have epilepsy, or diabetes, or they got hit by a car. Some are ordinary women, from middle-class backgrounds, who achieved what they thought was a respectable marriage, only to find that the man of their dreams was an alcoholic, or beat them, or went crazy, or went to jail.

Any woman can be deprived of money any time, if she is not independently wealthy. Granted, under the new family laws, if she worked and contributed money to the home, she is entitled to half. But if all she did was keep the home fires burning, she can forget a pension.[2] But she can keep the kids, usually. And it could happen to anyone: if not you, your mother, or your sister, or your daughter, or your friend.

As Adams points out, if you add all the poor women together, including those working for low wages and the elderly, "then you have a group five times the size of all the poverty-stricken racial groups put together. The majority of the poor in this country are women: it is as simple as that. By conservative addition, there are some three million of them in Canada, almost one-half the number of women over sixteen."[3]

But why us? There must be one main reason so many women are poor. There is, and I think I have found it. If you take an historical perspective on poverty, it is easy to see that it has always been women and children who were poor. Why? Because women and children are considered expendable.

Historically, women have always been expendable. Girl children were exposed to die, or sold for a pittance. They were regarded as worthless. They would not grow up to run the family farm. In fact, the parents would have to scrape up enough money to pay someone else to take them off their hands, eventually. In India today, brides are still being burned by their mothers-in-law if they do not come accompanied by a big enough dowry. Consider this quotation by Robert Mueller: "I asked a Burmese why women, after centuries of walking behind their men, now walk ahead. He said there were many unexploded land mines since the war."[4]

Except in certain circumstances, women have always been expendable. "Surely not here," one might exclaim. In the early years of this continent's European settlement, women, that is, European women, were scarce, and thus valuable. Indian women, on the other hand, were fairly plentiful, and they were still expendable. Western novels are full of the reverence for women folk. This actually lasted only a short time, and even when it existed, it was reverence for some women folk, namely white women. It soon wore off, and women continued to be worked and bred to death. Men may have died by violence in the Old West, by gunshot and storm and stampede, but women tended to die at home, in childbirth, or of old age at fifty. Pioneer graveyards are an excellent place to find out how women were living and dying then.

The legend, of course, is otherwise. "Women and children first," is the rule, supposedly, for lifeboats. But it was always only certain women and children, not the ones in steerage.

With the arrival of more immigrants, many poor women from Europe came as bonded servants, general household slaves. Then, of course, there were the black slaves. After emancipation, there were still some women condemned to do household work for nothing for others, these were generally the women who did not marry, or who had not entered one of the very few occupations open to women, chief of which was becoming a nun and slaving for God.

Then came the machine age, with factories and sweatshops: still not a pleasant existence for the majority of women, although seen through a haze of romanticism now. Always there were certain women who had it better. But let us remember that even queens were usually sold off to the highest bidder. Elizabeth I was the exception, not the rule.

We tend, however, to see history in the light of exceptional women, those who were lucky enough to come of well-to-do parents, marry well-to-do men, and produce well-to-do children. After all, those were the ones who could write, so the history passed down by those women is a history of themselves, not of women generally.

For most women, life was unending drudgery. For every Scarlett O'Hara there were thousands of women married to nobodies, working out in the fields from dawn to dark. We hear a lot about General Washington's wooden false teeth. How much do you want to bet Martha had no teeth at all?

Here are the words of "A Housewife's Lament" written by a Mrs. Sara Price of Illinois (one of the privileged women who could write) at some time around the the time of the American civil war. Presumably, since the nuclear family was not fashionable then, she had some household help:

One day I was walking, I heard a complaining, and saw an old woman the picture of gloom
She gazed at the mud on her doorstep ('twas raining) and this was her song as she wielded
   her broom:
Oh, life is a toil, and love is a trouble, beauty will fade, and riches will flee,
Pleasures they dwindle, and prices they double, and nothing is as I would wish it to be.

There's too much of worriment goes to a bonnet, there's too much of ironing goes to a shirt
There's nothing that pays for the time you waste on it, there's nothing that lasts us but
    trouble and dirt.
In March it is mud, 'tis slush in December, the midsummer breezes are loaded with dust
In fall, the leaves litter, in muddy September the wallpaper rots and the candlesticks rust...

There are worms on the cherries, and slugs on the roses, and ants in the sugar, and mice
    in the pies,
The rubbish of spiders no mortal supposes, and ravaging roaches and damaging flies.
It's sweeping at six, and it's dusting at seven, it's victuals at eight, and it's dishes at nine,
It's potting and panning from ten to eleven, we scarce break our fast till we plan how to dine.

With grease and with grime from corner to center, forever at war and forever alert
No rest for a day lest the enemy enter, I spend my whole day in a struggle with dirt.
Last night in my dreams I was stationed forever on a far little rock in the midst of the sea
My one chance of life was a ceaseless endeavour to sweep off the waves as they swept over me.

Alas: 'twas no dream, ahead I behold it, I see I am helpless my fate to avert.
She lay down her broom, her apron she folded, she lay down and died and was buried in dirt.
Oh, life is a toil, and love is a trouble, beauty will fade, and riches will flee
Pleasures they dwindle and prices they double and nothing is as I would wish it to be.[5]

But why were women considered expendable? Because, as Sir Thomas Beecham remarked, "There are no women composers, never have been, and possibly never will be."[6] Widening that, of course, to include all the other things women have never done, where are all the women geniuses to compare with William Shakespeare, Francis Bacon, and so on? Most of them, obviously, were being buried in dirt, buried at an early age. When little boys were out playing, little girls were learning how to deal with housework and nursing and child-raising and child-bearing and other nurturing duties.

But surely now that we have vacuum cleaners and washing machines and dryers and dishwashers and electric can openers, we have been emancipated. Not really. Robert Heinlein, in *The Door into Summer,* remarks that, "amazingly little thought had been given to housework, even though it is at least 50 percent of all the work in the world...the horse to jet plane revolution had not reached the home...housekeeping is repetitive and unnecessary drudgery; as an engineer it offended me."[7] But supposing all women were released from the drudgery of housework, would they be welcome in the work force? You know the answer to that. Speaking of expendability, who is it that is last hired and first fired? Who is paid the lowest wages? A pamphlet from the feminist action

44

collective in Ottawa says: "The employer can say he doesn't need us because there are lots of women out there looking for work. But he does need women workers as a pool of cheap labour. Our husbands and society say we don't do real work; they say their work supports our leisure…but we know that we work hard and that it is our housework that supports their leisure. Society needs the free work we do taking care of children because otherwise enormous amounts of money would have to be spent to replace our contribution."[8]

So we are regarded as expendable in the work force, expendable at home. How else are we expendable? Any reading of the newspapers will show the enormous numbers of women murdered every year. Think of famous murderers: Jack the Ripper, The Boston Strangler, The Zodiac Killer, Neill Cream, Dr. Crippen, The Yorkshire Ripper. These were all men who were mass murderers of women. But when retentionists talk about bringing back the death penalty, to whom do they want it applied? Do they want it applied to murderers of women and children? No, it is for killers of police officers and prison guards. If you assault a police officer, you go to jail. If you assault a woman, even a complete stranger, you might not. If you assault your wife, it is likely you will be able to walk around with impunity.

If we look at the rest of the animal kingdom, we see something curious. Other animals do not kill their females. In fact, humans do not generally kill female animals. In hunting season, you are allowed to kill stags, but not does. Farmers keep only one bull for a herd of cows. Bull calves get slaughtered for veal, but not heifers. In all nature, humankind values female animals, but this value does not seem to apply to human females.

So women are expendable. What can we do about it? For one thing, we can attach a value to ourselves. Most women put a value on our individual hides, but not on the collective, or, if on the collective, only within certain bounds. Those bounds generally do not include poor women. It is true that women are often the worst enemies of other women. All through history, while most women were dying in poverty and misery, some were not. But few of those women did much to help the others, seeing it as a matter of class, or caste. There were exceptions – Nellie McClung, Emily Murphy – but they were few. Most of them saw themselves as special people who deserved better, or they saw themselves as smarter or prettier, or abler in some fashion or another. They saw it as God's will that there should always be poor women to visit with baskets, while they should thrive. They saw it as a good work to patronize the local widow by giving her the family laundry to do, or giving her worn-out clothes nobody else wanted, dividing in their minds the mass of women into "us" and "them."

Much of the lady bountiful feeling is certainly gone. What remains, among

45

many fairly successful women, is a feeling that poor women do not have to be poor, that if they were not inherently lazy or stupid, they could be right up there with the other women. But think about the ramifications of that: are we really prepared to say, since almost half the women in this country over sixteen are poor, that women are so inferior that almost half of them are born subnormal? Again, from Ian Adams: "But hopefully, for the first time, the women who bear the real burden of poverty in this country are being listened to. And it all happened quite accidentally. When all those nice middle-class ladies with their associations and service clubs pressured government into the appointment of a Royal Commission on the Status of Women, they never thought for a moment that everywhere they went they would be hit in the teeth with the simple fact: the real problem with women in this country is that they are poor. The ladies were even less prepared for the tirades that came from women like Doris Wilson of Regina and Kay Dixon of Victoria, who blasted the nice service club women for treating the poor as a 'project': and asked why one of their own wasn't sitting on the commission. Chairman Anne Francis had to admit that poverty was one aspect of the status of women that 'all the women's groups who pushed for a commission hadn't spent much time thinking about'!"[9]

Obviously, they still have not. A group of poor women in Ottawa approached a political women's group to get support for women on welfare. Most of the "political" women did not want to support them. They wanted to fight against genital mutilation of women in Africa. The fact that there was not much they could do for women in Africa and a lot they could do for women in Ottawa apparently did not occur to them. In fact, when they were going to have a celebration of the fiftieth anniversary of the person's decision in the exclusive and expensive Chelsea Club in Ottawa, and some members pointed out that poor women would obviously not be able to attend, some members got quite snappy, and said that "the poor shouldn't expect that they can attend everything." One almost gets the feeling that it might have spoiled the occasion if women on welfare had turned up like ghosts at the feast.

And the women's media have not been terribly helpful. *Chatelaine* ran a story entitled "Up From Welfare" which, after eulogizing the welfare worker of the woman in question, and explaining how the worker helped get her into school, wound up with the heroine meeting a man in a bar, marrying him, and moving with her children into his trailer.[10] A modern Cinderella story: all you have to do is catch a prince, even if he is a toad with a trailer.

I noticed a story in *Ms. Magazine* some years ago, which was an interview on the women of Appalachia. What I remember most clearly about the story was not any touching account of their poverty, but the fact that every single grammatical error and dropped "g" was included. It seemed to be saying, in brackets, "This is the real thing, folks." The main feeling I got from both magazines was a definite impression that they were not being written for me and my friends, any more than we were being invited to the Chelsea Club.

I should note here that maybe I am being a little spiteful. I sent my manuscripts of the first two Chiclet Gomez stories to both magazines and they bounced back quick as a flash. In fact, when *Chiclet Gomez* was published,[11] and even it had been on cbc for thirty-one weeks, *Chatelaine* refused to review it. I am afraid I believe in my heart of hearts that it was because my view of poor women did not coincide with theirs, and I knew more such women than they did.

Most middle-income women want to believe the myths about women on welfare, because, if they do not, the result is too frightening. They realize that it could happen to them. Through no fault of their own, even though they have been good, they could find themselves on the very bottom of the social scale. Make no mistake: it is the very bottom. There is no one in Canada considered more disgusting, more sub-human, than the woman on welfare.

That is why some women will shoplift before they go on welfare, will bounce cheques, will almost starve themselves and their children before taking that last step. They believe the myth, that the women on welfare are the grasshoppers of the country, singing "The world owes me a living"; and they know they have always been good little ants, full of the Protestant work ethic. The assumption is always there that the woman on welfare wants something for nothing. Raising wheat is work, driving a gargabe truck is work, raising children is nothing.

A professional woman will tell you she has "earned her degree." Therefore, you are supposed to believe that she merits success. An older woman may say that she earned her money by putting up with an unhappy marriage for thirty years before "the stinker" finally died. But what has the welfare mother earned? Misery and grief, obviously. In spite of the fact that we know it is untrue, the mythology is that life is fair, and you get what you deserve. If you do not like the results, too bad. You should not have done whatever it was you did. There is never any feeling that the welfare mother has earned anything, including respect. They made their bed, let them lie in it. In fact, males often suggest that, if women on welfare want to earn money, they should do just that: lie on their backs. Women on welfare are influenced by this myth, too, sometimes to such an extent that they see themselves only by what they are not, not by what they are. "Well, at least I'm not a prostitute, bad housekeeper, child beater." They do not believe, because the newspapers and television and radio and magazines and popular opinion do not believe, that they are working.

Here are the words to "There Must be Something Easier" from the musical,

Red Tape, Running Shoes and Razzamatazz, by The Great Canadian Theatre Company, and based in part on stories from *Chiclet Gomez:*

I hear Johnnie screaming, guess he needs his diaper changed
And I just fed young Julie, but she's hungry now again
I forgot about the dentist, that's twice this month I've missed
And Johnny's skinned his knee, and wants his bobo kissed
And it looks like it might rain and the laundry's on the line
And the telephone is ringing, I'm about to lose my mind...

I've finally got the laundry down; I've waited for a year
For them to paint the living room, the sky is going to clear
And Frank called up this morning, says he wants to try again
But now I've got nine children, and I'd sooner not have ten
And Christ, I've missed my period, I wonder where it went
And the bank account is empty, and I haven't paid the rent
There must be something easier...

Jamie starts school Tuesday, and he needs some better clothes
Every month a couple of inches, my God how fast they grow
There's a tenants' council meeting, and I clean forgot the date
And I finished off a bag of chips, I'll never lose that weight
And Brenda's husband's left her, and she wants to come and talk
And Janet's gone to welfare and her dog still needs a walk.

The kitchen sink is dripping, and the baby's throwing up
I'd love to have a little tea, but I can't find a cup
And the vacuum cleaner's broken, and the kids are raising dust
And the priest is coming over, oh my God, in Thee I trust
Sorry kids, no time to play – go turn on the TV
Good news, at last my period has started, finally
And Frank has called me up again he says he'll pay the sitter
And I tell him to forget it, and he says that I sound bitter
There must be something easier...I'd love to have a job
I'm sure there's something easier, the answer is a job.[12]

Another widely believed story about women on welfare concerns their promiscuity. It is a funny thing, but movie stars can have a series of love affairs, and it is attributed to their beauty; but let a woman on welfare have a couple, and she is loose.

The myth says that women on welfare are prostitutes, fraud artists, child beaters, drug pushers, lazy, incompetent, ignorant and dirty, and, moreover, ugly. They do not care what they look like. They slop around all day in their dressing gowns, eating chips and watching soap operas. At night they go out and blow their welfare cheques on bingo. In order to stay on welfare, they will go right out and have more children. In order to get into public housing, they will go right out and have more children. In order to keep a boyfriend, they will go right out and have more children. And everybody in the country seems to have a close friend who knows a woman just like this.

Most myths generally have a grain of truth in them. There are women who are lonely, and will take love where they find it. Being a single parent is a lonely, exhausting job. You give, and give, and give, twenty-four hours a day, seven days a week, fifty-two weeks a year. No holidays, no one to give you a hug and tell you you are doing a good job. Sometimes they go home with someone they met in a bar, or even let him move in.

A lot of them do not seem to spend much time on their personal appearance. The young ones often look pretty good, but, once over thirty, they lose their bloom pretty fast. A lot of them are overweight, or underweight. A lot of them have no teeth. Their hair is straggly. They do not dress very well. They have a dumb look on their faces. What many people fail to realize is that these things are not a matter of choice. The weight problems are due to malnourishment and stress: too much macaroni and not enough fruit, too many rent raises and moves to worse housing. The teeth are gone for the same reasons. The hair is falling out. They do not have money for hairdressers. The dumb look is from exhaustion, and is a natural defence. In fact, these are the stigmata of poverty. This is what Bertholt Brecht says: "Oh, thoughtless rumour that the poor are base/You shall be silenced by their stricken face."[13] And here is another song from *Red Tape, Running Shoes and Rassamatazz.* It is called "Thirty-two Goin' on Seventy-three":

I used to think my life a bowl of cherries
Everything a girl could want was mine
I had a good man with a job and he kept me very well
Then one day I woke up and he was gone.

I get so disenchanted, and I get so damn depressed
And I never find the time I need to rest
And I'm only thirty-two, but friends, I'm telling you
It feels more like I'm seventy-three.

Well, I tried to understand what went wrong
Then I realized I'd have to push along
I'd have to make it on my own, bring the kids up all alone
Public housing was the only place for me.

And I get so disenchanted, I get so damn depressed
And I never find the time I need to rest
And I'm only thirty-two, but friends, I'm telling you
It feels more like I'm seventy-three.

I looked into the mirror again this morning
And I wondered who it was staring back
Well it soon came clear to me that a life of poverty
Was drawing lines on the girl I used to be.

And I get so disenchanted, I get so damn depressed
And I never find the time I need to rest
Well, I'm only thirty-two, but friends, I'm telling you
It looks more like I'm seventy-three.[14]

That covers promiscuity and ugliness. What about all these children women on welfare are supposed to have? I remember a couple of years ago I was on a talk show in Vancouver, pushing one of my books, and a woman phoned in and asked me how dare I have five children at her expense. All I could think of to say at the time was, "Lady, they were at my expense." But I sat bolt upright in bed that night, realizing what I, like many other people, keep forgetting. Birth control, that is, effective birth control, is a relatively recent phenomenon. When I was producing children, it was not that easy even to get information about birth control. It was, in fact, illegal. Even when I had my last child, and wanted a tubal ligation so I could stop, hospital rules required that my husband sign a paper giving his consent. Luckily for me, he did. But we tend to forget how recent effective birth control is.

The younger generation of women on welfare often have only one child; more than two is unusual. But a friend of mine, when her two children were ten and eleven, suddenly was pregnant again. And I believe that her subconscious did her in. Consciously she was saying, "Well, the children can take care of themselves now, so I'd better see about getting a job and getting off welfare." She got married at seventeen because she was pregnant; she had never worked, and had a grade eleven education. She had no extra training, and did not feel qualified to do anything. I know that she did not consciously decide to get pregnant and stay on welfare. But I think that many women, not just those on welfare, panic and get pregnant. I should say that, following this baby, she also had her tubes tied.

But what about all these teenagers getting pregnant and going on welfare? They do not all come from a poor background, but they certainly do end up on welfare. Do you remember this old rugby song?

50

Poverty: The Feminine Complaint

She was poor, but she was honest,
Victim of the squire's whim:
First he loved her, then he left her,
And she lost her honest name.

Then she ran away to London,
For to hide her grief and shame;
There she met another squire,
She lost her name again.

See her riding in her carriage,
In the Park and all so gay:
All the nibs and nobby persons
Come to pass the time of day.

See the little old-world village
Where her aged parents live,
Drinking the champagne she sends them;
But they never can forgive.

In the rich man's arms she flutters,
Like a bird with broken wing:
First he loved her, then he left her,
And she hasn't got a ring.

See him in the splendid mansion,
Entertaining with the best,
While the girl that he has ruined,
Entertains a sordid guest.

See him in the House of Commons,
Making laws to put down crime,
While the victim of his passions
Trails her way through mud and slime.

Standing on the bridge at midnight,
She says: 'Farewell, blighted Love,'
There's a scream, a splash – Good Heavens!
What is she a-doing of?

Then they drag her from the river,
Water from her clothes they wrang,
For they thought that she was drownded;
But the corpse got up and sang:

'It's the same the whole world over;
It's the poor that gets the blame,
It's the rich that gets the pleasure.
Isn't it a blooming shame?'[15]

All that is missing is a small, pitiful corpse on her bosom as she floats downstream. This is considered a very funny song, and is sung in a maudlin tone of voice, accompanied by loud guffaws. But it is not really funny. Recently, I went to an Irish pub for an evening, and the trio sang exclusively (if you can believe it) "love 'em and leave 'em pregnant" songs. They were quite annoyed when I mildly pointed out that there are other songs which qualify as Irish. They had picked those songs as being good pub material – good for a laugh.

But girls are still being "ruint." They do not generally end up in the river, or being driven away in a snowstorm. Now they end up eking out a miserable existence on welfare, instead. What about the males involved? You really could not expect to trap them into marriage and fatherhood before they are ready. And it was not their responsibility to think about birth control. And you cannot expect them to contribute financially.

Most lawyers and practically all judges are men. The penalties on defecting fathers, even if they were married, are not usually too harsh. But if they are, the fathers can always slip over a provincial border, and nobody will follow them. Bell Telephone would follow them if they owed a phone bill, but it is usually easier to harass the wife. If they owed a car payment, the company would follow them. But if they just owe child support, the courts cannot be bothered. Usually the wives or girl friends will not push it, because for one thing, they do not want an angry ex-husband or ex-lover turning up at their door with blood in his eye, and for another, if they are on welfare, they do not get to keep the money anyway. If a child support payment is made, it is deducted from the cheque.

But I am getting off the subject. Yes, even in this age of birth control, teenage girls are having babies. But I do not know why. Nobody seems to. Maybe it is some biological clock. Maybe it is preservation of the species. I often think that if young women can make it past their teenage years, the next dangerous period is not until their late twenties and early thirties. The last dangerous period is when they think they are past it. I think biology has a lot to answer for.

Finally, what about fraud? Yes, women on welfare are committing fraud. Let me tell you about it. How much money is the woman on welfare getting to raise her kids and pay her bills? It varies from province to province, but in no province does it approach the official "poverty line." There is always a shortfall. In Ontario, she gets about half what is defined as the poverty line.[16] There is never enough to cover rent, food, hydro, telephone, transportation, clothing. Certainly, there is nothing for recreation.

A couple of years ago, churches in Ottawa started screaming about fraud. They had found out that some families were hitting more than one church for food vouchers. Sometimes the families were not even parishioners. It did not seem to occur to the churches that they should be screaming "poverty," not "fraud." They did not seem aware of the fact that a fifteen-dollar food voucher does not go very far for a family. They called it "playing the system."

One difference between women on welfare and other women is that the money they receive is not theirs. It is a loan. The family allowance is every mother's right in Canada. But welfare is a loan, payable any time you have money. If you win $500 at bingo, they can take it. If you get a lump-sum insurance settlement, they can take it. If your husband sends child support, they take it. And if they catch you committing fraud, you lose the whole bundle.

Fraud is committed when an estranged husband or a boyfriend stays overnight every so often, even if it cannot be proven he contributed anything but a sunny smile. It is committed by welfare recipients working and not reporting the money. People on welfare are allowed to earn some extra money, but they can get into difficult pay-back situations. A recent case in Toronto involved a woman with six kids who worked part time as a school bus driver. She did not report it. She was thrown in jail for four months as an example. Her children were put into care, as the saying goes. The newspapers applauded the decision, as it would serve as a deterrent to other women. No editorials appeared asking why she should find it necessary to drive a school bus to support her family. Questions about the amount of rent she was paying, and whether welfare covered the rent and the food bills, were never asked. At the time this happened, the top allowance on welfare for rent for heated accommodation was $135 monthly. It has now soared to $185. Normal rents in Toronto are around $400. So she has a criminal record. I thought she should have received a medal.

Perhaps the trouble with women and welfare fraud is that the amounts are not big enough to capture the public's imagination. Or maybe it is that the acts of fraud lack imagination and flair. Almost always they concern either a woman who is working or who is living with a man. In the latter case, it is always assumed that he, *ipso facto,* must have been supporting her. After all, that is what males do. Right?

Now let us look at punishment. You remember that the school bus lady with six kids got four months. Do you remember Clarence Campbell and the sky shops affair? Convicted of conspiring to bribe a senator with the sum of $95,000, Clarence Campbell, former president of the National Hockey League, was sentenced to one symbolic day in jail, and a fine of $25,000. Even though his crime was not in the line of service, so to speak, the NHL Board of Governors unanimously voted to give him $50,000 to pay his fine and legal expenses. Of course, it helps if a former Governor-General turns up as a character witness.

How about Burton Cummings, the rock star? He was arrested in Winnipeg on a charge of possession of marijuana and hashish. The federal government decided to stay the charge against him, on condition that he donate $1,000 to a drop-in centre in Winnipeg. This was so as not to hurt his professional standing in the United States. Roland Penner, now Attorney-General of Manitoba, said this was "confirmation of the citizen's worst fears, that there is one law for the rich, and one law for the poor. It is possible for anyone with an extra $1,000 to buy his way out of a charge."[17] Of course, there was Keith Richards of the Rolling Stones, sentenced, on a similar charge, to play a concert for the blind the next time he happened to be in Toronto.

Well, we know things are different for the rich. Now how about this example? In Ontario, drinking drivers who are employed men are sentenced to weekends in jail, so they will not lose their jobs. Such weekends are from Friday night to Saturday noon.

Recently in Ottawa, a welfare mother was convicted of fraud. The judge said he felt compassion for her, and realized that she, being French, might not have understood she was committing fraud when she did not inform the welfare department that one of her children was in a residential school, and so continued to get support for that child. (The forms, of course, are all in English.) Out of the goodness of his heart, therefore, the judge sentenced her to spend her time in jail from 6 a.m. Tuesdays till 6 a.m. Fridays, every week until her sentence was up, so that she could spend her weekends with her children. A heart of gold has that judge.

Now, let us talk about the way welfare fraud is reported. Suppose a welfare mother is charged with earning $200 a month and not reporting it, and she is caught after two years. She is charged with one count of fraud for every month she did not report it. The papers say she is charged with twenty-four counts of fraud, which is pretty impressive. She is not charged on the basis of the amount she earned, that is, twenty-four times $200. She is charged with fraudulently getting welfare funds from the government, even though everybody knows she could not possibly have lived on $200 monthly. If she gets $5,000 yearly to support her family, therefore, she is charged with defrauding the government of $10,000.

Some years ago, nine thousand people committed fraud. They were all middle class. Maybe you remember this. The government was giving first-time homeowner grants of $1,000 to people who answered no to the question, "Have you ever owned your own home before?" Nine thousand people apparently found the question too difficult, and said no when they should have said yes. They included a Conservative Member of Parliament and a Liberal who worked for the Prime Minister. Nine million dollars was involved. Nobody went to jail. As far as I know, they did not even have to pay it back. The Conservative Member of Parliament is still a Member of Parliament.

Richard Johnson, who is running in Ontario for leader of the New Democratic Party, wrote a letter to the *Globe and Mail* about women convicted of fraud, in which he declared that the real crime was an inadequate welfare system which forced people to commit fraud. The maximum payment in Ontario for one adult and two children per month is $508; with the average rent in Toronto being $449, that leaves $59 a month to feed and clothe three people.[18] Businessmen have spent that much on lunches in a month, and declared it as a business expense on their tax returns.

It costs the taxpayers about $100,000 for every doctor who goes to a Canadian university. Every doctor is subsidized to the amount of $100,000. But if one wants to leave the country to get away from health insurance, perhaps go to the United States to make lots of money, he or she does not have to pay it back. This is called free enterprise.

"Subsidy" is an epithet often thrown at the poor. They are told, with scorn, that they are heavily subsidized. But most subsidized people in this country are not poor. They are businessmen. Pierre Berton, in *The Smug Minority,* points out that every businessman who enjoys a company car is getting government welfare, or everyone who enjoys a fancy tax-deductible pension scheme.[19] We have all heard the businessmen scream when the government threatens to take these subsidies away. Doctors going to conferences are subsidized. Roads are subsidized. Water is subsidized. Air travel is subsidized. The National Arts Centre is subsidized. Health care is subsidized. Public housing is the only housing always referred to as subsidized, yet most home owners have in some way been subsidized by the government. Michael Audain writes that, "In the area of housing, upper- and middle-income earners have benefited very significantly over the years from below interest market rates conferred in the form of NHA mortgages."[20]

Another interesting example of double-speak is the fact that, whenever the word "taxpayer" is used, it is thought to refer only to people who are upper or middle income. It is true that women on welfare do not pay personal income tax. But they are not exempt from provincial sales tax, and when property taxes go up, landlords raise rents. But just let a welfare mother try to tell someone who is screaming at her about welfare, that she pays taxes so their kid can go to university.

In fact, the taxpayer, that anonymous "everyman," is told daily what he will not stand for, and what he wants. He wants, apparently, bigger and better buildings. The new right-wing councillors elected in Ottawa to lower taxes and keep the socialists from throwing away money on pie-in-the-sky schemes, point with pride at the new police station being built at a cost of millions, and at the new super shopping complex. They point with equal pride at their fight against helping with a rent subsidy for the women on welfare. They eventually capitulated (with too little money), but first they wanted to pay for the subsidy by taking away the Christmas bonus or the back-to-school clothing allowance. Their real pride lay in defeating a plan to give single parents a holiday in the summer.

The Province of Ontario had returned 1.4 million dollars to the City; this amount was allocated as the City's share of the public housing subsidy. A group of poor women decided that it would be nice if that money still benefited poor people, and suggested some of it be spent on holidays for poor women. The media in Ottawa took on the job of convincing Mr. and Mrs. Taxpayer what a terrible waste of money it would be. It culminated in a truly awful public meeting. The director of the Children's Aid Society testified that the plan would save thousands of dollars because it would keep children out of care whose mothers, otherwise, would break down; other people who worked professionally with the poor supported the plan (including people from the major psychiatric hospital where these women get their only vacation). The general public, however, turned out and ranted and raved as they had been told they would, and women were the worst. Elderly women with blue rinses and their hands loaded with rings screamed at the young mothers about their morals, their characters, and their leisure habits. It was disgusting. It certainly proved the right wingers were out to save money. In fact, however, they have spent more than the left wingers ever did, but they have spent it on buildings, which the taxpayers can see. Pierre Berton says, "We are always prepared to repair or improve something we can look at, like a road or a causeway. Indeed, we insist on such repairs. But human repairs and improvements remain beyond our ken, and when someone suggests we initiate such a program of renovation on the human body and spirit, he is reviled as a do-gooder making free with our tax dollars."[21]

The women on welfare had made the mistake of assuming it was their tax dollar too. Of the 1.4 million dollars returned last year, and which will be returned every year from now on, not one alderman, no matter how much of a socialist he may be, has suggested putting aside a sum for the poor, even though the money had come from that source. It will be a long time before welfare recipients in Ottawa will feel like asking for anything again. They were humiliated and publicly demeaned. Yet they very rarely ask anything for themselves. When they ask, it is for the children.

At Christmas, there is something called the Christmas exchange in Ottawa.

People donate to it. It is for the poor, but only the working poor. Women on welfare cannot have any of it, because they get a Christmas bonus (thirty-five dollars) no matter what the size of the family. They also get a card in the mail. It tells them to present themselves to the Salvation Army on such and such a date, at such and such a time, to receive one present per child.

Of course, there is no birthday money for the kids. It is very moving to hear a young woman who is scarcely more than a child herself say, "I want a better life for my child than I had." She perceives her life as being over. Last year, I went to a meeting in Thunder Bay, where several of these young women spoke up to welfare administrators. We had shown a videotape of young women on welfare, and the administrators accused us of picking "Charlie's angels" to star in it. They were not familiar with the people they were administering, and did not realize that all the young women in the first four rows were young women on welfare. They had the old "Al Capp" version in their heads–fat, unkempt women, with naked babies under each arm. These young women were saying, "I realize I made a mistake, but don't make my child suffer for it." One of the incidents I thought most poignant was that of a young girl who married at seventeen, became a mother at eighteen, and was deserted at nineteen. When asked at nineteen why she had got married, she replied, "I was young."

Some of the young ones from middle-class backgrounds described their parents' reactions to them. Most of them had been treated like tools which contained some flaw, so were set aside. One of them had been interviewed on television about recreation needed for the children in their public housing. Her parents called her immediately afterward, not to offer congratulations on her interview, which went very well, but to say, "Will you never stop embarrassing us?" The idea, apparently, is that these young women are never to re-appear socially unless they snare some well-to-do male. Of course, as they do not go any place where they might meet such men, this is not likely.

What about work for these able-bodied young women? Well, if you ignore the fact that there is no work, and if there was work, there is no day care, you get pretty close to the Ontario government's thinking. In fact, the work incentive plan the government offered recently to single parents had some real flaws. Our organization tried the program out.

We hired a single parent with two children. The work incentive plan was supposed to allow her $2.50 an hour, plus keeping her and her children covered medically. (Actually, of course, the plan was subsidizing employers who wanted to pay the minimum wage. As we were operating on government grants, we could not pay a decent wage.) She arranged first for day care. This took some time, as it entailed leaving work, taking a bus to the other end of town, and waiting an hour or two to sign forms. Then she had to leave work to go to the welfare office to sign forms. This was also at the other end of town. Then a transfer from the housing authority came through. She could leave her one-bedroom apartment in a high rise for a house with two bedrooms for herself, her son and her daughter, but only if she moved the following Monday. Then she had to re-arrange day care because she had changed districts. She had to switch her children to another school, because they would take her four-year-old all day. Then she had to have an operation for cancer. When she got back from that, she got a phone call from the day-care centre telling her she could not work Mondays as no day care was available. She fought. Then the centre phoned her and told her it was all set, but she could not work Thursdays. Then she got a letter from the school telling her that, although her nine-year-old son had a lot of friends, he was not a sociable child, and the school recommended that she take him one afternoon a week to see a psychiatrist. The day-care centre insisted that, if the school said she should, then she must. Then the psychiatrist told her she seemed hostile!

Most employers find it just too much trouble to hire single parents. Ironically, the press release announcing the work incentive plan concluded with, "The success of the plan depends on the initiative of the women on welfare."[22] If it does not work, it is your fault. It is interesting, too, how many of the people giving her the runaround were women, everyone but the psychiatrist.

You may think, "Oh, well, this is an exceptional case." The only thing exceptional about it was the need for an operation. Otherwise, it is the norm.

If there is no day care and she goes to work, the single parent mother is accused of being an unfit mother, if not downright criminal. People write stories about latchstring children and juvenile delinquency. If there is no day care and she does not go to work, she is reviled for sitting around on her fanny and having no ambition. She never gets credit for doing a job in her home. You know, we have a "ladies' agreement" in this country which says it is strictly taboo to criticize the way somebody else raises her family – unless she is on welfare. Then anybody can get in on the act.

Public health nurses ask the children of the poor publicly what they had for breakfast. If they say they had cereal, then they hear that all children should have an egg, cereal, orange juice, toast and a glass of milk every morning for breakfast, or their mothers are not feeding them properly. Nobody listens when the mother tries to explain that she could feed her children only one meal a day on that diet. If the child does not have running shoes in gym, the teacher may deduct marks. If the child goes to school in gum boots because pay day is not for a week, the mother is going to hear about it. If the child misses school because there is no money for winter boots, the mother is going to hear about it. She is going to hear little lectures on the Canada food rules, and that peanut butter is a good meat substitute; but nobody is going to listen when she says she cannot afford peanut butter any more. She is going to get a lecture on budgeting from someone who has no personal experience with poverty. Nobody is going to tell her she is doing a marvellous job. Finally, she is going to stop answering, and just stand there with the dumb look on her face. Then people stop lecturing her, because they figure she is too dumb to understand, anyway. The dumb look is worn by a lot of poor people. It is a protection. Unfortunately, it works too well, and social workers often believe that the woman is stupid. Teachers think, if the woman is stupid, her children are, too, and treat them accordingly. Robert Bates, coordinator for the inner city schools from the Toronto School Board says, "Streaming begins as early as grade two. We are dead-ending these kids."[23]

Of course, the mother is also accused of discouraging her children from aspiring - and sometimes she does. If a middle-income kid wants a bicycle, his parents may say, "Well, you go get a paper route, and when you've earned half the money, we'll put up the rest." The welfare mother is more likely to say, "You don't want a bike. What do you want a bike for?" She knows she cannot afford to contribute toward a bike. Furthermore, if he gets a paper route, she knows that, if the kid is sick, she will not have the strength to go out and deliver the paper for him. She does not want him to go out and sell cards or chocolate bars for the school to earn credits because she is afraid that, if he loses the money, she will have to pay. If he goes out and mows lawns and shovels snow for pocket money, she knows she may take that money for milk and bread. She may allow her daughter to drop out of school and work behind the counter at some dead-end job because she knows she cannot dress the girl the way the other girls at school dress. She may not let one kid join a recreation program for only six dollars a year, because she has three kids and they will all want to join and she cannot afford eighteen dollars. She may not let her child have free music lessons because she cannot afford to buy or rent the instrument required for the lessons.

One of the reasons Ontario no longer builds public housing is that the authorities figured out that it was dangerous: because public housing was filled with women. One Toronto newspaper actually said these women might find out they did not need men, and that would be bad for the children. Public housing helped a lot of woman, apart from the affordability. If only one family on a street is poor, the kids figure it is all their mother's fault if they do not have a father, or a family car, or a bicycle. If they live with one hundred other families who do not have fathers, cars, or bicycles, they figure that is the way things are. Politicians call that killing initiative. Better to hate their mothers.

You know, people hate the poor. And they hate the look of poverty, but they do not hate poverty. In fact, they blame the poor for poverty. That is like blaming the blacks for the Ku Klux Klan, or blaming women for the fact that men rape them.

In the past thirty years, the percentage of the gross national income going to the bottom 20 percent of Canadian families has dropped. The bottom 20 percent used to receive 4.4 percent of the gross national product; since 1972 it has not risen above 3.9 percent. Income tax reports have shown that the poor families report an average income of $4,118 per year, while the average income of middle-class families is $20,102. The gap is getting bigger. In fact, the latest revised report from the Toronto social planning council, which takes into account the latest raises, shows that the purchasing power of the sole support mother in Ontario has decreased by $945 since 1972.[24]

I am reminded of a letter my son sent me from Costa Rica, where he was serving with Canada World Youth. He was employed on an ecological farm, kicking soil over soy beans. He explained that the soy beans went to feed the pigs and the people. The pig waste went into the pond to feed the algae, which fed the fish, which fed the pigs and the people. There was only one problem. There was a crocodile in the pond. So all the labour went to feed one crocodile. Sometimes I feel this country has a crocodile in the pond.

A Canada without poverty would be in a lot of trouble. This country's economy is based on the existence of poor people. Thousands of people have jobs connected with poverty in one way or another: social workers, public health nurses, clerks in discount and second hand stores, lawyers in legal clinics, doctors in medical clinics, welfare administrators, printing shop employees printing the thousands of forms, government clerks, fraud squad operatives, security guards, bailiffs. The list goes on. But there is never any public acknowledgement of this fact. Perhaps the most striking difference between the poor as employers and other people is that, with poverty, the workers, not the employers, get the raises.

As Herman Miller says in *Rich Man, Poor Man,* "Many people refuse to recognize a simple statistical fact. If a distribution has a middle and a top, it must have a bottom, and somebody must be there. The important question is why they are there and how much they get."[25] Women on welfare know why they are there, and how much they get. To them the important question is not so much, "How do we get out?" or, "Who should be here?" but, "Why does it have to be this bad?" Most of them are not insisting that they should be bank presidents, or even teachers or social workers. Most of them simply want to know why it is so bad to be doing a job they were taught to want, and are doing to the best of their abilities. They want to know why it is important to the country that they be miserable.

Were you aware that the federal government has pencils on which is written, "Misuse is abuse" and the message is "Do not waste pencils"? But there is no objection to wasting millions of women and children. Most women on welfare look forward to getting old, because then they will finally get enough to live on. But a lot of them will not make it that far. Poor women are still dying at a relatively early age. They have heart attacks at forty-eight or fifty-two. The reason is that the years of giving the kids the meat and the fruit and eating the macaroni themselves takes effect. They do not die right away, like the starving of the third world. They linger for a while. But as things get worse, and they are getting worse, there may not be enough for the kids either. We may see rickets come back, and yaws, and scurvy. In fact, I have seen scurvy; scurvy is one of the reasons a lot of these women have no teeth by the time they are in their mid-twenties. And vitamin deficiency diseases can lead to other public health problems affecting more than just the poor.

There are signs, ominous signs, that things are not going to get better for poor women. One such sign was an article which appeared in *Maclean's Magazine* last May; it was a profile of a Sarnia landlord. He was quoted as saying, "What I and other landlords would like to see is these welfare mothers and their families sentenced to dig nuclear waste on Three Mile Island."[26] Sentenced for what crime? Even murderers get parole, but not welfare mothers. They spend their entire lives serving a sentence for poverty. I read the letters column for months after that, looking for some letter which would say that he was a fascist, or one which would ask why he was given national coverage. But I did not see one. I wrote one myself, but it was never published. There were letters questioning where *Maclean's* got the blue candy for a gingerbread house on the cover of one issue, but not one about a man who was proposing genocide.

There was another article recently in *Maclean's* about a new game which comes from the United States and is selling briskly in Canada. In it, a middle-income earner is pitted against a welfare recipient. The middle-income earner is stuck in a dentist's office paying bills, while the welfare recipient stops merrily on the way to the welfare office to sell drugs, turn tricks and hold up banks. The State of New York has banned sales of this game, but apparently it is all right in Canada. The welfare recipients, by the way, are defended by ethnic lawyers. One assumes that means they are not Anglo-Saxon, Protestant, white males.

Those of us who live near the border of the United States and are exposed to their television shows, get ads saying, "turn in a welfare cheat," even though the Department of Health, Education and Welfare in the United States has testified, according to the *New Statesman,* that the incidence of fraud among welfare recipients is about four-tenths of one percent. That is nothing compared with estimates by the Internal Revenue Service that 34 percent of private interest income goes unreported. An ad for an investment company states: "Smith and Barney get money the old-fashioned way– they earn it." Who does not? "Ah," your mind replies, "those bums on welfare." We are back to the idea that they have only earned poverty.

Even the children of the poor are somehow held to the idea of having earned their poverty. Talks about recreation for the children of the poor invariably end with politicians and others saying they have not earned it. Yet what middle-class kid has earned the right to ski lessons, ballet, piano lessons, access to a swimming pool? The answer is apparently that they have earned it with their marvellous pre-birth ability to choose parents with decent wages, who will not fall ill, divorce, die, get hit by a car, or go mad. Many remain complacently assured all their lives that fortune has smiled on them because they earned it.

Many government people say the poor should not have more money because it would kill their initiative. If they were too comfortable on welfare they would not go out to work. It is funny nobody says that of the children of the rich.

One of the arguments poor women hear most often is, "There's only so much pie to go around. Wait until the pie gets bigger." Well, being women, they want to know, if there is a pie, where is Mommie? Because Mommie, we all know, is the one who says, "No, you can't have another piece of pie, Billie, your sister hasn't had one yet," or "Don't take the biggest piece, Philip, that's not nice." With no mommie in control, they know it does not matter how big the pie gets. By the time it gets to them, there will be only crumbs left. And the crumbs do not get any bigger.

The other argument we hear is about responsibility. I do not know if you have ever heard the elephant joke that goes like this: there were these four politicians who had to produce a talk on elephants. The French politician prepared his on the love life of the elephant. The British one spoke on elephants and the empire. The American's speech was entitled "Bigger and Better Elephants." The Canadian wrote: "Elephants: A Federal, Provincial or Municipal Responsibility?"

Anyone attempting to get more money for women on welfare encounters these arguments: it is not good for the women (which is ridiculous); it is not the responsibility of whichever government you are talking to (which is a lie); and there is not enough money (it is true that there may not be enough money allocated to tackling poverty, but there is lots of money). In 1933, governments spent 14 percent of their total expenditures on social welfare programs. By 1960, they were spending 14.1 percent, and 1960 was a good year.[27]

What do these women want? They want proper day-care centres for their children so they can get out and earn a living. Or they want respect given to traditional women's work, so they can stay home and raise their kids properly. They want a guaranteed minimum income. They want human rights legislation. In many provinces, landlords can refuse to rent to women on welfare, even if they cannot refuse because of race or colour. They want enforcement of equal pay statutes. They want better protection under the law and from the law. They want re-training programs so they can find decent jobs. But most of all, they want help for their kids. They know they probably will not find a way out of the poverty trap in their own lifetimes, but they desperately want to find an escape hatch for their children. And it would be nice if these women could get holidays. It would be nice if, on International Women's Day, women paid tribute to poor women. It would be nice if a poor woman was declared "mother of the year" in those magazine contests, and if poor women got a little respect and liking now and then.

Poor women are not generally feminists. By playing up the right to work, and the right to leave the home, and by not acknowledging that some women think that homemaking is their work, I think the feminist movement has helped to down-grade women who do not choose to, or cannot, work outside the home. Some women feel contempt for those who stay at home.

The feminist movement in general seems to me to be elitist. Feminists and poor women are often on completely different tracks. I am reminded of a program run by the Women's Credit Union in Ottawa for training women on welfare to work in money institutions. When their first trainee got a job outside the credit union, she was asked how it was going. "It's wonderful," she said, "three men pinched me." Those women fighting sexual harassment at work would not have thought it was wonderful; but this woman had been unnoticed for so long, she thought it was marvellous.

It is the same with rape crisis centres. Most poor women are not very interested in them, or in "take back the night" marches. That is not what their worries are about. Some of them may even make jokes like, "Rape? I should be so lucky." I am not saying that sexual harassment and rape crisis centres are unimportant. They are important. But to a woman who cannot afford to buy her kids underwear, they seem irrelevant for the moment.

If she were financially secure, she could turn her mind to other concerns. Contrary to what one might expect, it is easier to organize low-income women to fight for change when times are relatively good. When going to a meeting means you have to pay a babysitter, which means you may be short a loaf of bread and a carton of milk the next day, you do not go. There is also a natural reluctance to read a brochure that warns you that times are getting worse. You do not want to hear about it, because today was terrible enough. You may remember Cassandra, who went around prophesying doom. Cassandra was always right, but never listened to. She was not exactly what you would call popular, either.

A few years ago, a friend and I, who were doing a lot of agitating, realized that we felt we lived in a village next to a sleeping giant, and we were deliberately going up and kicking him, saying, "Move over!" The neighbours did not necessarily appreciate the fact that the giant might wake up and notice them. Most of them really wanted us to shut up and leave things alone.

Sticking your head in the sand, however, does not really make you invisible. On one International Women's Day, we managed to get forty low-income women to march on Parliament Hill. It was the first time we had been recognized as a women's group, and we had been invited to participate by the Women's Centre. In the planning sessions we had tried to point out, as delicately as we could, that poor women do not necessarily want to be allied with any other group that is not popular. We thought we had got our point across, but we almost lost the whole group, which was the largest contingent there, at the gates to the Parliament Buildings. Every sign they could see said, "lesbian rights now." The only way we could get them to go up on the Hill was to tell them to hold their signs up in front of the others. This was not exactly solidarity.

Another group of women held a political meeting right outside Toronto's Regent Park, the largest public housing community in North America. Ten thousand people live there. I was invited to be a guest speaker. I tried to tell them nobody from Regent Park would come. The other speakers were from "Beaver" (a feminist organization for prostitutes), a lesbian mothers' group, and one concerned with child abuse. There was no way that women on welfare were going to ally themselves voluntarily with these groups and thus justify, they thought, the public image of women on welfare. It was a good conference, but nobody came.

So when I talk about women not supporting other women, it is not a one-way street. A lot of work has to be done. But I am convinced that we can all work together. Elizabeth Cady Stanton said: "Social science affirms that a woman's place in society marks the level of civilization."[28] I have a sign in my office which says, "I swear it to you...I swear on my common woman's head... the common woman is as common as a common loaf of bread...and will rise."

I am asking you, therefore, to help the rest of us common women rise.

Help us by fighting prejudice against women on welfare. Help us by asking politicians when they are going to raise the subsistence level of these women, and argue with them when you get a stock answer. Lobby for a return of the subsidy on powdered milk. Ask questions about obscene profits in the food industry. Lobby for more money for social services. Lobby for more jobs for women. Attack any cuts in social services, or unemployment insurance, or training allowances. Remember us when you ask for raises in your own field.

Whenever there is an increase in welfare payments, the minimum wage goes up. Helping women on welfare, therefore, may help all women in low-paying jobs. An Ontario cabinet minister was honoured a couple of years ago by the restaurant industry for his help in keeping the minimum wage for waiters and waitresses in licensed establishments down. He once made an unthinking remark in the House of Commons, about women, "as a race," not being well informed. He got jumped on. But sometimes I wonder if, for once, he did not hit on something.

Maybe women are a "race." Maybe the ability to reproduce, and the glands and emotions that go with it, is a more important difference among people than what colour your skin is, or whether or not your hair curls. Maybe every woman who contributes to discrimination against other women is guilty of racial discrimination against her own race.

I would like to close my presentation with the words to an old song, "Bread and Roses." Many people say it is old fashioned. I remember a piece of washroom graffiti that says, "Forget roses, give us raises," but I think the words still pertain to many of us who are straggling along behind:

As we come marching, marching, in the beauty of the day
A million darkened kitchens, a thousand mill lifts grey
Are touched with all the radiance that a sudden sun discloses
And the people hear us singing Bread and Roses, Bread and Roses.

As we come marching, marching, we battle too for men
For they are women's children, and we mother them again
Our lives shall not be sweated from birth until life closes
Hearts starve as well as bodies, give us bread but give us roses.

As we come marching, marching, unnumbered women dead
Go crying through our singing their ancient cry for bread
Small art and love and beauty their drudging spirits knew
Yes, it is bread we fight for, but fight for roses too.

As we come marching, marching, we bring the better days
For the rising of the women is the rising of the race
No more the drudge and idler, ten that toil where one reposes
But a sharing of life's glories, Bread and Roses! Bread and Roses![29]

5

Native Women and the State

Marlene Pierre-Aggamaway

When I became involved in the native women's movement and in the general native movement fifteen years ago, I, like others, believed that anything I could imagine vividly and that I desired ardently-like equality and justice for native people in this country-would come about. I believed in this so much that I worked every moment of my life for it. I slept it; I ate it; I greeted every obstacle with optimism; I believed that all those things that I was fighting for must come to pass. After fifteen years, from my own perspective, very little has happened.

Through the enactment in 1953 of Section 12(1)(b) of the Indian Act, by which native women lost their legal status as Indians if they married men without status, the government provided an issue to divide the people.[1] Our native leadership continues to deny the legal rights of native women. And, much to our dismay, our own women have become entangled in this legal dilemma. What better way is there to destroy a people than to take away the rights of women?

In 1972, I was involved in a study of the housing needs of native people in the community of Thunder Bay. We found that 51.8 percent of the people interviewed were single parents. The average size of their families was five persons and the average income was $5,000 a year. These families were dependent on some form of social assistance, lived in substandard housing, and tended to live in the poorer parts of the city. Today I am involved in a study of the employment needs of native women and the statistics have not changed that much; 51.2 percent of native women are single parents, the average size of their families is 4.2 persons, the average income is $8,000 and these families are still dependent on some form of social assistance. In our community then, despite all our efforts and those of a government supposedly committed to creating a better life for native people in this country, there has been no real change.

Reports such as *Indian Conditions,* from Indian Affairs and Northern Development, document the economic and social conditions: the poor and overcrowded housing, the polluted water supplies, the alcohol and drug abuse, the suicide rate, the number of people in jails, the number of people who do not complete their education.[2] When we look at such reports, we have to question our present relationship with the government. We have to question who we are, why we are here, and where we intend to go.

In "Indian country," it is the women who pass on the ways in which we are to arrange ourselves as families, the ways in which we arrange ourselves in our communities. Passing on the ways was always our responsibility. In clan societies, in a matriarchal society, it was also the women who selected the leadership. But one of the sad facts about the condition of native women today is that, although we have the responsibility to pass on that which makes up the Indian system, we ourselves do not know our heritage. Anthropologists may know more about us than we know ourselves. Some of us do not know our language; we do not know our culture nor do we understand how it can be lost.

We have not begun to address these basic issues in our own world and yet we are expected to respond rationally to a government that has created these problems for us. We have to say, "Well, this is how it should be," when we have not been able to put the whole story together and believe in it. We, as native women, have also to contend with the attitude of almost all of the Indian leadership in the country: our place is at home. We are supposed to be ten paces behind men, not beside men or in front of men or wherever we want to be.

Out of our own concerns, therefore, and out of our recognition that nothing would be done until we became involved in a discussion of our own affairs, we began to organize. In Ontario, we formed *Anishinabequek* locals of native women in the communities. We had tea parties, bannock-making sessions, knitting sessions and beading sessions. Women started talking, not about their beading designs, but about what was happening in their families and in other families in the community. In time, these locals across Canada came together at the provincial level and then at the national level in the Native Women's Association of Canada. We tried, through groups such as Indian Rights for Indian women, to disentangle the disorder created by Section 12(1)(b). We attempted, while fighting a legal battle, to find answers for ourselves to the economic and social disarray of our own and our families' lives. We began to speak in public forums as well as amongst ourselves. About two years ago, recognizing that we seemed always to be reacting to the government rather than planning a good future for our children, we decided that we had to become more political and much more organized in the ways we presented ourselves to the government and the people.

Now, as an association and as native women, we face the consequences of the patriation of the constitution. When I was the president of the Native Women's Association of Canada, I was criticized by some for the stand I took, which was that Section 12(1)(b) must be removed from the Indian Act, but there is something more integral to our survival, and that is the entrenchment of aboriginal and treaty rights in the constitution. Many of the women in our movement, however, did begin to pay more attention to the issue of patriation of our constitution because native women had more to lose than the denial of their status through marriage. If Section 12(1)(b) was to be removed, how much would that help a people – men, women and children – who had already lost their rights? If every court in the country could take away my rights, I could be a status Indian in Ontario and not in Alberta. What kind of confusion would that create in our own Indian world?

Although we have attempted as an organization to be more political and to bring our concerns about aboriginal rights to the public, we have encountered many problems. I think that Canadian society in general has been determining our needs as it has perceived them. Non-native women's organizations do not seem interested in native women's concerns. And native women have had even less opportunity to express their concerns than have other women. The Indian leadership still says that it is representing the views of native women and it is not. It continues to exclude one of the most vital elements in the native movement, that is, the native woman. More discomforting and terrifying to me is that the status Indian leadership will speak only for the status Indian constituency. You are a "real, true-blue Indian" only if you have status and live on a reserve.

Having been classified as a Metis, as a non-status person, and now as a status Indian, having lived in a city all my life, and having had to deal with discrimination whether I was or was not a status Indian, I believe that all native people, including women, have aboriginal rights in this country no matter where they live, no matter what distinctive category has been assigned to them. I should be able to travel the world and still have the right to be recognized as a member of the Ojibway nation.

Thus, while native women are trying to assume their own rightful place in the home and in the community, they are also trying to assume their rightful place in the decision-making process of the country. Because we thought the native leadership was not saying what we believed in, the Native Women's

Association of Canada appeared before the Senate Committee during the constitutional hearings. Even we were surprised that we did it. But once we had started talking about the constitution, once we had started talking about patriation, once we had started talking about Indian government, we realized that these subjects, although abstract and intangible at the present time, have roots in our history as a matriarchal society.

Some of us are already telling our Indian leaders that they are not our leaders: Indian leadership comes only when leaders have demonstrated to us their capabilities to make wise decisions and to speak to every need, not only to their own need. That is a form of power, to be able to say, "You cannot be my leader. I will not let you be my leader. I want to choose someone who will speak for the majority of the native people in this country." I still believe that the majority of native people in this country have not yet spoken about their ideals and beliefs.

I believe, however, that native women are moving ahead. Their sensitivity to the family, to who they are, convinces me that we are going to win this battle of aboriginal rights. I believe that many more of the native people are beginning to understand the political process and are beginning to question our relationship with the provincial and federal governments, are beginning to question whether we should establish our own government. There will be much discussion in the next five years about the form which that government would take.

What are the issues that we, as native women and as native people, must deal with in the future? Central to everything is sovereignty: the power to make decisions for ourselves, whether we are Indian or non-Indian. For many of us, the ultimate solution is in the exercising of our people's sovereignty according to our culture and traditions. It was to this end that we spoke out on the Canadian constitution. It is our belief that only with the return of our sovereignty will discrimination be lessened. We have confidence enough in our traditions and culture to know that native women will then be able to take their rightful place in the future of our people.

We are, at the present time, at least in my province, organizing "down-in-the-home" or "up-in-the-home" discussions, because we believe that our power is in our homes. We are preparing easily read interpretations of what the constitution is, what aboriginal rights mean, and we are encouraging native women to talk about these issues. We are gathering dollars to allow our women to meet on a regional basis. We do not want native men or the government to tell us what aboriginal rights are. We want to say for ourselves what they are and we believe we can do that through a quiet, organized approach and a demonstration of our willingness to learn.

In the political context, one cannot deny the impact of the Indian Act in terms of defining who is, and who is not, an Indian. On behalf of the three-quarters of our people who are not governed daily by the Indian Act, we must continue to put pressure on the federal and provincial governments to end their squabbles over, and their denials of, responsibility for jurisdiction. There are those who call for the withdrawal of the Indian Act and who want instead aboriginal government for all native people. Native women, like myself, who are concerned with obtaining rights for all native people, are attracted to this proposal.

Provincial governments have a particular responsibility to come to an agreement with the federal government because the people of the provinces benefit directly from the use of the land that belongs to us. Many non-natives become angry at our saying that the land belongs to us. They think they bought it from us, and, therefore, they have no further responsibility to the people who were here before they came. They, the non-natives, say that we are not contributors to the economy, that we are always "on welfare." My answer to that is, "You are only paying your rent. In some cases, you are not even paying your rent. You have destroyed the houses you are living in. You have destroyed the lakes from which you drink. It is about time for you to give us some answers about what you are going to do. Being an Indian, I am not going to, nor do I want to, throw you off your land; but I want you to assume the responsibility you took when you first began to live on the land, and that is to care for it."

This is my premise: The length of our future as a recognizable race of people depends upon our will to survive and, ultimately, on an order of government which encompasses the principles and beliefs of our culture and, thereby, the arrangements of our economy, our social life, and our system of justice. That is the base from which I work; I cannot trust any other government to decide for me how I must live in the future. We must, therefore, take hold of the future by beginning now to determine who we are. We must focus our attention on the native communities, not only within the physical boundaries of the reservations, but wherever we may find ourselves whether it be in a rural, isolated village, or in a large, urban centre. There is as much a role for native women in this as there is for native men, and we must work quickly as the government of Canada has given the aboriginal people one year to examine and produce a definition of aboriginal rights.

Once we understand our history and the Indian laws that governed us in the past, we must consider our future. If sovereignty is central to our survival, then economic development is central to the success of sovereignty. What kind of economic development are we talking about? Some forms of economic development involve technologies which are not only dangerous to the existence of native cultures but also affect the physical quality of life. How does economic development affect native women? Who should benefit from our efforts? In the historical past, native women had an integral part to play in economic development. Today, native women are expected to be concerned with the family and with the social and cultural development of the community. They are not perceived as being direct and full participants in the economy; they are only adjuncts to the economic and political structures of Indian and Inuit societies. Economic development is often seen as a process into which native women can be integrated at specific points; these specific points are identified out of a perspective of native women being primarily concerned with the family and with the social and cultural development of the community. There seems to have been an acceptance of the myth that women's roles are limited, and, in the economic sphere, directly related to the roles of their men.

The change in status of native women began with the arrival of the Europeans and with the subsequent imposition of dependency on Indian and Inuit societies by the Canadian government. Prohibition of traditional culture and of religious rituals, alien social systems, and the introduction of non-traditional coping mechanisms such as alcohol, placed incredible pressure on the community, seriously damaged the family unit, and altered the roles of native women. A major factor was the introduction of the wage economy. Native women's work began to resemble women's work in general. Recent economic strategies, particularly those instituted by Indian Affairs and Northern Development, have provided little job security and a poor standard of living.

Native women are concerned about the water pollution from industrial waste and the air pollution from factories. We are concerned about land being flooded to create lakes for hydro-electric energy for everyone but us, and pipelines being built for the benefit of other countries rather than for our country. We raise these concerns, not to indicate a lack of confidence in the strategies proposed by our own people, but to point out the need to reconcile the various objectives of economic development with the pressures of a modern technological society. We realize that our development does not depend on a return to the past or an out-of-hand rejection of non-native technologies, but on a blending of our cultural, economic, social and political aspirations with the appropriate tools of today. We want to take from the past, blend it with the present, and come out with something that is acceptable to and can be carried out by native people.

If we argue that social development can also find positive examples in the traditional economies, then people shout that the day of the buffalo has ended and that such thoughts belong in the romanticist's archives. Many native communities now suffer from an almost total dependence on federal funding for their very existence. If the funders can claim any success at all, it is in the acculturation of the native people. Communities which were once self-sufficient are now virtually assimilated into the Canadian economy or, more correctly, the welfare economy. This has been brought about by a government policy – and I believe it is a policy – of acculturation and its administration by Indian Affairs and Northern Development. Federal funding has brought our people money but it has also purchased our dependence.

Culture and economy are inseparable. Many people today have come to accept culture as being the music, dress and language of a people. (This, in my view, is the definition used by Indian Affairs and Northern Development.) But cultures are inconceivable without an economic base. Even spiritual life revolves to a considerable extent around the ways people see their lives supported. Indeed, people's relationships to others and to their environments may be moulded by the ways in which they meet their needs, and a manifestation of those ways may be what we call culture. People who only promote music and costume making are not promoting culture.

One of the alarming aspects of the loss of a culture is that, in the absence of processes which meet a people's needs, social disintegration takes place. That is why acculturation can be associated with alcoholism, suicide, family disintegration and all the other social ills for which the federal government has programs. This is a model of colonialism: first, one creates the problem through the destruction of the native economy and then one offers welfare programs as a remedy. The logical answer to that destructive process is for the native people to develop or re-develop their own economies. The technologies must be low cost and ecologically sound; the tools and skills should be under the control of local communities and should use locally available resources.

Many people are looking to the Canadian government for assistance with their economic problems, but people cannot invoke native sovereignty in one breath and demand that Canada enact its trust responsibility in the next. The native people cannot enact sovereignty when they are dependent on federal dollars for their every need from housing to education to the food on the table. These issues are intertwined. To develop economic self-reliance, a people must exercise sovereignty and to exercise sovereignty, the native nations must achieve economic self-reliance. The value of appropriate technology is that it can provide the means for controlling our own lives. Returning to native people real control over their own lives must be the primary goal if we, as a native people and as native women, are to survive, and perhaps even to prosper.

But that is in the future. Today, as one may gather from this presentation, native women are angry, frustrated and full of an inner turmoil about the condition of their lives. There is a sense of urgency evident among us. As women, we are dealing with a double stereotype – of Indians and of Indian women. We are facing daily the discomforts of being at the lower end of the social and economic scale. We are constantly defending ourselves, in the streets, in the courts, and in the government, from the more powerful gentry in this country. Our frustrations are furthered by our lack of a sense of self, by a lack of self-recognition. Perhaps the most frustrating, and possibly the most insistent and devastating problem is our inability to cut across status lines. We must do away with the notion that only those holding status are Indians. The Indian leadership, by accepting this notion, is encouraging assimilation of many of the native people, and is actively denying the aboriginal people their rights and heritage.

When I am really angry, I usually go into a corner and write. Recently I read an article by one of our native leaders in which he blamed the Metis and the non-status Indians who were attempting to represent the interests of those without legal status in this country for the loss of a minor battle during the period of the patriation of the constitution. I became very angry and wrote this poem, with which I should like to conclude my presentation:

Who do you think you are to say or not to say
I am me
Who are you to say, my brother, that I am not me
My blood is the mother of me, no one not even man
Can tell me I am mother,
For it is I who bear the child
And the child becomes the father of man
Laws – fake laws – you cherish
White laws you cherish and Indian laws I cherish
Indian laws, my brother, you abandon
My right to my heritage, you abandon
My link to the original
You deny my being to create and me.
Who gave you the power?
If blood does not speak, I cannot speak
Nor can you.
Nor can you, my brother – only if I have borne you.

6

Feminist Counselling:
Approach or Technique?

Helen Levine

Rather than dealing with the question of "approach or technique" directly and immediately, I am going to weave my comments in and out of my way of looking at various aspects of feminist counselling. I should say that when speaking about feminist ways of working, I usually insist upon a critical analysis of the condition of women in a patriarchal society, because I consider it fundamental. However, in the context of this conference, I have a sense that I can consider the oppression of women as a given, and move on from that base.

I want to comment briefly on how I became a feminist counsellor and how feminists view the commonality of girls' and women's lives. I came to this approach by way of trying to combine my experience and skills as a social worker with my awareness and experience as a woman. It began as an attempt to translate into practice changing perceptions of myself and other women in this society. As with most of us, this development did not arise apart from changes and crises in my own life.

It is important for me to state that I have been on both sides of the institution and the desk, as provider and consumer of service, at different times of my life. I emphasize this, not to be glib about crackups, breakdowns, depressions, or the kinds of pain and hurt in women's lives, but to share "the personal" with you. Some of us here may seem to have been more fortunate than others but, as women in a sexist society, not one of us is safe, not one of us is fully confident, not one of us has made it, and not one of us is an exception. The point in sharing one woman's experience, any woman's experience, is to get at the commonalities in every woman's life, to link personal and political in the service of change.

Several years ago, during a time when I was barely coping with my life, I spoke on a panel at Ottawa University. Inside, I was feeling, "My God, I won't be able to open my mouth. I'll cry or choke or break down on the spot." I managed, just. Three women came up to me afterwards and said, "We really liked what you said. But, you know, we'd never be able to do it. You've got so much confidence, a kind of security or 'togetherness' that we don't have." My response was to share with them the insecurity I was feeling, how scary that whole task had been, how difficult it is for women to speak in public. I think it is important to talk about our real fears openly, because otherwise we miss the connections between one woman and all women; this is absolutely fundamental to feminist counselling.

Beginning with my own experience, connecting my struggles with those of other women, is central to being a feminist and to feminist counselling. What I am going to say is based on the premise that what happens to other women in this society can or does happen to me, and vice versa. Despite class and individual differences, despite uniqueness of temperament and personality, the broad outlines of women's lives are strikingly similar. We have been taught, for example, to define the central and primary task of our lives as marriage and motherhood. We have been conditioned to view happiness and contentment within restrictive and limiting contexts. Often, the absence of severe problems with a mate, rather than the presence of a rich and challenging life, is seen as the good life for women. Men become husbands, fathers and workers. Women are not supposed to aspire to such an integration of life if it is in any way disruptive to others, if in any way it impinges significantly on men's needs and aspirations, or on the lives of children. This is partly what patriarchy is all about. Women have been directed to be loyal, first and foremost, to individual men in their lives, and to blame themselves or other women when trouble emerges. Under such conditions, solidarity among women in pursuit of change has been profoundly undermined.

Contemporary feminist thought, building on feminist movements of the past, describes the world as having been historically defined by men and for men, with women seen primarily as property, as servants within and outside the home, and as marginal to the fundamental issues of historical struggle and change. Many women reject this perception of the status of women in society, one of the reasons being, perhaps, that we have been well trained to police one another's conformity to the status quo. The ways in which women direct their anger and energy is a very important question that has to do with power differentials between women and men in both private and public spheres.

Feminists no longer trust knowledge or theory that lacks a clear connection with the daily reality of women's multi-level struggles to survive in, let alone change, a male-defined society. Dorothy Smith has this to say: "The practice of ruling is largely if not exclusively the prerogative of men....Our means of knowing and speaking of ourselves and our world are written for us by men who occupy a special place in it....In learning to speak our experience and situation, we insist upon the right to begin where we are, to stand as subjects of our sentences, and to hear one another as the authoritative speakers of our experience."[1]

The consequence of woman's subordinate place in a sexist society, where we are used as handmaidens to men, as cheap or unpaid labour, is a mass schizophrenia among girls and women. We grow up with opposite pulls within us: on the one hand we want to grow into full, vital human beings; on the other hand, we are required to control and contain our lives and define them in terms of others. When I say *schizophrenia,* I am not applying an over-used and abused psychiatric label. I am using the term in relation to the very real splits in our lives. The inevitable conflicts engendered by our growing up female and second class frequently create severe personal difficulties at one time or another in women's lives. It is then that we are most frequently perceived by the helping professions as inadequate, irresponsible, sick or abnormal, as objects (called patients or clients) who must be assessed, diagnosed, treated and, in fact, often controlled, blamed and punished.

We are not seen, and we have not been seen, by those very same helping professions as one of the major oppressed groups in this society, struggling with the poverty, subservience and indignity built into the very structure of our lives. I give tremendous credit to the contemporary women's liberation movement for having forged a new and important link for women between personal pain and political oppression. The women's movement asserts that the ways in which women and men share their labour, money and decision-making power at the domestic level are intimately linked with our lack of power, in shaping the societal structures, institutions and goals that affect each and every one of us.

A feminist critique of conventional counselling includes the serious charge that its theory and practice have left us a legacy of scapegoating women. Under the guise of expert and sophisticated definitions of normalcy developed primarily by men, women have been kept firmly tied to the traditional institutions of marriage and motherhood. One woman, who had been on tranquillizers for ten years, said, "I use these drugs for one purpose, and one purpose only, to protect my family from my irritability."

How is it that a woman's health is permitted to be sacrificed for others in this way? Why do we train women to drug themselves into a denial of their own needs and aspirations on the altar of family well-being? What happens when women try routes other than drugs or docility? The following is an example of the dangers lurking within the medical profession and elsewhere (social work is no exception) in relation to defining the struggles women present when we seek help. This is an excerpt from "The Angry Woman Syndrome" by psychiatrist Nathan Rickles. (Note that we are not only blamed for our anger, but have also become a "syndrome.") Rickles writes: "Specific common denominators in the angry woman syndrome set it apart from any present-day classification. These symptoms are periodic outbursts of unprovoked anger, marital maladjustment, serious suicide attempts, proneness to abuse of alcohol and drugs, a morbidly oriented critical attitude to people and a contrary obsessive need to excel in all endeavors, with an intense need for neatness and punctuality."[2]

This diatribe against women, under the guise of diagnostic classification, is a chilling example of how women themselves are clinically blamed for the anger, desperation and even excellence that are part of our lives. The political and personal context of our lives in marriage or beyond is not considered. The Catch-22 of women's lives comes clear: submission, dependency and conformity create hazards for us, as do our anger and desperation.

Be they concerned with incest, wife battering, rape, chemical dependency or whatever, the helping professions – reflecting patriarchy – manage to zero in on female, rather than male, culpability. As a result, the search by women for help in clinics, hospitals and agencies has frequently been disastrous. By and large, women have found that helpers stress adjustment rather than change; individual, not collective or political solutions; personal pathology; weakness rather than strength; the psyche, unrelated to economic and social hazards in women's lives; and the authority of male experts, male management, and male decision makers in and beyond the home. I would suggest that the goal of ensuring that women remain in their place, servicing others and sacrificing their own separate, adult, human rights has often been found lurking underneath the subtle and sophisticated surface of therapy, counselling and treatment.

I want to share two of numerous examples from the literature that may have particular meaning to those who are in the helping professions or studying the social sciences. Erik Erikson's work is considered basic to the curriculum of many schools of social work, psychology and psychiatry. Erickson says that young women often ask whether they can "have an identity" before they know whom they will marry and for whom they will make a home. He thinks that much of a young woman's identity is already defined in her kind of attractiveness and in the selectivity of her search for the man (or men) by whom she wishes to be sought.[3]

In *Childhood and Society,* Erikson devoted seventeen pages to the identity development of the adolescent boy, and one paragraph to the development of the adolescent girl.[4] *Obstetrics and Gynecology,* a text used in sixty American medical schools in 1977, says that the normal sexual act entails a masochistic surrender of the woman to the man, there is always an element of rape, and that the traits that compose the core of the female personality are feminine narcissism, masochism and passivity.[5]

It was out of an analysis of such theories and presumptions midst a new grasp of the substance of women's lives that the search began for radical alternatives to the predominately sexist, chemical, adjustment-oriented services offered to women when we needed help. Out of the women's movement came the realization that, embedded in the standard approach of the helping professions, there was a double standard of mental health for women and for men. Moreover, the double standard was, directly or indirectly, reinforcing and adding to the very situations with which women were struggling and for which they were seeking help.

Feminists hold the traditional helping professions responsible for negatively defining, categorizing and labelling women's struggles and behaviour outside a political context, whilst frequently finding good reasons–legitimate causes–for men's and children's difficulties. Even regarding such questions as wife battering, rape, incest, sexual assault, the question is most often put in terms of what women do or do not provoke, what women should or should not have done.

Before the contemporary women's movement began, professionals did not consider these questions worthy of attention, in theory or in practice, other than from a highly individualized and pathological perspective. It was feminists who first exposed issues of rape and wife battering; who connected and made visible the personal and political implications of men's violence against women in and beyond the family; who demanded and frequently set up the crisis centres, the transition houses for battered women and children, the support systems of various kinds, and often without money, buildings, staff or status. The women's movement has demonstrated that, in dealing with such issues as marriage, the family, paid and unpaid work and violence against women, a clear and active feminist framework is essential.

In addition to being held to be subordinate as a sex, women, as a group, cross-cut all other disadvantaged and oppressed groups in our society: the poor, the elderly, people requiring public assistance, native people, the unemployed. Women, in fact, are the major users of social and health services. The first question to be asked is, "Why?" And the next question to be asked is, "What is to be done?"

Feminist counselling is one response to these questions. It is a positive wrought out of a negative, an opportunity created out of a crisis. It rests on a critical analysis of the sexism embedded in the theory and practice of the helping professions, and on the search for radically different kinds of help for women. It is the antithesis of the various forms of "treatment" and therapies that have left us a legacy of the cult of the individual and of the supposedly decisive role played by the individual psyche and personality in shaping human behaviour. By contrast, I like a sentence from the brochure of the Carleton University School of Social Work describing a structural approach to social work practice. "Human behaviour is seen to be rooted primarily in the structures and institutions of a given society, not in the individual person or in the individual family." This idea, the emphasis on the dominant effect of both structure and ideology in shaping the internal and external experience of women, is central to feminist counselling.

I am often asked, "Isn't feminist counselling just good counselling?" My answer is a firm no. By defining personal problems from a political perspective, feminist counsellors define, think, act and react in new ways. For example, when women are paralyzed by depression, they are often on strike against killing roles and expectations. When women end up in psychiatrist's offices or become dependent on drugs and alcohol, they may well be political refugees from narrow and suffocating lives. And when women are poor or on public assistance, seem resigned, apathetic or explode with anger, their responses are seen as normal – not abnormal – responses to untenable life situations.

This feminist approach to counselling reflects the linking of personal and political in the lives of women. Studies have compared female former mental patients who returned to hospital with those who did not. The researchers found that the re-hospitalized women had refused to function domestically in terms of cleaning, cooking, child care and shopping.[6] Feminist counselling assumes that women's work – paid and unpaid – is frequently a fundamental factor in the creation of what is labelled mental illness, and that very serious occupational health hazards are rampant in the home and paid workplace for women.

I found my own health improved considerably when, after twenty-five years of marriage, it was agreed, following crises, conflicts and serious negotiations, that my husband would do the cooking and the shopping in our household. I no longer have responsibility for those areas of domestic life. I think now that my so-called psychiatric problems at the time had a great deal to do with the overload of responsibility and absence of genuine authority reserved for women, and the presence of authority and minimal responsibility on the homefront enjoyed by men.

The mandate for feminist counselling includes a healing process, an educational process, and a political process, and is based on a feminist understanding of society. It is based on the premise that, as women, we have a vested interest in changing our situation and a potential power to do so; that we need to reclaim actively the strength and power and talent that lie dormant and hidden within us; that women can best help themselves and each other in the healing process, and in fighting back; and that it is time for men of goodwill to listen and learn from women, to contribute time, money, resources and concrete housekeeping labour in order to free women for the political and personal tasks that are facing us.

I do not say this lightly. When men consider taking women's studies courses at the Carleton School of Social Work, I tell them they are welcome in the class, but my expectation is that they will do a great deal of listening to and learning from women. They will not be permitted to take over, to dominate the discussion, to define women's oppression. A handful usually remain.

Feminist counsellors refuse to blame the victim or to define women's personal struggles as individual pathology. We have been helped by the women's movement to address these issues in our own lives. As providers of service, we make no separation between our own experience and the experience of those who come to us for help. We use the commonality between us as a way of understanding, sharing and working together.

Feminist counselling is an integrated form of help at its best. The political aspect of the work - an essential part of the counselling - is, however, often the least understood and most difficult to implement. Some may imagine from my previous comments that my approach to working with one woman (or a group of women) mainly involves my presentation of a feminist analysis of the situation, and advocating radical changes in her life, preferably outside the institutions of marriage and motherhood. Not so. I want to underline the fact that if a feminist analysis of women in society is not connected to a fundamental respect for the consumer in relation to where she is, what she wants, how she works best at coping, moving on, making changes, then there can be no worth-while process or product. Whatever I would not want or tolerate for myself, I try very hard not to expect of others.

This means that for feminist counsellors there is a sharing of, a redefining of the personal and political struggles in women's lives. The point I wish to make is that a feminist analysis of women in society - shared with women, in some way, at some level, and at all stages - is a vital and critical part of the helping process.

The analysis is not imposed, it is not an intellectual exercise. It is connected with the kinds of feelings, pain, work and struggles that every woman experiences in some way. Consciousness raising is at the heart of feminist counselling and it provides a dynamic social context within which the provider and consumer of service together determine the work to be done. Although we have been taught the opposite, the answers to personal dilemmas do not lie in therapeutic blueprints. They most often lie in a redefinition of the struggle itself. This redefinition of the problem, from a feminist point of view, constitutes the critical missing piece in the helping process for women.

The essence of contemporary professionalism is rooted in the claim to power, authority and expertise vested in the professional by virtue of her or his specialized knowledge and training. Regardless of intention, contemporary professionalism places the emphasis in practice on personal weakness, faulty communication, defective personality, family relationships and, ultimately, on change at the personal level alone. Feminist counselling, in part, is a means of lifting the unjust burden of blame, guilt and individual responsibility from the shoulders of individual women who have been made scapegoats at many levels in society. Accordingly, it is an approach geared to releasing the energies and abilities of women to change their lives individually and collectively.

A social work student in a hospital on field placement described the following situation to me. A woman patient was very depressed and had been admitted to a psychiatric ward. She had once been a teacher, had two children, was at home full time and was pregnant again. She wanted an abortion and then to return to teaching. Her husband refused to consider either possibility. She became depressed about having no control over her body, her work, her life. No wonder. Yet the message from all concerned was that there was something wrong with her. These are the "treatments" she received while in hospital, as an answer to her problem: *in vivo* desensitization for phobias, bio-energetics, individual therapy, group therapy. This and countless other more grisly examples remind us how essential it is to locate women's responses within a political context, in relation to the subordination of women as a sex.

Feminist counsellors encourage women to "shop around" for help before making a decision. In particular, the consumer needs information regarding the counsellor's views of women in society, and whether the counsellor views female unhappiness and conflict as sickness. Shopping encourages a woman, right at the beginning, to assert her control and decision making in seeking help, and sets the stage for a more egalitarian working relationship. A woman needs to be free to enquire about the counsellor's ways of working, to ask questions such as, "Do you have children?" Exploring the counsellor's work experience and training, asking whether or not she or he has ever received counselling or therapy, is heterosexual, is divorced or married, for example, can help show what the counsellor has to offer.

There is an awareness of the high rate of negligence and malpractice in law, medicine and the other helping professions. Referrals are made selectively to individual women in individual settings in these professions, primarily to people who are clearly concerned with women's issues. I personally make non-specific referrals to agencies or institutions only as a very last resort. No referral at all may be less hazardous, in the long run, than an unspecified referral.

The alternate services for women in the community are usually well known from the inside by feminist counsellors. For example, instead of referring a woman to the Manpower office, a counsellor may introduce her to a women's career counselling service. The counsellor is usually able to make a personal referral to known people in day care centres, interval houses, rape crisis centres, and so on.

Feminist counsellors try to work in cooperative, collective or group arrangements, although we do not always succeed in doing so. The emphasis is away from hierarchy, away from knowledge being maintained by individual practitioners as a commodity. There is an appreciation of the support, creativity and strength of working together, of sharing both ideas and personal vulnerability.

Feminist counsellors assume that keeping the conditions of women's lives private only serves to perpetuate the status quo for women. So there is an emphasis on generalizing such seemingly individual experiences as wife battering, incest, depression among women, the high rate of drugs prescribed for women, the responsibility women currently carry for using dangerous chemicals or technology to prevent conception. One of my concerns about current discussions regarding teen-age pregnancies is that little is said about the responsiblity of boys and men in terms of contraception.

In feminist counselling, it is considered very helpful for women to work in groups, though not exclusively so. Sometimes women need a private, quiet space of their own. But women learn a great deal from sharing the lives we have been taught to keep private. Women in small groups learn that it is all right to share their struggles, to offer one another support, friendship and mutual aid, and to begin solving problems cooperatively.

A feminist counsellor uses her own life experience, her own sorrows and joys, her own traumas and knowledge if they are relevant to the consumer's life situation. The sharing helps to de-mystify the sense that the counsellor is an omnipotent professional and to universalize, in a visible, concrete way, the efforts of human beings, especially women, to survive and to change. We present ourselves as imperfect human beings, not as professional experts in a one-up, one-down relationship. It is like a peer relationship, with the focus necessarily on the consumer because she is the one who has arranged to get help.

It is understood that, without conscious reciprocal learning between the counsellor and consumer, there can be no authentic respect and trust – whatever else is said or done. I feel very strongly about this. It is true that the feminist counsellor brings experience, certain knowledge and skills to the counselling situation. But if we are not actively learning from the people with whom we work, with the ones who are sharing their particular dilemmas and struggles with us, then an essential ingredient is missing.

There is an absence of jargon, of professional mystification in feminist counselling. There is a presence of simplicity, clarity and sharing, with the simple acknowledgement that the consumer, at this time, has contracted for help. It may well be the provider who, in some other place, is, has been, or will be, the consumer, and this is made explicit.

There is no formal diagnosis, assessment or treatment; one of the central assumptions of feminist counselling is that individual problems are not to be equated with pathology. This approach does not deny the validity of one woman's personal pain, her right to express and to act upon the hurt in her life as she chooses to or needs to. But the structural roots of her fear, pain and anger are shared, and may be translated into some form of action, in whatever way, at whatever pace the consumer decides makes sense to her.

Fees are geared to income. I want to make some comments here, comments which are critical of some of the developments in feminist therapy and, perhaps, in feminist counselling as well. Women, in trying to work outside traditional structures, often open private practices. We certainly have the right to make a living (we have to eat too) and we are separate adult people who deserve incomes just like anybody else. But I feel strongly that, if we have a political commitment to women, we have to struggle to find ways to structure our work to help low-income women. Whether we work in traditional agencies, in private practices, or in cooperative groups, we have to consider how we can reserve a significant percentage of our time to help women with little or no money.

This resolve came to me recently when I was asked to give a short course at a house for battered women and children near Ottawa. The women from this house who came to talk to me said, "Well, what's your fee?" (This service for battered wives and children is struggling to survive and salaries associated with it are characteristically low.) I said, "Well, look, some of us consider this to be our political work and we don't expect to be paid all the time. That's our way of contributing to the women's movement, among other things that we do." I guess what the women in that house were struggling with was an abstract principle that women should no longer be cheap labour, should no longer be asked to do unpaid work. That is an important principle which I think needs to be balanced with a serious political commitment to share time, money, skills and whatever else we may have to offer to the women's movement.

I do not think it is enough to develop alternate ways of working with women and then proceed to "market" the service in the same old ways.

There is a sharing of information and knowledge with consumers in feminist counselling because there is a recognition that knowledge is power and must be shared. Literature is not seen as the private preserve of the professional, but as material that can be of direct value to the consumer. With the permission of the consumer, the counsellor may invite a woman who is experiencing, or has experienced, the same difficulties as the consumer to a counselling session. Sharing relevant experience or knowledge about day care, lawyers, lesbianism, or work experience, for example, helps put women in touch with each other.

Feminist counsellors are very much aware of the dangers of exceptionalism. Women, in our relative powerlessness, in our primary dependency upon men, often have difficulty rejecting the temporary and illusory rewards of exceptionalism. It is a time-honoured strategy and divides women from one another to the advantage of the dominant sex.

Files and reports, if kept, are open and actively shared, and the consumer's input is considered especially valuable. "Case" conferences are attended and information is shared, with permission, and on the condition that the people whose lives are being discussed are in attendance, with advocates of their choice. (I am not referring here to the conventional signing of consent forms. I have seen that done in psychiatric hospitals, and I know the pressures, the controls, and the intimidation that are used in "persuading" women to sign. I am talking about authentic permission, about women having advocates of their choice.)

Feminist counselling recognizes that a form of bilingualism and bi-culturalism exists between women and men. Treated as a minority, women are expected to adopt the values, observe the rules, and share the assumptions built into the ideology of the dominant sex. There is an acute awareness of the politics of language as a symbol of oppression. The daily process of editing one's thoughts, censoring one's statements, remaining silent, withholding ideas or anger, is seen to be part-consciously or unconsciously-of most women's experience. Feminist counsellors understand this. It is a common survival stance of oppressed groups.

We are conscious of how most women interact with men in integrated groups and public forums. In many instances women are silent, subdued, fearful of looking or sounding foolish. The emphasis, therefore, is on organizing women's groups, on bringing women together as the main task of counselling, so that they can discover their talents and strengths together, free from male control and dominance. The threat to traditional agencies, institutions and professionals in organizing services to women in groups by themselves, rather than with men (which is deemed more "normal") is incredible. Such services for women only are very often simply disallowed.

It is understood in feminist counselling that women are ordinarily expected to lubricate social relationships and social occasions: to smile, to charm, and to listen to men while they explain the world. Women are helped to understand and to refuse this role, and to develop alternate ways of participating in and enjoying social occasions.

Feminist counselling recognizes women's need and right to be full, functional, decision making persons in this society, publicly and privately. Thus, there is a recognition of the importance of significantly increased public participation for women and significantly increased domestic and child care responsibilities for men.

Feminist counselling recognizes women's need and right to be full, functional, decision-making persons in this society, publicly and privately. Thus, there is a recognition of the importance of significantly increased public participation for women and significantly increased domestic and child care responsibilities for men.

I think it is important to zero in fairly early in a family situation, with such questions as, "Who does the child care? Who really controls the money? How is domestic work divided? Who decides? Who feels responsible? Have you thought about paid and unpaid work, or the double work load of women?"

Women are traditionally taught to submit and conform, not to demand and protest. Confidence and assertion, therefore, must grow in different ways if things are to change. Assertiveness training is one valuable approach when used from a feminist perspective. However, if workers or counsellors view this way of working as a rare, precious, and highly professional technique, and worry about women learning to be assertive rather than aggressive, they are, I think, missing the point. Women need to experiment with the whole spectrum of human emotions. We need to claim the right to make mistakes, to try things out, to carry on without guilt and self-blame, and to assume that all of this is part of the human capacity to learn and change.

Feminist counselling attaches value to action, decision making and risk taking, because it recognizes that women have been trained to talk and react, rather than to act; to be, rather than to do; to feel, rather than to decide. So women are encouraged to act upon the problems facing them, individually and collectively, and not to be satisfied with talking, taking drugs, or finding a temporary release from tension.

At the same time, feminist counsellors understand that taking the initiative in changing or expanding our own lives is particularly difficult for women because we have been taught dependence and passivity in relation to men and the world at large. We have had to learn to adjust and adapt in order to survive. Jessie Bernard, in *The Future of Marriage,* points out that when two people marry, it is the man's life that remains relatively unchanged. It is the woman who is expected to adjust and submerge her needs and aspirations to his.[7]

A feminist counsellor is aware that girls and women have been trained to be good and to be careful. We are wary and fearful of making mistakes and being penalized for them. This is a major source of disabling guilt. Again, what feminist counsellors try to do is to offer conscious support to women to try out new ways of being, of acting and of deciding. Counsellors encourage women to claim the right to fail, to be wrong and to move on.

Both in feminist counselling and in consciousness-raising groups, there is a validation of women's life experiences – as we tell them, as we feel them and as we react to them. That validation is significant for women because it implies respect, dignity and trust. It is a rich experience for women. We are not accustomed to being accorded respect, dignity and trust, and they are important ingredients in all our lives.

Feminist counsellors believe that a key to regaining and retaining our dignity, energy and self-esteem is the anger that propels us to fight back and to join together in acting to change our lives. Anyone who has read *Women in Psychiatry* knows that the apt sub-title of the book is *I'm Not Mad, I'm Angry.*[8] Most women, consciously or unconsciously, live with a profound sense of rage in relation to a society and a dominant sex that keep us down individually and collectively.

We recognize how devastating misogyny is in women's daily lives and relationships. Feminist counsellors understand the economic and ideological base of misogyny, and how much physical and emotional energy is drained from women's lives because of it; we know about the pain and hurt in women's daily existence because we live in a sexist society.

We understand that marriage and motherhood are authentic choices for some women. We know that other options are equally appropriate and, in this society, need support and reinforcement. For example, the decision by a woman not to marry, to be a single mother, to remain childless, to be lesbian, to be celibate or sexual in ways other than the state and its institutions have defined – all these choices need equal validation and support from a feminist counsellor. There is the assumption that there are many ways for women to live and love other than in marriage and the nuclear family.

Feminist counsellors recognize that women are especially deprived of nurturance. Traditionally, we do the nurturing. We do the entertaining, the nursing, the cooking and shopping and cleaning, the appointment keeping, the tension management, the child care, the worrying. The fact is that women need wives, need to be on the receiving end of much, much more nurturance and giving. Instead of helping a woman primarily devote herself to others, the counsellor works with her, her family, her friends, or whomever, to recognize her essential needs and entitlements as a person. The consumer is not seen as an adjunct to her family, but as a separate person in relation to the whole world, sharing – and only sharing – responsibility for work and nurturance with significant others in her life. When I get depressed these days, one of the "cures" I have discovered is to zero in on my own immediate needs, to nurture myself. It took a long time to learn that giving to myself makes me feel better, and also to be able to ask for nurturance from those around me, whether it is particularly convenient or not.

One key strategy of feminist counselling is helping women re-assess the importance and value of relationships with other women. Traditionally, women have dreamt of and sought happiness and fulfillment with one man. In encouraging women to validate and like themselves as persons, to appreciate their own significance, the counsellor also helps women to enjoy, respect and seek out other women as primary friends and companions. A support network of women friends is seen as crucial.

Feminist counselling is particularly concerned with the political and personal questions arising from lesbian relationships. We know that lesbian women have to cope with a particularly virulent form of misogyny, that the helping professions have most frequently perceived lesbian women as sick, and that lesbian women often need help in coping with the common struggles and problems of being women in this society, of being couples, of coming out, of being different. Feminist counsellors have the added advantage here of harbouring few illusions about what heterosexuality means for women in a sexist society.

Feminist counsellors see the traditional nuclear family as one in which men and children are encouraged to concentrate on their own needs and aspirations, and women are expected to submerge theirs. This is considered to be mentally unhealthy for all concerned because it is recognized that many men, in the family and other places of power, are particularly self-centred and adolescent in their behaviour. The emphasis, therefore, is on helping men and boys to grow up into more adult behaviours where they can begin to take responsibility for the basics that women have learned throughout their lives, of sharing, nurturing, cooperating and learning from others.

In summary, I consider feminist counselling to be an approach, not a technique. It is a way of linking women's personal struggles with the political context of our lives as both providers and consumers of service, and working towards change together.

7

Women as Providers and Consumers

Helen Levine

Dorothy O'Connell

Marlene Pierre-Aggamaway

DOROTHY O'CONNELL I want to talk about some of the thoughts I had after listening to Gloria Steinem last night. One of the points she made that really stayed in my mind concerned terminology, and the importance of creating our own terms and positive ways of saying things. She said "reproduction freedom" was a positive way to say "population control." Our chair, in introducing the subject of this panel, said "users and deliverers of service"; the brochure says "givers and receivers of services." Once you look at that title, you say, "Oh, yes, the social workers give, and the welfare mothers take, and there the welfare mothers are, taking, getting something for nothing, getting something done for them, being waited on." So even quite simple titles, which look perfectly inoffensive, can rub people the wrong way, and that is one of the wrong ways that I got rubbed.

Somebody asked me this morning if I minded being called poor. *Poor* is a term I use on purpose, all the time, for political reasons. Many other people on welfare, people who are not part of the movement yet, object to it and ask, "Why do you call us poor? It comes out in the papers and people look down on us. In the English language, poor can mean bad, like poor housekeeper, poor budgeter or poor manager." They feel there is a lot of ugliness that goes with the word poor. But I say that if you are drowning, you do not yell, "Help, I'm damp!" If you go around saying you are "low income," people say, "That's interesting." It is important to use the word *poor*. We do it on purpose, so I do not mind being called poor.

Another word that I would like to talk about is the word *client*. I know that this seems like an inoffensive word, but I wish there were some other word – like *people,* or *friends,* or *sisters* – that did not separate us again into "us" and "them." I think that, as women, we cannot let ourselves be separated, divided and conquered.

Another concern is that, of all the people in the world, there are only a few people who have to prove that they are respectable. Most people assume, unless someone does something to prove otherwise, that people are respectable. But women on welfare always have to prove that they are respectable. And one of the unfortunate results is that they think they have to prove they are respectable by pointing to someone else who is not. That is dangerous, and we try to fight it. We try hard never to say anything that would reflect badly on our neighbours, or our friends, or ourselves. That is why, when somebody asked me yesterday if there were particular feminists who did not do enough for the poor, I did not want to respond. That is saying something about other women, naming names and pointing fingers. But without pointing a finger, I think we have to recognize that the rule of divide and conquer has worked extremely well among women. We are divided. I think it is beginning to change – and I am delighted – but it is not changing fast enough.

Gloria Steinem also talked about how we have to build our own institutions in this anthropological revolution. I am counting on some of you people in the social work field to help us construct those kinds of institutions, humanistic institutions, where people work together to make things better. I am not saying to the people who will graduate this year that I expect it to be done by next year. I like the term *anthropological revolution* because it implies that it will take some time. Certainly, as Gloria Steinem said, we do not want to take one thousand years, but we cannot expect an overnight revolution.

In my past as a poor person, I have noticed that some social work students come bounding out of the schools yelling, "To the barricades." They expect the women on welfare to pick up arms and follow them, to be ready to fight for their rights. But it is hard, very hard, to get women on welfare to fight – because they have so much to lose. Not financially, certainly, but when that is all you have, it is everything. And, if you think, as a result of rebellion, that you might lose your children, then it is everything. Their children are the hostages that keep the women on welfare under control. When you think, if you speak out that the teacher might point out your child in class, if you speak out your cheque might be held up, if you speak out you might get evicted, then it is very difficult to have the courage to do any of these things. So for those of you who may feel that the women on welfare are not pushing hard enough or not fighting hard enough, remember that this is a very expensive action to consider when you know what the consequences could be.

You might say, "No social worker would hold up a cheque," or, "No housing authority would evict a person for this." But it is rather like slavery. You might be lucky enough to have a nice master who does not sell you down the river, but, as long as he has the power to sell you down the river, you are still a slave. Women on welfare have a lot to break loose from and it takes a great deal of courage for them to stand up and fight. I should explain that I am not patting myself on the back for taking action; I am not a woman on welfare. I am one of the very few poor women who is married. I speak about single parents, however, because most of the women are single parents. As I represent a group, I speak for most of the women, not just for myself.

There is another word I would like to look at. A few years ago, a local newspaper took a whack at public housing and called it a ghetto. I wrote a very angry letter to the newspaper saying, "We are not a ghetto. If we are a ghetto, then the condominium down the street is a ghetto, because it is built the same way." Then a couple of years later, I thought about it. I thought, "What am I saying? Yes, we are a ghetto. What's wrong with ghettos? Ghettos are good places. Ghettos are places where you can bond, where you can establish close ties. Ghettos are just groups of people of the same kind who live together." There are many ghettos. Rockcliffe in Ottawa is a ghetto; public housing is a ghetto. Some ghettos are nicer than others, and I happen to live in a nice one. But there is such a stigma attached to the word, that your first reaction is, "Not me. I don't live in a ghetto."

I think we have to examine terms like this and we have to, if necessary, turn them around and use them in other ways. *Culture* is another one. At one time, we applied for a grant available to various cultural groups. The administrators said, "You can't have one because you are all from different cultures." I tried to convince them that poverty was a culture. I believe it is a culture.

I also believe that when you are poor, you learn how to deal with problems, and humour is definitely one of the ways to deal with problems. Humour is a very good weapon, and it sure beats crying. I believe that a lot of poor people use humour. If you look at the great humourists of the past, most came from disadvantaged groups. They were Jewish, Puerto Rican, female, or black, and they learned to laugh at problems and to deal with problems through laughter. I think that laughter is a natural part of poverty. Sometimes, there is nothing you can do except laugh.

With the preceding in mind, I should like to offer some suggestions about what we can do to help people who are poor. The biggest thing is to listen. That is why I am so glad that I had the chance to come and talk here, because I have a captive audience, and you have to listen. But in other situations as well - listen. Poor people generally have a very good idea of what it is they need and how to get it. One of the ways people can help is to provide information and help to spread the word to other people. One of the best ways a social worker can help is to provide the people receiving benefits with information about every single penny they could get. Do not let someone find out five years later that she could have been receiving an extra five dollars a month because she was diabetic and required a special diet. Make sure that people on welfare have all the information they need. That is very important.

The other area I wanted to talk about concerns band-aid solutions and long-term solutions. We need both of them; we absolutely have to have both of them. So often a group of poor people proposes something and hears, "You're just helping the system; you're just propping up the system; that's just a band-aid solution." There is nothing wrong with putting a band-aid over a cut until you can do something more about it. I have assisted in a lot of band-aid solutions myself. For example, I helped start legal clinics in Ottawa, because lawyers, at least in Ottawa, often do not have the foggiest idea of welfare rights, or of landlord-tenant laws. Eventually, of course, we want to change the system. But that is in the long term. In the short term, you do not let people die for lack of care because you have only long-term goals. Keep in mind that the system has to change, but, in the meantime, make sure that it is the best system possible at the time.

I was on an open-line show once on which I was talking about changing the system. A minister of finance phoned me and said, "So, you want us to be communists." I said, "Well, you know, humankind is very inventive, and I cannot believe that there can be only two monetary systems: capitalist and communist. I think if we spent some time putting our minds to it, we might come up with a third one." Any world that has as many languages as ours does should certainly be able to devise some different methods of distributing wealth. I do not think capitalism is the method and I do not think communism is the method. Perhaps some of you here are in economics and can figure it out. I am not good at that. I have never understood why, when our dollar bill is prettier, it is not worth more than the American dollar bill.

The last comment I want to make is that I loved hearing Marlene Pierre-Aggamaway say this morning, about Indian women on welfare, that the welfare payments were just rent. How I wish that other women on welfare could say something equivalent and as perfect as that. We have been saying welfare is a salary; it is a lousy salary, but it is a salary. It is for work that we do. I think that is one of the facts that everybody has to realize. Women who raise children are doing work; we are working not only for ourselves, and for the children, but also for the benefit of the country. We would be more confident of our work if our children were being given a decent chance of growing up to fit into the country. But they are not. I think it is ridiculous to import people from other countries to do jobs our kids could do if they could get the training. We are working right now in Ottawa to try to change the system insofar as the kids are concerned, but it is not happening easily or quickly.

As an example, we brought a videotape to a school. The videotape is called "Cul-de-Sac" and it is about poor kids in the school system.[1] I, personally, found it a very disturbing film. In it were all kinds of kids who said they wanted to quit school and get a job. When asked what kind of job, they said, "Well, body mechanic, car repair, garbageman." When the film ended, teachers in the school said that it was a very positive film. These kids were full of the work ethic and should be permitted to drop out and go to work. That I found disturbing.

I was disturbed, also, by the twenty-one-year-old in the film who could neither read nor write. Towards the end of the film, he more or less jokingly said that his future would be that of leaping off a building. Not one of the teachers even remarked upon it, even asked, "Where's that kid now?" or "What happened to him?" One of the children in the film said, "Well, easy come, easy go," meaning anything but that, judging by the way he was saying it. The teachers responded by saying, "You can hear the mothers in them, eh? Easy come, easy go—always wanting something for nothing. Some of these women won't even take budgeting courses." I tried to explain to them that any woman who can manage on the money received from welfare is an expert in budgeting and should be teaching other people about it. In closing, I want to leave with you two thoughts: first, listen to what the poor say they want; second, try to work together to build a better life for all Canadian women.

MARLENE PIERRE-AGGAMAWAY I feel, somehow, that I have robbed you of a good conversation. While having our break, Dorothy O'Connell and I had the opportunity to share feelings and thoughts about the similarities between native women and poor women, and some of the ways that we could work together at some future time. Native women are in no way different from poor women. Native women and their families suffer the same kinds of discrimination that poor people do, but I believe to an even greater degree because we are natives.

Dorothy and I talked about a number of things. One of them was the way in which social policy really affects people. There has been a great hullabaloo about the government's policy on make-work programs such as the Local Initiatives Program—how they were being operated, the great amount of money being spent and misspent. But in the early 1970s, when those programs were being instituted, they provided an opportunity for native women who would otherwise never have had a chance to involve themselves in something of their own making and design. The criteria were easy enough to fit into, whether we wanted to start a day-care centre, wanted to start this, that, or the other thing. I tried to ensure, however, that we were working on something we wanted as a group. If nothing else, these programs helped us, as a native women's local, to demonstrate – at least to ourselves – that we had the where-withal to do something and no one could criticize us for it.

There was one great drawback to all of those programs. They were not long term. In most cases, they did not have a long-term effect, and there was no coordination. We soon came to be adept at taking one program and using it to continue what we had been trying to do earlier, then taking another make-work program and using it, until we achieved our own long-term objectives. A lot of us used our genius, I suppose, and made those programs work for us, although they did not solve anything in terms of long-term development. And so we fought in our community to meet with government officials, to change the direction of government policy.

As you can see from this, social work does not mean just working on a one-to-one basis with people, but it also means helping to change those things that have caused people to be poor, and legislation that has been created to keep people poor. I also believe that social workers, as social animators and social innovators, have the responsibility to look at creative ways of bringing people dignity, because poverty has its own stigma. Someone asked me this morning, "How does one work with native women who find themselves in touch with social workers?" I think it is most important to examine your own attitudes. Ask yourself why you are working with native people or native women. Is it because you have to satisfy your own social curiosity, or do you have to satisfy your own need to help the more disadvantaged? Would you drop out when you are not needed any more, when you have given me the skills to do what I really want, and that is to gain control of myself and my life. (I say "me," because I was a single parent. I became a parent at age twenty and am now thirty-seven and have three children, whom I basically raised on my own.) Most non-Indian people working with native people have a hard time dropping out and letting us experience our own mistakes or our own strengths or successes.

You must try to understand that I, as a native woman, have to be able to feel good about myself, that the public image native women have borne, unjustifiably, is that we are "easy" and that we bear babies "like minks bear minks." All the negative imagery created about native women has not only had its effect on me personally, but it has had its effect on you – it has given you an image that some of you have grown to accept as true. I must say that this image does not include me at all; that was never me. I was allowed dignity by my social worker when I was on welfare. She did not question who I was; she let me be me; she did not let the system try to tell me who I was. She really pushed

93

me along. Together, seventeen years ago, we organized the first single parents' group in Thunder Bay. I think it was that kind of relationship that spurred me and many other women on to realizing our own capabilities. I cannot say enough about the kind of human understanding and warmth that we can draw on and that helps to develop the best in us.

I hope that I have since been able to help develop understanding in ourselves as women; that we can have our own crisis centres; that we can have our own legal counselling clinics; that all of the skills I have learned, and others in our community have learned, can contribute to the development of the programs that will become the foundation of whatever form of government native people want to develop.

I want to end by saying that you do not usually see native women coming up to the front to speak about these issues. There are a few who do, but, by and large, we are quiet-a quiet nation-and that is good. I think we can build faster underground. But four or five years from now, you will see many more native women taking their places on the platform, and showing themselves and their children that it is worthwhile to come before audiences like this. In the meantime, if you are really sincere about working with the socially disadvantaged, do not go back to work or school at the end of this conference and continue to do the same things you have always done. Start to think and ask the people with whom you are working about how they feel and how they want to be treated.

HELEN LEVINE I am going to talk about myself as a consumer of service. I am really uncomfortable with language sometimes, and so have shifted from *client* to *consumer* and then to the idea of *user*. There must be another word. But for the moment, my term is consumer of service. I want to focus on my own experience because social workers and helping professionals tend to project the image of being "all right" and "together," of managing their lives. It is the "poor" clients or patients who have not been able to do so well. I want to explode the myth.

One of the ways in which I began to challenge the myth was to write a paper entitled "On Women and on One Woman as Provider and Consumer of Social and Health Services."[2] In it, I used the diary I had written while I was a patient in a psychiatric hospital, both to share my own struggles and to comment on the experiences of the other women whom I came to know in the institution. I had been asked to do a background piece on women in society. It was two years after that painful period in my life, and I was steeped in the subject matter, yet I could not seem to get my ideas together. The turning point came when I decided to write about what had happened to me in

94

hospital. The paper began to fall together in totally unexpected ways, to include and to go beyond my own experience.

The paper was to be presented to a seminar of women who were addressing the need for separate drug and alcohol services for women. I remember being quite terrified about what I had written. I thought, "They're going to think I'm crazy, it will be embarrassing, the stigma will be unbearable." All kinds of unpleasant and scary things could happen. However, that was only part of what was going on inside of me. Another more determined side of me was saying, "This is part of the human condition. This is part of what happens, especially to women. Why do we tip-toe around and pretend otherwise? Why can we tell only our best friends? Why can't we refuse to hide the fact that this is a political issue for women as well as a personal crisis, and claim the experience, without in any way glamorizing what happens to women when we break down and disappear behind the walls of faceless institutions? Why can't we claim the experience as something that may potentially help us, in the end, to grasp what women are up against in a sexist society?" So there was a feeling of claiming, as well as of fearing the consequence of public disclosure.

I want to comment on some of the things I learned as a social worker because I was a patient in a psychiatric hospital. In a way, I lost my pride. That may sound like a negative, like a loss. But being on a ward with other women who seem very different at first and have had a wide range of life experience, I began to realize that I am just one human being among many, that I am nothing special, and that I rate a membership in the human race just like everyone else. Professionals, in particular, are taught to highlight the distinctions between "us" and "them," to feel superior to some others, at least, so we will not feel as inadequate inside as we sometimes do. Authentic membership in the human race is precious, but it has to be worked at and learned, sometimes from pretty tough experiences.

Recently I tried to obtain my medical files from the hospital I had been in. It was an interesting experience. The hospital refused my requests; they were unwilling to release files to an ex-patient. (One remains a psychiatric patient, or ex-patient; one never loses the label.) Hospital staff and administrators say they will not release files because of their professional concern with the potentially fragile nature of your psyche, and with how reading "their" files might affect your mental health. I know that this particular rationale reveals more about the way patients are judged and dealt with by staff and the common fear of exposure on the part of professionals who keep records to themselves for very dubious reasons. I finally went to a civil liberties lawyer, who threatened court action and got the files. That was satisfying because I felt the records were really mine to know about, to think about, to evaluate in terms of institutional practices that seriously affected my life at the time.

When I was writing that paper in 1975, I asked, "Where am I now as provider and consumer of social and health services?" These were some of the answers I gave:

As a consumer, I know how important it is for me, together with others, to struggle for women's rights, women's dignity and women's potential. As a consumer, I recognize that I am only one of all womankind, with more similarities than differences with other women, and with more to be learned and gained from working together rather than separately. As a consumer, I know what a thin line there is, if any, between being a provider and consumer of service, and how the experience of one can profoundly affect the other. As a consumer, I know now what it means to be helpless and dependent upon culture-bound and sometimes destructive practitioners in institutions. As a consumer, I now recognize – in my gut, not just in my head – the dangerous power of social control that providers of service potentially have over a consumer's very existence. As a consumer, I have also learned how very limited my perceptions and actions were as a provider of service, and how much I, and others, must learn in an on-going way from consumers.... I am aging now and the process is a tremendous hurdle for women. It is, in a sense, the end of my life as a sex object, full-time mother, needed child-care worker, housekeeper. I am fortunate to have had some training and work experience, and by sheer luck as well as struggle, to have found work that involves me personally, politically and occupationally. (I want to stress the luck. When things come together, it is not necessarily because we are so smart, or so competent, or because we have taken advantage of opportunities. It is sometimes just getting a break.) And I would also still be trapped and lost in a profound sense, if I had not, with the support of other women, struggled bitterly for my own personal and occupational needs, both within and outside of the family.

I now have an intense sense of urgency about my work in the paid labour force, a whole area of life that I missed out on earlier as a woman. It can never be made up and I am limited by a fifty-two-year-old [in 1975] physical and emotional capacity to invest myself in my own goals. The wisdom of age tells me nothing in life is absolutely equal, but for the rest of my active years in family and community, I want primary consideration (here I am speaking about the family) in my choice of pursuits, and I need the personal support system my husband can provide as I once did for him, to make that possible.

The women's movement has been an important countervailing support system for me in a culture heavily weighted in favour of men. It has helped me to struggle for a sense of centrality and importance, both personally and politically. The struggle to maintain one's fight, one's confidence, and one's global perceptions is a daily one for any second-class, powerless minority in this society. I consider my anger and my rebellion, my patience and my determination to be precious, hard-won achievements (though I have been taught the opposite all my life as woman). I am no longer willing to collude in the oppression of myself and other women – half the world – in the name of any profession or any political movement that does not actively, visibly and effectively promote the full and unequivocal citizenship of women.[3]

DOROTHY O'CONNELL I do not know how anyone can respond to something as moving and as honest and as important as what Helen has just said. I think it is an impossible task. I am impressed with the insight that she has about herself, with the guts with which she faced problems, and with the guts with which she opened herself to what could have been destructive to her, professionally, in talking about mental illness or in talking about nervous breakdowns or the kind of thing that happens to so many women. One of the statements I made at another social work convention was that most of you students have a right to hear the consequences of speaking out for low-income women. Parading around with signs might be a good way to get fired; certainly there are financial consequences to bucking the system that you are working within. So I am sure that you were moved by Helen's efforts at bucking the system.

I would just like to say one thing, and that is about files. Poor women have been trying to get their files from public housing and welfare for a long time. They want to see what other people are saying about them, particularly since those groups exchange files all the time. There is nothing as intimidating as going into an office where somebody has a big file on you that they keep tapping while they are talking to you. The intimation of what might be in that file and the intimation that anything you say is somehow magically being taken down and entered into that file, can almost render you speechless.

One of the fights that many low-income women have been involved in, therefore, is the right of access to their own files. That right would include medical files, and, for some of us, RCMP files. (Those of us who live in Ottawa get our picture taken every time we go up on the Hill to protest, and that can become quite amusing. There have been times when I have even searched behind pictures for possible bugs. One of my friends once said to me, "I'm not paranoid. There are people following me.")

All I can say about the other two speakers on this panel is that there is no conflict among us. I think they are both marvellous, I am privileged to be up here with them, and I support them with all my heart.

MARLENE PIERRE-AGGAMAWAY I find it difficult to pose a question or comment when I see the understanding and empathy of two women who have also been through trials and tribulations in their own lives. Questions like, "How did you do it?" seem unimportant. But I can comment that (what did Gloria Steinem call it last night?) there is a "psychic turf" here, and not just because we are poor or we are Indian. And all of us here, on the platform and in the audience, must continue to bring people together on a similar psychic turf, not only in an educational institution, but also out in the real world. I guess that is a comment that can be reinforced, and has been reinforced, by your presence.

This conference will mean more to me than just having been able to sit up here and say a few words. I will go home and think about what Dorothy means when she said this or that. I have to think a lot more and I have to feel a lot more about what she has said, and about what Helen said. We must learn from each other; we must not forget each other.

HELEN LEVINE One of the most exciting parts of this conference, one that has been referred to over and over again, is the "click" that Gloria Steinem spoke of last night. Clicks are really important because making connections is the stuff of life. This has been an important panel for me. It feels good. It is, somehow, like joining hands across some of the gaps that plague us, and it is sharing in a way that counts.

I just want to mention a couple of clicks of my own. One was the idea of welfare as a salary, mentioned by Dorothy. I have heard that definition before, but somehow it got lost. When I heard it again, I thought, "Yes, that's it. Why did I forget it?" The concept of welfare as salary can take us in different directions, both as consumers and providers. A consumer who is getting a salary for essential work will think, feel and act differently than if she knows she is getting a handout.

The second click occurred when Dorothy spoke about listening to the poor, listening to consumers. I do not know whether I need to say it again, but I think that helping professionals are desperately in need of much, much more humility. I realize it is hard to come by, because we are taught the opposite. We are told that we are the experts, that we know better than others about their own struggles, because we have a title and a status and a mystified form of expertise. But listening to, that is, real listening, not just looking as though we are listening-and learning from consumers of service could result in our being able to begin to work in a totally different way, based on combined human experience and mutual respect.

I would like to make one other point in relation to what Marlene had to say. She touched on something dear to my heart when she said that the definition of social work is not just that of working with individuals. I was glad to hear that important statement made because there is a strong tendency in many schools of social work, and I am sure in schools of medicine and psychology, to assume that work with individuals or individual families requires a range of techniques and a repertoire of therapies that are considered the be-all and the end-all in terms of being effective. I want to explode that myth. For me, the definition of a social worker necessitates taking social and political action against service delivery systems and societal structures that oppress women, and working together with women in terms of imperfect, joint, human efforts rather than applied technological knowhow.

8

The Electronic Sweatshop

Judith Gregory

Amy works as a word-processing operator for a major industrial firm in Cincinnati. One day, she paused briefly from word processing just as her manager walked in. "What are you doing?" he demanded. "Oh, I'm just thinking for a minute," she replied. "Well, get back to work," he snapped. "You're not paid to think. I am."

Amy's experience is typical of the problems that are made worse by the rapid introduction of office automation, and by the attitude of her manager. "Get back to work. You're not paid to think," is at the core of the creation of the electronic sweatshop. Yet, in business and trade journals, we read rave reviews of the wonders that the new office technology is bringing us. We are told that the technological revolution is easing the drudgery usually found in America's paper factories, through creating more stimulating careers for office workers. We are all children of the micro-millenium. One magazine boasts that portable terminals will allow workers to work at home, on the road, or in a mountain cabin. "This will be a special aid to home-bound mothers with children," so declared *U.S. News and World Report.* [1] We are then shown a picture of a stockbroker lying on a beach in Florida with his terminal beside him on the blanket. He can follow the stock market while he works on his tan.

The widespread use of the computer made possible the introduction of micro-processors in the 1970s. A single computer on a chip today can have twenty-five times the capacity of a computer which in the late 1960s filled an entire room. The wonders of these micro chips are staggering. If I had a chip here, it would barely cover one-third of my fingertip. The memory capacity of a chip increases by 15 percent a year, while the cost plummets. The rapid change in office technology is extraordinary. Computer companies have to come up with new products every eighteen months to stay competitive.

Again and again we hear from employers about how much their employees love the fancy new equipment. The office automation director for Avon products says that if you tried to take the word processors away from his secretaries, "They would chop your hands off!"[2] Employers extol the virtues of office automation to convince us that these changes are bringing benefits to all of us, clerical workers, secretaries and executives alike, and that we can appreciate and share in these benefits equally. But in private, among their peers, businessmen and managers often talk differently.

Last fall, I sat in on a small seminar for banking managers on office automation. To begin with, the moderator proclaimed, "Banks and insurance companies are already factories. In fact, they are most similar to the electronics industry." The keynote talk was given by a manager from the Chemical Bank in New York, which employs some thirty-seven thousand people. He estimated that half of certain types of transactions are handled today by automated teller machines (ATMs) rather than by "human tellers." That is what they now call us. The banking industry estimates that 50 percent of all bank transactions in the United States will be handled by "non-human tellers" by the end of the decade.

In the discussion, several managers from medium-sized and smaller banks were hesitant about automation. It seems that, in their towns and cities, customer resistance is often an obstacle. Many of the customers are not so wild about the idea. The big banker's remedy? Charge people extra if they insist on seeing a human being; a little pressure helps the public adapt to these new systems. An impatient executive from a major Detroit bank laid his views on the line: "I have never heard such squeamishness about automation," he said in disgust. "The way I look at it, you've got your choice. You can have your two Susy tellers over here, with their vacation days, their sick children, their annual demands for cost-of-living raises, and their desire for promotion; or you can have your two automatic teller machines over here, which can work all night, never get sick or take a vacation, and which only need to be upgraded every five years. It's your choice."

In 1980, 9 to 5 (then called Working Women) issued the report "Race Against Time."[3] In it, we identified major problems with office automation as it is being introduced today. Office automation allows for the de-skilling and devaluing of our work. Office automation causes the potential for job loss in the future on a large scale. Office automation increases risks to office workers' health, associated with increased stress and strain from working with video display terminals (VDTs) in repetitive jobs, under high pressure.

Today, in the 1980s, in the United States, there are about ten million people working at VDTs. We predicted that increased automation would mean an increase in shift work and piece-work pay per line of information processed, and increased rationalization of work, sometimes known as "Taylorization," or "Taylorism" or "scientific management." That is the kind of re-organization of work where the work is broken down into its component parts so that each person works faster on a smaller fragment of the job, doing it over and over again. The less thinking, the better. Managers are using production quotas and constant monitoring of work performance to carry out speedups of awesome proportion in large clerical operations. These trends lead us to conclude that management's idea of the office of the future is really nothing more than the re-creation of the factory of the past. Instead of dying down, the problems we identified are on the rise. The age of the electronic sweatshop is upon us.

Rose Cirk re-entered the work force after twenty years away. Her excellent typing skills quickly landed her a job as one of twelve VDT or CRT operators in a downtown publishing company in Cleveland. She found that office work had changed a great deal during her years away from the work force. "The chairs were good and the machines adjustable too, but I have never been confined to one spot doing key entry at such a pace," she explained. "The computer at one end of the room keeps track of the keystrokes you do. The more keystrokes you do, the more money you might get. At the end of the day, the figures for all of us were posted. You look at your speed, you look at everyone else's, and you say to yourself, 'Tomorrow, I'm going to do better.' They get you thinking just like they want you to. You're really pushing hard."[4]

It is not only re-entry women like Rose who experience these problems. She describes a co-worker, who is much younger, who began doing VDT work right after high school. She says of her co-worker, "She's been running a CRT for close to ten years and she's as fast as the wind. But it has really affected her personality. I used to wonder if something was wrong. She just had no exuberance. One morning, she said to me, 'Rose, as soon as I sit down at that machine, I feel like I am going to cry.'"

I want to make it clear from the beginning that we do believe that new office technology, including computer technology, has a great potential to truly benefit all of us, to upgrade our skills, to upgrade our jobs and to upgrade our standard of living. New technology could, and should, be used to make our jobs easier, less tedious, more enjoyable and more skilled. Some secretaries would probably chop your hands off if you tried to take away their beloved Wangs or their Lexitrons or their Laniers; some genuinely love their machines and have good situations to work in.

Amanda works in the resource department of a large university. She uses a new word processor about three or four hours a day, as she needs to, and she does a variety of jobs at the terminal, entering and editing documents for four

101

writers. Overall, she enjoys it as an aid to her job, but she adds that on the days that she has to work at the terminal under pressure for six to eight hours a day, she develops problems, going home with a headache and muscle strain all over.

One long-term secretary, who did all-around secretarial work for thirty years, was forced to decide four years before retirement to make the switch to word processing or to retire at that point. She told writer Barbara Garson, "... I'm very glad I learned this word processor. If only I could have had it while I was a secretary....I want you to take this down: I love my Wang. It's not the machine that gave me the shaft."[5]

We know that our productivity is vastly increased with the addition of new equipment. These increases can, and should, be reflected by more rest breaks, more pay, or shorter work weeks, or a combination of all three. But the truth is that, today, office automation does not benefit managers and secretaries equally. For women in the office, office automation raises new workplace pressures and concerns about the future of our jobs. Many of these problems have been with us a long time in office work, and sometimes the question is raised, "What's so different?" Many of the predictions about job loss and the problems of automation have been made before also. And again, the question is raised, "What makes this wave of automation different?"

This time, computerization in offices is meant to computerize the very flow of work, to computerize procedures in the office, rather than just to give the worker something with which to do particular tasks more quickly. Because of this, there has been a revival of the idea of rationalization of work, and hence there is greater potential for major job loss in the near future. This happens because, in order to take office automation to a higher state, the jobs as they now exist must first be broken down; then it is necessary to extract from us the knowledge and the decision-making we have today on the job, so that our knowledge can be translated into a computer program. The worker is thus reduced to being an extension of the terminal and is tied to the computer system. With the growing use of micro-processor technology combined with telecommunications technology, we are seeing a qualitative difference in this wave of automation compared with earlier ones.

When we say that we are concerned about the de-skilling and devaluing of jobs tomorrow, it makes sense for us to pause a moment and think about the position of clerical workers today.

In the United States, almost one out of five workers is a clerical worker. Clerical jobs are among the lowest paid in the economy. Nearly one in three women clerical workers in 1979 earned less than $8,500 a year for full-time work. Now, in the early 1980s, the average pay for clerical workers across the board is about $11,000, which is close to a low-income budget for a family of four, according to the Bureau of Labor Statistics.[6] Clerical jobs are notorious as dead-end jobs and they offer even fewer opportunities than they promise.

Now let us look at de-skilling. In a 1977 study of five major New England companies, sociologists Evelyn Glenn and Roslyn Feldberg found that when computerization occurred, the portion of low-level clerical jobs remained about the same, and the clerical workers were rarely upgraded to fill new skilled jobs.[7] The study found that the automatic clerical jobs were more mechanical and narrow, and that the main avenues for clerical workers were either horizontal or down, but not up. Legal secretaries are among the most highly skilled, and have the highest prestige jobs among clerical workers. Mary Murphree, in a recent case study of the effect of word processing on Wall Street legal secretaries' jobs, found that, as new technologies came in, the skills and the jobs were split both upward and downward, with new professionals being hired as para-legals, and new lower-wage workers being hired to work at the word processors. This turned the legal secretaries into "telephone gate-keepers," in limbo except as a status symbol to their bosses. Then one day everyone came into a particular law office and found that on each of the desks was a dictation machine (transcribing machine) and each was hooked into the word processor centre. As well, the secretaries had been arbitrarily clustered, two to four to a group, and the number of lawyers each supported was increased across the board. All of this was done with absolutely no consultation with the secretaries![8]

I recommend the book, *Women and the Chip* by Heather Menzies, to all of you.[9] It includes case studies on the effects of office automation technologies in several companies in Canada, and discusses labour force trends for Canadian women in clerical work. What Menzies found was an increasing polarization of the work force. Highly technological jobs were being placed at the top in managerial positions with some room for expansion, but there were more and more de-skilled jobs and dead-end jobs at the bottom, and there was a "skills gap" in between, which was almost impossible to bridge without conscious strategies and policy efforts.

One executive describes the polarization process quite boldly in an interview with Barbara Garson. He said, "We are moving from the pyramid shape to the Mae West. The employment chart of the future will still show those swellings on the top, and we'll never completely get rid of those big bulges of clerks on the bottom. What we're trying to do right now is pull in that waistline [expensive middle management and skilled secretaries]."[10] His description is a wild one – it hints of other well-known problems in the office – and it gives us cause to be alarmed about what is happening to career paths in office work.

Jobs are being devalued; women are getting paid less to do more. For the majority of women office workers, office automation means working harder and faster for more people at once, without being paid commensurately. In 1979, full-time VDT operators in the United States made only $7 more per week than did conventional typists.[11] This occurred despite claims from computer vendors that productivity soars from 50 percent to 500 percent, depending on the type of document produced.[12] In some sun-belt cities, where automation is more likely to come in on the ground floor, VDT typists actually earned less than did conventional typists.

In law firms, we have seen a variety of ways that word-processing technologies are introduced, related to wage rates and trends. Quite often, the introduction of word processing results in the company hiring new workers at a lower wage rate to specialize in the new system in a word-processing pool. Other times, the secretaries themselves are split up, some remaining as administrative assistants serving more lawyers or more managers at once, others going into the word-processing pool. There may be a short-term increase in pay as an incentive to go along with the new system, or a step increase because a new skill is being used. However, the new wage rate, one notch up, continues over time, and wage ceilings stay low. We need, therefore, to look at both short-range and long-range effects on wages.

A third way that word-processing technology has come into corporate offices is by training secretaries to use new technologies in their current jobs, and giving them an increase in pay for the new skill. However, many other secretaries are trained to use the new system but get no raises. There is tremendous resentment about skills being taken away and about new skills not being recognized, either in respect accorded the person, or in pay cheques.

In 1981, a team of Swedish researchers came to Cleveland and did a tour of one of the big banks. They recorded the young vice-president of international operations during the tour of the large computer operations centre. He was enthusiastic about how everyone loved the new technology, ". . . especially the secretaries, they find it really enhances their job. You know, in my job I spend about one-third of my time travelling around the world. Now when I am away, my secretary can handle just about everything while I am gone. With the new technology, all the secretaries who use it are finding that they are able to take on more and more responsibilities." One of the Swedes asked, "And are the secretaries finding that they are being paid more and more?" There was a very long pause. After about twenty seconds of stunned silence, the bank vice-president mumbled his answer: "Well, I guess eventually they will be."

What are the consequences of all of these trends? Some of the major ones are, potential for job loss, continued sex and race segregation of the work force, increased health risks, and negative effects on personal, family and community life. The potential for job loss on a large scale is becoming an increasing concern for unions, for policy-makers, and for office workers. The Siemens corporation of Germany predicted that 40 percent of office work today will be suitable for automation by the end of the decade.[13] A study done in Britain estimates that office and other computer-based forms of automation could contribute to a structural level of 20 percent unemployment in that country.[14] Menzies, in her study of Canadian women workers for the Institute for Research on Public Policy, estimates that, "With fast diffusion and high productivity, female clerical unemployment in 1985 could reach as high as 16 or 26 percent...if the present proportion of working women continues to seek clerical employment. Under the same conditions, by 1990, the unemployment rate among female clerical workers could range from 25 to 41 percent."[15]

In the United States, clerical work is still the fastest growing occupation. It is estimated that some four to five million jobs will be created in clerical work in the 1980s.[16] We know that it already takes fewer people to do more work. We believe it is just a matter of time before the labour-reducing tendency of computer technology overtakes clerical employment growth. In American Banks, between 1973 and 1976, for example, employment growth slowed down compared to growth during the previous decade. The number of jobs continued increasing in banks, but the growth rate slowed down, while the number of transactions continued to climb sharply.[17] In other words, the labour require- ments were reduced although the absolute level of employment increased. We believe that in another ten to fifteen years the two trends could change positions in the United States. We hope it will not be any sooner than that.

Based on Menzies' research, my sense is that this is happening more rapidly in Canada. According to her report, clerical employment in insurance dropped by 11 percent between 1976 and 1980. She compares growth in the female work force with the growth in clerical work in the 1970s, and finds that between 1971 and 1975 the female work force increased by 24 percent, while the clerical work force increased by 33 percent, which meant that there was a very great demand for clerical workers. Between 1975 and 1979, although the female work force increased again by 24 percent, the clerical work force grew by only 12 percent.[18] That is still a large number of workers - still a growing area of employment - but the rate of growth is slowing down.

We must face two questions. First, where will the new jobs come from if employment growth is slowed in the service industries which have absorbed some of the people who have lost jobs in manufacturing? And second, where will women who are moving back into the work force find jobs? In the United States, since the early 1970s, women have moved into the paid labour force at a rate of one million a year, and one out of three of all women who work do clerical work. If there is significant slowing, and there will be a long-term slowing, then we need to study questions of public policy as soon as possible. To say that we have five or ten or fifteen years to consider these questions is to say that we do not have much time at all.

Office automation is also perpetuating sex and race segregation of the work force. By homogenizing many different clerical jobs into data-entry types of jobs, office automation extends the characteristics of what is called a "dual-labour market." Secondary labour market jobs are dead-end jobs; they are low paid, with high turnover and are semi- or unskilled. These are the jobs traditionally done by women and those from minority racial groups. The jobs in the primary section have formal requirements which do not allow one to move easily from the secondary section to the primary section. Many companies maintain or encourage deliberately high turnover rates in certain clerical operations. It gives them greater flexibility to re-organize work. As jobs become more interchangeable with automation, companies can continue to bring in minimum wage clerks to do the jobs. High turnover benefits management by keeping the work force unorganized and unstable. It allows greater use of part-time and temporary workers, and reduces what management pays in benefits since workers do not stay long enough to qualify for pensions. In one office, where the job rate had shifted from 80 percent to 45 percent clerical, with the same number of employees, but including many more professional and technical jobs, the manager was asked why clerical workers were not put into training programs to move them into some of the new jobs. After all, they were completely familiar with the work of the department. The manager's response was, "Well, you can't make a doctor out of a nurse, can you?"[19] We believe this means that affirmative action and equal employment laws and policies are more important than ever. We will have to fight for women and minority workers to obtain advancement in the new opportunities created by computer technology.

There are also increased health risks in the computerized work environments in offices. Increased stress and health problems are associated with particular design problems of the machines. More important, health problems are related to issues of whether or not people have control over the speed of their work, how they do their work, and whether they have some control over the volume of work they are expected to do. A study done as part of the Framingham Heart Study in the United States was released in February, 1980. It found that over an eight-year period women clerical workers developed coronary heart disease at twice the rate that other women workers did, and women clerical workers with blue-collar families developed coronary heart disease at almost twice the rate that men workers did. The factors the researchers found which predicted coronary heart disease among the women clerical workers were: an unsupportive boss; a lack of job changes in a ten-year period; an inability to or difficulty in expressing anger or frustration, which we see as very much related to the unorganized nature of the work force; an absence of procedures for grievance; a lack of power to challenge a problem and get it solved; and, the very arbitrary nature of supervision in offices. The researchers believe the relationship to blue-collar families is an indication of "socio-economic stress."[20] These problems, we believe, will be exacerbated in automated offices. The computer becomes the ultimate unsupportive boss. Promotional opportunities are reduced and dead-end jobs become more prevalent. Finally, the kinds of economic problems women office workers face today are perpetuated because of the way the technology is being introduced.

An especially bad combination of working conditions leading to job stress, researchers say, occurs when workers have too much work to do in too little time. This is called "quantitative overload." When the work holds too little interest for workers, it is called "qualitative underload." Swedish researchers point out that this combination, which we call "too much boring work," is more and more common with growing automation.

The National Institute of Occupational Safety and Health (NIOSH) in the United States released a report in February, 1981, in which it found higher levels of job stress reported among VDT operators at Blue Shield insurance offices in San Francisco than they had found in any occupational group they had ever studied, including many air traffic controllers. The NIOSH study also compared three groups of workers: VDT clerks, conventional clerks (doing the same work, but with typewriters, pen, pencil and paper), and professionals using VDTS (in this case, mostly newspaper writers and editors). The research team found that the highest stress was among VDT clerks, mid-level stress was found among conventional clerks, and the lowest stress was found among the professionals using VDTS.[21] The differences, they believe, were due to the conditions of the professionals' jobs, compared to the clerks' jobs. The VDT professionals had more control on the job, more likelihood of satisfaction and pleasure from their work; they could decide how to meet a deadline and got credit for what they did. The VDT clericals' jobs were completely rigid. They had extremely high production quotas. Not only did they get little recognition and satisfaction for what they did, but they did not even see the end results: they were inputting the information onto the screen, it disappeared into the electronic file, and it did not stop. Finding that the professionals using the VDTS had lower stress underscores the view that it is not the technology *per se,* but the way that managers introduce the technology, the way they let us use it or force us to use it, that creates new levels of job stress, and health risks, and threatens our job satisfaction.

The fourth consequence of computerization has to do with the effects on personal life, home life and community life. Researchers have observed a social withdrawal and depression among some word-processing and VDT operators.[22] In one woman's words, "The two years I worked in that law firm, I felt that I had no attitude, no feelings. It was like being in a coma for two years."[23] Comparing VDT workers under a piece-rate system, paid per-line-of-information-processed, with VDT operators working at an hourly rate, European researchers found that there was an increase in negative health symptoms and there was a decline in the sense of self-esteem of workers at the end of the work day. Shift work (evening and night work) is increasing to maximize use of the machines. It also causes disruptions in workers' personal lives. A black woman working on the night shift for a New York City bank remarked about her white supervisor, "...he doesn't seem to think we're the same kind of people he is. Like, he's got two kids and a wife in the suburbs and he goes to the PTA, drives them to the Scouts. Me, I got three kids, but he wants me to stay till ten p.m. With all the late nights, I haven't helped them with their homework once this year. I don't even know what's in their notebooks."[24]

Now we hear a clamour for a "cottage industry" of office work, called "office homework," "telecommuting," or "remote office work." Office homework may benefit some people, but it depends on who controls this trend. We consider office homework to be a dangerous trend; we must be sure of organizing to ensure that women doing such work will have fair wages and benefits. If you are working alone, by yourself, under a piece-rate pay system, and your only contact is with the boss, you are more vulnerable to unfair treatment.

Margrethe Olson of New York University has done one of the few studies on office homework.[25] Her findings provide some disturbing insights into what it may be like for women clerks working at a computer terminal at home. Among more than thirty homeworkers (men and women, mostly professional or technical workers, with a handful of data-entry workers), those who were best suited to this type of work had few social contacts and few interests outside their work, and they tended not to be involved in community life or political activities. Another important factor was whether the office home-workers were able to exert discipline over their family, whether they could control interaction in the family so they did not have too many interruptions.

The idea that it is somehow magically possible to solve child-care respon-sibilities at the same time as mothers are working is based on false notions about the kind of attention mothers need and want to give their children. Women who can afford to do so will place their children in a day-care centre or hire a babysitter to come in and take care of the children while they work. Office homework must not be seen as a substitute for available, quality child care for working mothers.

There is some research in Scandinavia which shows that when people work in jobs where they have very little control, they are more likely to withdraw from social and political activity. There is the possibility that soul-destroying jobs, if they are not challenged, can create vicious political and sociological circles. We have many reasons to fight to make jobs better than they are today, and to keep intact jobs that have variety and meaning.

Finally, we can consider the effects of office automation technologies on what may be called "the culture of work," including the ability to have social interaction on the job. Steven Sauter, an industrial psychologist studying the occupational health effects of VDT work, says he was not surprised that VDT operators in clerical jobs reported higher stress levels than other workers. VDT work that is constantly monitored by computers can actually be more stressful than assembly line work, one reason being that the worker cannot work ahead or delay if production is always "on-line" to the supervisor.[26] As alienating as assembly work is, in most situations you can still work fast for a bit, have a few seconds' breather, and then catch up. On a display terminal, if all the keystrokes are monitored and measured, if there is a prompter inside the machine bringing up more work immediately as the final key on the last form is hit, then the faster the worker works the faster she or he gets more work. The worker cannot work ahead, or delay the work for a few seconds. The supervisor has constant access to the production rate and to whether or not the equipment is being used. At any time, the supervisor may obtain a printout to analyze the worker's time on and off the keyboard. In many assembly-line situations, if workers are working closely enough, they can spell each other off, or help each other out if need be. On a terminal, it is just the worker and the machine; in many cases, workers cannot talk to each other. The more demanding or intense the work in terms of attention to detail, the less likely it is that there will be communication between workers. One woman gave as the reason for leaving her job in an insurance company, "What finally got to me was that I didn't even have anyone to say 'goodbye' to at the end of the day."

In trying to organize these issues, it is useful to remember that we are subsidizing the implementation of office automation. The bank I used to go to increased its charge for chequing six months ago. When I called to ask why the charge went up, I heard, "We're undertaking major office automation, so we need to increase the charges to pay for it." As the public and as consumers, we need to think about the influence we might exert on behalf of workers about these issues, because we are paying the costs of technological changes.

We should also be aware that when people work under extraordinary pressures, with very high production quotas, there can sometimes be unexpected effects on productivity. Studies have found that error rates increase anywhere from 40 percent to 400 percent when the control over the speed of work is taken from the person and given over to a machine-controlled system.[27] It makes a lot of sense to us. If the incentive is to increase the number of keystrokes, workers lose some of the incentive to go back and correct a mistake. One clerk who worked in "exception handling" (where a claim cannot be processed by the standardized procedure) in the claims division of an insurance company, told 9 to 5, "When I first started, I really cared about the work. I would study each claim, and I would try to decide on the basis of our rule book whether or not the claimant deserved the payment. Some days now, I just give everybody the money."

Shoshanah Zuboff of Harvard Business School described a department in a retail operation of a large department store in New York City, where work is rigidly controlled. She found that some workers were so angry at the production rates they had to meet that sometimes they made up customers out of desperation in order to meet their quota.[28] You can imagine how this made the books go haywire, because the company would then try to get money from customers who did not exist!

Workers do these kinds of things only out of sheer frustration over the way they are treated on the job. Increased office automation all too often attacks the pride office workers take in doing their work; it can also attack the dignity we deserve on the job.

It surprised me when I first heard about increased error rates and inefficiencies in automated workplaces, that management would introduce new systems regardless of the detrimental effects on productivity. After all, the most basic argument for office automation is to improve efficiency and productivity for the public good. What the real picture means to us is that certain types of managerial control can be counter productive as well as health threatening. It also means that our employers are willing to sacrifice the quality of service provided to their customers for the sake of the quantity of work they wrest from, and the control they gain over, the work force.

In summary, I would like to ask, "What are management's goals in introducing office automation? Its public goal is to increase productivity and efficiency for the public good. That is something we would all agree with, but we don't want it at our expense. We know now that productivity is not really at the top of management's list. At the top of the employers' list of goals is their desire to maximize their profit margins by reducing labour costs, and they plan to reduce labour costs in a number of ways: first, by taking the skills out of our jobs, so that wage ceilings stay as low as possible; second, by increasing our work load and speed, without increasing our pay; third, by making employees more interchangeable so that high turnover becomes a policy, rather than a problem; and fourth, by reducing future labour costs through reducing the number of employees needed.

What can we do about all this? It sounds pretty grim, but I believe there are a number of things we can do. The resistance to office automation is becoming more organized. Unions in the United States and in Canada are bargaining for and including clauses on technological change from the beginning of contracts. They are challenging management's prerogative to set production standards unilaterally in new contracts from the beginning, and are seeking work influence in current contracts. Boston 9 to 5 recently learned that the John Hancock Insurance Company suspended an order for VDTS so that they could shop around more to find equipment which meets 9 to 5's demands for safe, high-quality terminals.

Office automation is still in a transitional phase. In this phase, companies have to listen to what we have to say. Managers know that the crucial factor in the pace of change from the social office to the electronic office is how people respond, that is, what we will and what we will not do. Informal resistance of many office workers slows down office automation and influences it. Companies are beginning to compete over who has the safest or most "friendly" equipment because of the attention derived from health complaints. We influence the type of technology created to some extent. An IBM executive told 9 to 5 that word processing would have to be considered a failure because it managed to capture only 6 percent of the market. "We plan to emphasize electronic mail in the future," he said. "Who can complain about getting their mail faster?"

Nine to 5 has called for a moratorium on the further production of VDTS until safer equipment is designed and manufactured, and until managers stop abusing new technology by using it as a new tool of power in the office. Managers and computer manufacturers go crazy when we call for a moratorium. But they cannot deny that they have the ability to make safe equipment and that the improvements in working conditions which we need are within the ability of management today.

I want to put the demand for a moratorium in perspective for you. In Europe, unions have virtually imposed partial moratoriums on badly designed VDTS and some forms of VDT work. In Sweden, where workers refused to work with certain low-quality equipment, IBM markets a different line of display terminals that are better and safer in ergonomic design. The Viennese government mandated four hours of work per day on VDTS, because studies showed that eye strain is much worse after four hours, even with rest breaks. In

111

Norway, the government has proposed legislation that goes even further. The proposed regulations would limit VDT work to 50 percent of the working day. The remainder of the time is to be spent doing more integrated work, that is, work related to the work done on the terminal. That way, workers get to know more about the line of service provided or the overall work of the company, rather than just entering abstract data into a machine. The Norwegian regulations include a clause on the use of data gathered by computerized monitoring: such information cannot be used for discipline against workers, or to set standards without negotiations with the unions. Representatives of the workers have some control over how the data will be used.

There are major differences between conditions in those countries and ours. Eighty to 90 percent of all office workers in Sweden are unionized, so their governments have to respond to their proposals and so do their employers. These examples show, though, the effect that we can have if we put our feet down and say, "No, we won't work with this terrible VDT. No, we won't tolerate these terrible conditions any longer." And they show the effects we can have when we articulate and demand the changes we want in the office of the future. The Swedish Insurance Union, looking at the new capabilities that computer technology presents, called for the creation of more insurance centres, particularly in rural areas, so people would not have to travel as far to a service centre. They called for more training and understanding, a wider variety of the insurance lines offered, and increased time with customers to explain the services to the insured.[29] The technology allows for the paperwork and records processing to be done faster, so more time can be spent in customer contact. Because computers and telecommunications systems make work very mobile, it is possible to have offices in more locations, more convenient to people.

Nine to 5 has worked to change the nature of public debate about office automation, and we feel we have had an effect. We have drawn attention to the concerns of women office workers, but we must remember how far our employers are willing to go, and how far they want to go. Now, more than ever, we need more decision-making and control in our jobs – not less. We *must* organize to influence the shape of the office of the future, because in doing so, we are organizing to protect the future of our jobs, the quality of life on the job, and our health. During this transitional time, when the extent of office automation can still be influenced, we must organize on a very large scale, before it is too late. We are truly in a race against time; the clock is ticking.

9

Women, Families and the State

Margrit Eichler

I would like to talk about changes which have been occurring recently in families and what these changes mean for policies. When I say policies, I am referring primarily to government policies, and specifically to federal policies.

It seems to me that families have been going through very fundamental changes in the last one or two decades. Although there have been many changes, there are two that I think are of particular importance; they change the very essence of what it means to be married or to be a member of a family. These two changes are the rapid increase in the participation of wives in the labour force, and the rapid increase in the divorce rate.

Today, more than half of all Canadian wives are now in the labour force and, therefore, earn an independent income.[1] This means that wives-the majority of wives-are no longer totally dependent economically on their husbands. The fact that there is a second income makes a big difference in the relationship between a husband and wife. It also means, because many of these wives are also mothers, that we now have an even greater need for high-quality day care, a need we have not begun to meet at this time.

Between 1969 and 1979, the divorce rate more than doubled.[2] That is a rather stunning rate of increase. Before 1969, we had a constant slight increase, but it was not of this proportion. A rough estimate is that about one marriage in three is likely to end in divorce. If this trend continues in the next decade, one marriage in two could end in divorce.

This means that we can no longer necessarily consider marriage as a life-time union. And it also means that, *de facto,* the character of marriage has

Note: Margrit Eichler has written further on this topic in Margrit Eichler, *Families in Canada Today: Recent Changes and their Policy Consequences* (Toronto: Gage, 1983).

changed. Earlier, we had tended to think of marriage as a voluntary union. Once we were married, however, it was really an involuntary union, because divorce was very difficult to obtain. This increase in the divorce rate, I think, has changed the character of marriage to a voluntary-or, at least, a more voluntary-union. The fact that the divorce rate is so high has an effect on all marriages, including the marriages that continue.

Divorce also changes the relationship between parents and children. The mother-child tie tends to continue since custody usually goes to the mother. Counter to some current thinking about custody, I found that in Canada between 1970 and 1979 there was no increase in the proportion of fathers getting custody.[3] There is a relatively high possibility, however, of the father-child tie being disrupted. Another aspect of divorce that may change the relationship between parents and children is re-marriage. In 1979, just over one-quarter of all marriages involved a previously married partner.[4] I think the trends I have just mentioned are going to become more pronounced.

Given this contemporary background, I should like to ask the question, "How do our government policies address themselves to the present situation?" To give a very short answer, my summing-up would be that our policies address themselves to our present world in a very inconsistent manner.

I want to explore the main features of these inconsistencies, and I want to comment on their effects on women, men, and children, and on society as a whole. I should, however, like to make one more introductory remark. I am going to criticize government policies because I think they are totally inadequate. On the other hand, we must recognize that we are in a transitional stage and that it is going to be very difficult to devise policies that are equitable for everybody. Since we have different types of families co-existing at the same time, we have to strive to implement future-oriented policies rather than to look backwards to what was, but is no longer. When I speak of "future-oriented policies," I am not necessarily speaking of "a family policy."

Canada does not have an explicit family policy and I want to make it totally clear that I am not arguing for or against our having one. I mention this because we will be talking about family policies, and because there is an assumption that it is a good thing to have a family policy. That depends on whether it is a good or a bad policy; there are some family policies that are quite terrible. Let me give an example. Most provinces used to make a legal distinction between illegitimate and legitimate children. The rationale behind this was that we wanted to protect the family, meaning the "real" family, the legitimate family. The problem was, of course, that the unmarried mother and her children also formed a family and, by protecting the one type of family, we were thereby discriminating against the other type of family. It was and is a

114

two-sided measure, and not necessarily a desirable one. At this time, Ontario, New Brunswick and Quebec no longer make any distinction between children born within a marriage or outside a marriage.

Here is another example of why family policies are not necessarily desirable. In Ireland there is a regulation restricting the sale of contraceptives to married couples, and a woman has to get a prescription from a doctor to buy contraceptives. That is one indicator of how a family policy could develop, and I would not consider it very desirable. Whether a family policy is desirable or undesirable depends very much on what type of policy we are talking about. The problem with family policies is that they tend to be based on a notion of what is the "right type of family." That is the family that will be supported, and therefore, by definition, other families will be faced with impediments or discrimination.

Let me give you one more example. The Saskatchewan Commissioner on Child Welfare wrote in his Annual Report of 1930-31 about the Child Welfare Agency: "We, like all child-caring agencies working up to the approved standards, avoid falling into the error of trying to assist children in their own homes or relieving parents of their responsibility for sentimental reasons. We must be hard-headed as to why we do it."[5]

It is very clear from this example that certain types of families are defined as being in need of support and other families are not, and it does not really matter whether the need is the same or not. It seems to me that we urgently need support for *all* families and not just for a particular type.

Although we do not have an explicit family policy in Canada, we do have a social security system. It is a system marked by inconsistencies, by confusion over provincial and federal rights and obligations, by a very cumbersome administration, by lack of clarity and comprehensibility, and by a lack of fit between the various components. This description is quite independent of what our social security system does for families; it simply characterizes the overall system at the present time. These comments are, incidentally, taken from a government report and constitute the assessment of the various provincial and federal governments themselves; they incorporate their basic conclusions about the current system.[6]

To understand our current system, we must extract the notion of the family that lies behind the system. Social security in our time is still very much tied up with a particular notion of the family, that is, the notion that families are there to support their own. Our social security system goes back, at least partially, to the Elizabethan Poor Laws. This aspect has been called the "residual concept of social security." It basically means that people are not entitled, as a human right, to financial support. What is considered normal is for people to look after themselves and their family members. Only when the normal channels fail will government agencies step in to provide some maintenance of income.

By the end of World War I, we find the first federal legislation that provides pensions for war widows, and we also find some provincial legislation that provides financial assistance for mothers with dependent children. Different provinces had different laws, but all of them accepted the residual concept and gave out money as a form of charity. It was not a right. It was always tied up with some sort of moral judgement about whether we had earned this type of assistance or not. If we did not display the right type of moral behaviour, then we might be disentitled from getting access to the assistance.

One of the best systems we had at the time was in British Columbia, which had a mother's pension administered through the Workmen's Compensation Board and was, therefore, less demeaning than many of the other schemes. But, even in this relatively non-demanding and relatively generous scheme, an applicant for a mother's pension still had to be of good character in order to qualify for this pension.

I want to read you one example of a woman who first made it, and then did not make it the second time around, to give you an idea of what it meant to be of good character: "A woman with three children, one of whom was crippled, was granted a pension after the death of her husband. Three years later, she remarried and her pension ceased forthwith. Although she had married her second husband in good faith, it turned out to be a bigamous union. Her second husband was jailed and on his release disappeared from the scene. With no means of support, the woman re-applied for a mother's pension, but was told that in view of her bigamous marriage she was not a 'fit and proper person' to receive a pension."[7]

There is another concept of social welfare. In Canada, we have at this time a mixed system; some of our policies are based on the residual concept and others are based on what has been called the "institutional concept of social welfare." This is a notion which assumes that there are certain risks attached to living in a modern society and that these risks have to be shared. If there is a lack of money, therefore, we will get some money as a right and as an entitlement from the state. Our Old Age Security, which everybody receives, is an example of the institutional concept of social welfare; the Family Allowance is another.

I should like to provide a criticism of the network of our programs. I am going to focus on federal programs because this is meant to be an overview for Canada. I have divided these programs into those that are oriented towards children, those that are oriented towards marital status, those that can be called "income maintenance" programs (which are money transfers to people), and indirect subsidies (which are money transfers to institutions).

116

What I want to do is to look at these programs and see whether the entitlement to benefits is on an individual or family membership basis, and whether or not they are based on a means or needs test. I am including two factors that are not often mentioned in a consideration of social security, but that I consider to be very important: tax provisions and indirect subsidies. People tend not to include tax provisions, but I feel that tax money is money like any other money. It seems to me a great omission not to consider tax provisions as a transfer of money. Also, we tend not to look at indirect subsidies as part of our social security, and again, it seems to me that is a great omission.

PROGRAMS ORIENTED TOWARDS CHILDREN

There are four major programs oriented towards children: the Family Allowance, the refundable Child Tax Credit, the Income Tax Exemption for dependent children, and the Child Care Deduction. Family Allowances have been in existence since 1945, and every mother receives the Family Allowance irrespective of income. The procedures vary a little from province to province, but basically the money goes to the mother of any child under the age of eighteen who is still dependent, and it is taxed to the parent who claims the child as a deduction, which tends to be the higher-earning parent, usually the father.

The refundable Child Tax Credit is a very interesting type of instrument. We used to receive more money in Family Allowances. The Allowance was reduced in 1978, and the money saved was put into the refundable Child Tax Credit. The Child Tax Credit pays an additional amount to the mother, depending on family income. There is an upper limit on family income, and if we earn more than the limit we either get less or nothing. The Child Tax Credit is therefore available to the mother, but on the basis of her income as well as that of her husband, if she is married.

The income tax exemption for dependent children reduces the amount of money a taxpayer must pay by the number of dependent children he has. (I am saying "he" because it is usually the father who is the higher income earner, and therefore claims this deduction.) The tax exemption for dependent children is available only to those parents who qualify because their income is high enough, and the higher the income, the higher the exemption is. The distinguishing characteristic of all tax exemptions is that the more money one has, the more money one receives, up to a certain ceiling.

In contrast to the tax exemption for dependent children, the child-care deduction can be claimed only by a "working mother." Fathers can claim the Child Care Deduction only if they can prove that the mother was not available,

117

if she were in an institution because she was sick, or he had custody of the children and the parents did not live together, or if she were infirm for more than two weeks and he could prove it with a doctor's certificate, to give some examples. Since the eligibility for the Child Care Deduction hinges on the labour-force status of the mother, one can get very interesting asymmetries. For instance, when the mother has a paying job and the father is a student, they can claim the Child Care Deduction, but if the father has a paying job and the mother is a student, they cannot because she does not have any income. It does not really hinge on whether the mother works, but on whether she makes enough money to qualify.

PROGRAMS ORIENTED TOWARDS MARITAL STATUS

Our marital status-oriented programs are the married exemption, the equivalent-to-married exemption, the possibility of transfers of deduction between spouses, and the Spouse's Allowance.

The married exemption is available to those who have a "breadwinner" marriage. It allows a tax-filer who has a dependent spouse (usually a husband who claims a dependent wife) to reduce his taxes by a certain amount. The equivalent-to-married exemption is available only to people who are single, divorced, separated or widowed. They can claim somebody who is a kin or in-law and lives with them and is dependent on them. It is not applicable to a common-law spouse or to a dependent adult who is not a relative. It does not provide a benefit simply because we support somebody, but depends on marital status. With both of these exemptions, the more money one has, the more money one gets.

Certain types of unused deductions can be transferred between spouses and allow taxes to be reduced in the family, for example, a spouse's age exemption and the educational exemption. The transfer of deductions between spouses is not stated as if it were available only to breadwinner marriages but, in fact, it is worded so that the income of one spouse has to become "zero" in order for any transfer to occur. It is again a device oriented towards a traditional marriage where the wife is the dependent (or the husband, but this very rarely happens), and the higher the income, the more exemptions received.

The Spouse's Allowance is a direct transfer, that is, one actually receives a cheque rather than a tax deduction. It is a monthly payment to a needy spouse (usually a wife) who is married to a pensioner in receipt of an old-age security pension. This benefit is based on an income test and is available only to spouses between the ages of sixty and sixty-five. However, if a woman is needy, but was either divorced or widowed before she turned sixty, she does not receive the allowance. Or, for instance, if a single woman is on welfare or on a very low income since she does not have a husband who is an old-age pensioner, she is not eligible for any federal support until age sixty-five.

INCOME MAINTENANCE PROGRAMS

Within this typology, we have income maintenance programs which are financial transfers to individuals. Of these, the major ones are the Unemployment Insurance Program, the Old Age Security System, the Guaranteed Income Supplement, the Canada/Quebec pension plans and welfare. All of these are federal programs with the exception of welfare, which falls under provincial and municipal legislation, but it is so important that we must talk about it here.

Unemployment Insurance is a universal program, federally legislated, for eligible wage or salary workers. If somebody loses a job (under certain specified conditions), that person gets a portion of her or his salary replaced for a certain amount of time. The time varies; the maximum is a year. How much one gets, therefore, depends on how much was earned before. The more one earned, up to a certain maximum, the more one receives. Unemployment Insurance is based on previous labour-force status, and is, at the present time, totally independent of definitions of parental or marital status. The level of payments depends on the previous level of earnings, and not on need.

Old Age Security is a public pension which is paid to every Canadian, irrespective of income, once she or he reaches the age of sixty-five.

The Guaranteed Income Supplement can be added to Old Age Security payments, but is based on an income test, which means only those below a certain level of income can receive it. It is paid either to a single person or to a couple. If it is paid to a couple, the amount received is less than these two people would get if they were two singles. Marital status, therefore does play a role here, but not to the degree present in the marital status-oriented programs.

The Canada/Quebec Pension Plan provides a retirement pension based on employee-employer contributions. It is a compulsory plan and is meant to be a replacement for only 25 percent of the average industrial wage. (This is under discussion at the present time, and we can expect that the system we have is going to be changed. It is not clear in what way it is going to be changed, but it is very likely to be different in the next few years.) Since the Canada/Quebec Pension Plan reflects previous earnings, we have the same situation as we have with Unemployment Insurance: up to a certain maximum the more money earned, the more money received in a pension. In December, 1980, the average pension for a male from the Canada/Quebec Pension Plan was $143; for a woman it was $99.99.[8]

There are two aspects of the Canada/Quebec Pension Plan that are of importance to us in this context. They are pension-splitting and survivor's benefits. Survivor's benefits are paid to a dependent spouse, and, under certain circumstances, to dependent orphans according to a complicated formula. The benefits are paid for as long as the children are considered dependent, or to the widow for as long as she does not re-marry and does not get a job. The pensions are small.[9]

In July, 1977, the Canada/Quebec Pension Plan was amended to allow for pension-splitting between a husband and wife in the event of the break-up of the marriage. What this means is that the benefits for the number of years that one or both of them contributed to the plan during the marriage may be split between them. The pension is only payable, of course, once they reach pensionable age, so we are talking about very, very small amounts of money, taking inflation and a limited period of entitlement into account.

The Canada/Quebec Pension Plan is thus based on previous income in the case of earners, but on the income of the spouse in the case of dependent spouses. So when we say, for instance, that we only want to replace earnings, and one cannot have pensions for housewives or for people who are not in the labour force, we are implying a watering-down of our current system. We tend to forget that our current system, or at least a very important part of it, is not based on earnings at all, but is based on family status.

The last of the income maintenance programs I am going to mention is welfare. Welfare is under provincial and municipal legislation, although the federal government has, so far, paid 50 percent of the costs under the Canada Assistance Plan. This is up for re-negotiation, also. In Ontario, which is my example here, we have two different types of welfare: general welfare, which provides short-term assistance; and family benefits, which provide long-term assistance. (In fact, short-term assistance tends to become long-term assistance for many people who do not qualify for family benefits.) Family benefits are available to mothers who raise dependent children by themselves, and do not have a common-law relationship or a marriage. They are available also to families in which the male breadwinner is disabled, but not to families in which the female is disabled and the male is not. Social welfare, in both its forms, is based on a "needs" test. In the case of an individual, it is based on the income and the assets of the particular individual. In the case of the family, the welfare payment is based on the income and assets of the entire family.

INDIRECT SUBSIDIES AND TAX PROVISIONS

Having looked at the major programs in Canada involving direct transfers to people, I should also mention indirect transfers. They tend to be forgotten when we talk about social security, as I said earlier. For example, two very important programs in Canada are public health care and public education. They have been so accepted as rights that we do not even tend to think about them as social benefits but as the way things are. Of course, that was not the way things were for a long time, and we are, in fact, dealing with benefits. Health care and public education are basically available to everyone. If we did not have public health care and public education, we would have to pay for them directly. Two other examples of transfer programs are subsidized day care and subsidized living arrangements for the elderly. Day-care subsidies are available to parents of pre-school children based on income. The same applies to homes for the elderly; subsidies are based on income.

As you can see, our programs are mixed. Some of them are available to all people, some are available only on the basis of marital status; some are available to all children, some are available to some children; some require a means test, some do not. With this type of background information, we are in a position to look at the notion of the family that underlies this medley of policies.

The prevailing wisdom in all of the programs that include family status as a relevant criterion seems to be that public support systems must not usurp the support function of the family. The rationale is that if we transfer money to so-called "intact" families, it would sap their initiative and start them on a destructive cycle of dependency. Existing programs and services are, therefore, typically geared towards families that, according to some organizational criteria, are in need of help, such as families that have one parent. The irony of this approach is that it often has the opposite effect from what it intends. I want to suggest that this effect is implicit in the policy, not only an atypical aspect of the specific examples I want to give you. The following three examples have been taken from the mass media. There is really nowhere else one can get this information, even if one goes to the ministries, as I have done.

In one example, Emily and her paraplegic husband, Matt, age twenty-seven, have been married only a few months. Now she is afraid she may have to get a legal separation and let the province take care of her husband in a $120-a-day chronic-care hospital. Emily wants to work three days a week as a registered nursing assistant because the couple cannot live on Matt's pension alone. But Matt requires extensive daily care and they would therefore have to hire someone to provide care while Emily is at work. If, however, she earns $600 a month at part-time nursing, her husband's $536-a-month disability allowance will be cut to $137 monthly. If she works full time, her husband's allowance will be cut off completely. This means his pension is reduced on the basis of her income. If Matt is transferred to hospital, the province will pay (instead of $536 a month) between $3,000 and $4,000 a month and he would get worse care.[10] This is justified, however, on the premise that we cannot usurp the support function of the family. Right?

In another, similar, case, a couple actually had to separate in order to be able to survive financially. A couple in Canada has filed for a legal separation in their three-year marriage because the terminally ill husband, formerly a heavy equipment operator now too ill to work, will be denied his veterans' pension if the marriage continues. The man, age fifty-two, who served fourteen months during the Korean War, was told by the Veterans' Affairs Department that he is not eligible for his $365 a month pension as long as his wife works. His wife says she cannot afford to quit her $14,000-a-year job as a government clerk, but is worried because her husband cannot take care of himself. "It's all very cruel," the wife said. "I thought we could get an annulment and live common-law, but they told us no. If we legally separate, he gets the money, and he would have enough to live. But we haven't been able to figure out how to provide care for him."[11]

In another example, a man and woman had to decide whether or not they could marry. She was employed; he was disabled and received a pension. If they did not marry, they could live on the two incomes. If they married, his pension would be reduced to a level which would not allow them an adequate income.[12]

These three cases all involve handicapped people and that simply makes the situation clearer, the points more pertinent. Recently, we have had three convictions in Ontario of what have been called "welfare cheats," and in all three cases the mothers were actually jailed. In each case, a woman claimed family benefits for her dependent children and was paid these benefits for a number of years. In each case, there was a man in the home. In one case, it was a legal husband and the woman simply said he was not living at home even though he was. The problem was that he did not earn any money and could not support the family.[13] The other two cases involved common-law relationships which were not stable. In neither of these cases was the man able or willing to pay any money for the family. The women who received the benefits, however, were accused of cheating the department because they were not living as single women. The law says one has to be living as a single woman in order to get family benefits, irrespective of whether the woman actually gets any money from a man.

What I am suggesting is that as long as we have families and have policies that take marital status as a relevant criterion, we are always, in one way or another, going to come up with what I have called the "familism-individualism flip-flop paradox." That is, we justify our policies in the name of supporting the family, and the effect may be exactly the opposite.

There are two reasons for people arguing that we must consider family status a relevant criterion. One is that we do not want to sap the initiative of the existing family, whether or not the family needs the money and whether or not we may, in fact, then drive the family to split up. The other argument is that it is inequitable to ignore family status. I want to look now at the notions of equity that have been used for defending social policies.

There are two concepts of social equity: horizontal equity and vertical equity. Horizontal equity means that we want to treat people in similar circumstances similarly. Vertical equity means that we want to reduce income disparity; we do not want to grease a fat hog, we want to give the money to the poorest, to those who need it.

The problem is that in order to determine whether a particular policy is equitable or inequitable, analysts typically consider the family as the unit and not the individuals within it. I want to give you one example, one of many, of how this works. It is taxation. Depending on whether our reference point is the family as a unit or the individuals within it, and using exactly the same logic, we can come up with opposite conclusions.

Different countries use different taxation systems. Some countries have family taxation, some countries have individual taxation.[14] If the country has family taxation, it usually means that two people who are married are taxed together. Most countries, however, also have some sort of progressive tax system in which the tax percentage increases as the income increases. This means that two people who are married pay more tax than would two people who were single and had their individual tax payments added together. In general, therefore, family taxation discriminates against married people, and individual taxation does not.

Now, I will take two concrete examples. Canada has a system of individual taxation (more or less, with the one exception of the Child Tax Credit, which we will ignore for the time being); the United States, on the other hand, has a system of family taxation. Both these types of taxation systems are defended in terms of equity. If we want to argue that the only way to tax people is on a family basis, our argument is the following. In one family, a husband earns $20,000 and the wife earns $12,000; their combined income is $32,000. In another family, one spouse earns $32,000; the other does not have an income. We then argue that we have two families and they both earn $32,000. As they are both families, they should pay exactly the same amount in taxes. This argument can then be extended to say these families must also have the same tax liabilities, the same tax deductions, and so on, so that the overall disposable income turns out to be exactly even for both couples.

If we then look at these examples from the perspective of the individual, it becomes very interesting. If we are arguing for joint taxation, we are also arguing that the person who earns $12,000 in one family will pay a much higher amount of tax than another person who earns $12,000 and is not married. This is because the lower income earner (who tends to be the wife) is taxed at what is called the "marginal tax rate" of the husband: that is, her income is taxed as if her first dollar were the last dollar of the husband. The rate of taxation becomes progressively higher. This also means that if the couple saves a bit of money and then separates (and as you recall, we said before that marriage is no longer necessarily a life-time union), then the partner who had lower earnings and paid higher taxes is doubly disadvantaged. At the time of the separation she is going to have that much less in savings because she has paid more tax.

There is another aspect of the argument for equity on a family basis that I find very interesting. Analysts will usually say that if a person works forty hours a week, she or he gets paid for that amount of work. If a person works eighty hours, then she or he should get double the amount of money. If we argue for family taxation and say the tax liability should be the same whether we have one income earner or two, we are basically saying that eighty hours of work are worth exactly the same as forty hours – which means we count the work of the second earner as nothing. Now these same analysts, the ones who argue for family taxation, do not rush forward in large numbers to say that we should also have tax benefits that would absorb some of the costs incurred, such as child care when both parents are working. If we argue for family taxation, we basically mean that the work the wife does, both for pay and without pay in the home, counts for zero.

Another problem with using the family unit as the measure is that we assume that two people live more cheaply than one person (which is, of course, not true.) Because we are married, therefore, our benefits are going to be lower for the two people than if we were not married and were receiving benefits as a single person. This applies to any system, without exception, if we have income-testing on a family basis.

Overall, it seems to me that any program using family status as a criterion is going to discriminate against people on the basis of their family status. At the same time, the program is going to be justified in terms of helping and supporting families.

As I stated earlier, vertical equity is concerned with reducing income disparity. Over the last fifteen years the income disparities in Canada have changed very little, although we have programs now that we did not have in the 1950s and early 1960s. This is, I think, explained partially by the fact that our policies are so inconsistent. Some provide more money if we are poor, and some give more money if we are richer. Basically, all deductions are always regressive, meaning that any deduction always gives more money to those who have money than to those who do not have money. In fact, taking a 1980 example, if our income was under $1,000 and we paid $100 for charitable donations, the government paid zero. If our income was over $200,000 in 1980, we actually paid only $48 of the $100 charitable deduction and the government paid $52, which was more than fifty percent of the $100.

Overall, in Canada then, our social security system displays a mixture of both regressive and progressive elements, some of which penalize people on the basis of family status, and some of which do not.

There is one other issue I would like to introduce and that is the difference between universal and selective programs. Selective programs are those that are aimed at a particular population, in effect, to try to get money to the poor. Universal programs give money to everybody within a particular category, such as to every person over sixty-five. Our Family Allowance is a universal program, is attached to the child, and goes with the child. It is ordinarily given to the mother, but it is really dependent on the child. If the child moves to live with the father because the parents separate and the father gets custody, the allowance will go to the father.

Some people believe that selective programs are more desirable, and are more "target efficient" than universal programs because, of course, we do not want to give money to the rich. The problem with that argument is that it ignores tax, and if we ignore tax, we simply do not get the full picture. I want to give you a very illuminating example from Jonathan R. Kessleman, an economist from British Columbia, who talks about the difference between selective and universal programs: "Imagine an economy with one rich person and one poor person. For now, assume that the programs do not influence individual behaviour. Suppose that the government decided to increase the poor person's income by $1,000 and transfer this sum to the poor person. Alternatively, the government could tax the rich person by $2,000, and transfer $1,000 to each person. The former program would be called selective, the latter program, universal."[15]

If we do not take tax into account, we simply do not know what the effect of any transfer system is. In fact, there have been a number of studies showing that selective programs, which are ostensibly geared towards the poor, can be more regressive than universal programs, depending on the where the cut-off point is in the taxation system that is being used. Depending on the tax, a selective system may, in fact, transfer less money to a poor person, than would a universal program. This point is very important to keep in mind, because I think that it negates the most powerful political argument being used against universal programs. If we argue for universal programs, we can also argue that we not use family status as a criterion because, when we are rich, we are basically paying the money back again through the tax system. The real difference between selective and universal programs is that one requires a means test before we receive the money, and in the other program, the means test applies after we receive the money.

It seems to me that, in order to come up with more equitable policies, we need to avoid any programs geared towards family units and have - always and under all circumstances - the individual as our administrative unit. To prevent discrimination on the basis of family status, we should abolish families as an administrative unit. This may get people's hackles up, and I think it is very important to emphasize the phrase, *as an administrative unit.* I am not talking about the family as a *social* unit. If we use families as administrative units, we tend to end up discriminating against them. To avoid penalizing people for living in whatever type of family they choose to live in, we should not use family status as an administrative criterion. I am, as I said, not talking about the social unit, where I think there should be a range of arrangements made according to people's choice; these arrangements should be the people's choice and not the government's business.

In arguing for individual units, we encounter the problem of women who have been raising children at home and who, therefore, are totally dependent economically. Some of these women would be left out of everything because we would take away some benefits. I think we must recognize the people who care for dependent people, either dependent children or adults who cannot look after themselves because they are handicapped or aged, and we should consider this care a socially useful service.

What I am suggesting is getting rid of the distinction between "housewife" and "working woman," and looking at what people who do not earn money actually do. I am suggesting another distinction that looks at the part of what they do that is socially useful, versus the part of what they do that is privately useful. If somebody renders services to another adult who is physically and mentally fit to look after himself or herself, that is of service to the particular person and the person should pay. If somebody looks after another person who needs care, such as a dependent child or an elderly or handicapped person, she or he is rendering a socially useful service. If that person (who tends to be a wife or a daughter) did not do that job, the government would have to pick up the tab. That is so because we have a social security system that takes over care of people when the family is unable or unwilling to provide it. It seems to me crucial to recognize the social aspect of the work being done without pay and to treat it as being socially useful and, therefore, to provide financial and other types of benefits for the people who do the work for the time that they do it.

Then, of course, we have to recognize that producing children is a contribution to society, and that parents – fathers as well as mothers – share equal responsibility for the upbringing and the well-being of the children. Then, in order to move towards getting rid of the notion of families as administrative units, we must at the same time also move towards eliminating the structural disadvantages for women in the labour market and elsewhere. While we do that, I think it is also important to recognize that not only at the present time, but for the next generation, no matter what happens, we are definitely going to have a "mix" of families in terms of economic patterns. We are going to continue to have families in which there are two earners (as I said, that is now the predominant mode in Canada) but we are also going to have families where the women will drop out of the labour market for a portion of time. That being the case, I think we must make a distinction between long-range and short-range policies.

When somebody has been doing a socially useful service, I think we have to compensate them for it for the time being: we should, of course, attach some kind of age limit concerning dependent children. We should expect children to be economically responsible for themselves at a certain age, as do our family laws. In Canada, family laws generally now assume that parents share equal responsibility for the upbringing of the children and that parents share equal responsibility for their own economic well-being. Our social security system does not.

We truly are in a period of transition. There are many discrepancies. The parts obviously do not fit together, either within the various social programs, or between other aspects of the state and the family and the individual.

In conclusion, I recommend that all government policies should be universal and progressive, and that the progressive element be brought in through the taxation system. This means that in the 1980s we must develop a much closer match between our taxation system and the social benefits provided through government policies.

10

Romantic Love and Reproductive Rights

Deidre English

I am here today to talk about romantic love and reproductive rights. This conference might seem like an odd place to talk about love because, at first, love seems to be a soft subject and these are hard times. In the United States, for instance, we are looking at what is clearly going to be the defeat of the Equal Rights Amendment (ERA). This will mean that we now have to fight, state by state, law by law, every issue that concerns discrimination against women, with no overriding principle to help us. We shall be doing that in the context of the growth of the religious Right, the growth of the Right to Life Movement and the pro-family movement, all of which have dedicated themselves to stripping away women's rights.

We are looking at a Congress in the United States that is actually about to consider a bill called the Family Protection Act, a bill that has been around for years and that, before the election of Ronald Reagan, was long thought to be simply a joke. This is a bill that would see fired any teacher who presented a positive image of homosexual lifestyles in the public schools. It is a bill that would call for committees of parental review of all curriculum materials and then would dictate the way in which these parent committees would judge them, and that says that the federal government would ban federal funding for any school materials "that would tend to denigrate, diminish or deny the role differences between the sexes as they have been historically understood in the United States."

You can imagine this being said about blacks, for example, that there could be no curriculum which would denigrate or deny the traditional role of the races, as historically understood in the United States. You can imagine the outcry. But there has not been a similar outcry over the fact that the United States Congress, after Prayer Breakfast, is debating this legislation.

The anti-abortion movement has become one of the strongest and most effective political movements of our time. It has as one of its adherents the President of the United States, a man who sent a message to the annual convention of the Right to Life Committee (which I attended incognito). His message was that he would go much further once in office than anyone had predicted, in helping the movement to achieve its aims. Fortunately, however, the movement is somewhat stalemated right now. I think it unlikely that the members will be able to bring about the kind of sweeping anti-abortion legislation they would like to see. I think so many people in the United States oppose the legislation that Congress will not enact it.

Nevertheless, the anti-abortion movement is successful because it has been so effective in electing people, solely on their stand on reproductive rights, to Congress and to every state legislature. Whether or not the members of the movement gain approval for their anti-abortion measure, they certainly have filled the government with people who are fighting for it, and therefore, of course, will fight for everything associated with it. That means they will support every attempt to keep women from having control over our own bodies, from having access to the contraceptive technology that we need in order to plan our pregnancies, or the federal funding for the abortions that we need when our ability to plan our pregnancies fails.

So that is the news for American feminists. It is a very depressing time for us. We know, historically, that periods of conservatism always coincide with periods of anti-feminism, and we are now experiencing the backlash.

The news is not much more encouraging for Canadian women. During the 1970s there was tremendous social change and there were enormous changes in the consciousnesses of women. I think that they were permanent changes, but they did not add up to much in dollars and cents. This is what I read in a Canadian magazine: the average Canadian woman earns 63 percent of the wage of the average Canadian male. In 1978-79, 67 percent of working Canadian women were earning less than $10,000 a year. By contrast, 70 percent of male workers earned between $15,000 and $20,000 a year.[1] This is at a time when Canadian women can expect to face a worklife in the labour force of some thirty-three years, and that is taking into account the fact that many women take years off for childbearing and when their children are young. The women who do not have children can expect to face a worklife of about forty-five years, the same as that of men.

One in three mother-led households in Canada has an income of less than $7,000 a year – that is really a poverty-level income.[2] Going to college will help in terms of increasing the amount of money one can earn, but it will not help women's salaries relative to men's. In fact, the difference is greater; the female college graduate will earn about 50 percent of what her male peers will earn.[3] What can be done about these discrepancies? Judy Erola, the Canadian Minister responsible for the Status of Women, predicted that progress in ending wage discrimination would be slow and painful.

Of course, to the corporations, Canadian, American or multi-national, that employ women workers, this idea of progress is a painful one. They have been underpaying for so long that fairness would cost them a lot now. When feminism begins to hit them in the pocket book, these companies will rebel. Suddenly the token woman in the boardroom is no longer the smiling face of corporate feminism.

The service sector, where most women work, is the most rapidly expanding section of the work force, at least in the United States.[4] Unionization is beginning to take hold, and unionization in the service sector of the work force, especially among clerical workers, may be in the 1980s what it was among auto and steel workers in the 1920s and 1930s. So that is what corporations are afraid of, that is what they feel they really have to fear from feminism. Let us make no mistake about it. Women who unionize, women who demand equal pay for equal work, are very much coming out of the consciousness of themselves as women with a new approach to their rights. They are not just organizing as workers; they are organizing as women who want to be treated as equal to men.[5] So feminism is as threatening an ideology to corporate capitalism as unionism is.

That is why the conservatives love the pro-family and anti-feminist movement. It does their work for them. It keeps women from demanding their due. And the great irony is that it does all this with such beautiful words: words like *pro-life* and *pro-family*. The secret of its appeal is its positive image. The pro-family movement appeals to a traditional ideal of romantic love. It harkens back to the day when every story had marriage as the happy ending. (We did not know what happened afterwards.) In the old ideal, women were swept off their feet by chivalrous men. These men then protected and supported their women in return for sex, smiles and service.

Phyllis Schlafly continually refers to the romantic ideal in her talk about marriage. She speaks of her husband, Fred, as a prince and says that it was a storybook romance, that he came along on a white charger, and she has been happy ever since. When she speaks around the country for the Stop the ERA Movement or for the Eagle Forum, the pro-American, defence-oriented organization she first founded, she often begins her talks by thanking Fred for letting her leave her housewifely duties for the day in order to address the group in the University or wherever.

Phyllis Schlafly is an excellent example of the coincidence of conservatism and anti-feminism. She was a conservative long before she was an anti-feminist. In fact, the Republican Party was pro-ERA until the last Republican convention when they overturned a forty-year history of being in favour of the ERA amendment. And so Phyllis Schlafly, as a good Republican, was pro-ERA, as well as being one of Barry Goldwater's strongest backers. Now she is a leader of the pro-family movement, and I believe, one of the most significant political figures of our day.[6]

This kind of appeal to return to the old, traditional family is working. We have to look at that, and take it seriously. The fact is, for instance, that the Right to Life Movement is overwhelmingly a women's movement. When I was at the convention, about 80 percent of the people present were women. Yes, the speakers were men, and yes the leaders were men, but the women were there. I do not think anybody forced them to be there. And they willingly placed men in the leadership positions of their movement. The women were the ones who were mailing the letters, making the phone calls, merely running the movement. The same is true of the anti-ERA movement. It is a women's movement. And I think we feminists can no longer say that the women who participate in these movements are simply robots, brainwashed or forced into these movements by men. That is obviously not true. These women believe that there is something in these organizations for them.

I do not think there is any great mystery, or anything that we should shy away from, in the positive response of many women to the pro-family movement. The answer is in the labour statistics that I gave you just a few minutes ago. I think it is very clear that many women today have no optimism left about what is going to happen to them in the work force. I think that a lot of women know in their guts that if they are on their own out in the work force they are going to sink like a stone. They are beginning to get the message that neither feminism, nor the federal government has the clout to help them out, and they should attach themselves to men, and quickly. Fear is what it is all about. It is about the terror of being stuck with the sole responsibility for one child, or two, or more, in an economy in which most women are earning much less than it takes to raise those children with any decency. That is what it is all about.

When we first became involved in the feminist movement in the 1970s, it was a period of economic growth. We still saw an expanding economy ahead of us, and we talked about a kind of feminist Utopia. That spirit resulted in many women taking risks, and changing their lives in very dramatic ways. Some women went back to school, or got a job; some women gained the confidence to walk out on a bad relationship. People talk about the high divorce rate of the 1970s as though it were a tragedy. I do not think it is a tragedy when a bad relationship breaks up. These changes said a lot about the fact that women had

131

some hope of being able to sustain themselves. They believed there was a women's community that would give them support and spirit. They believed there were jobs available. They believed there was training available. They believed there were women's centres opening up. There were resources for them; they could take a risk; they did not have to stay in a situation where they were being beaten, being humiliated, or simply not being taken seriously, which is bad enough.

Some women had the nerve to get involved in a sexual relationship with another woman because, for the first time, they had a sense that they could do so in a way that would not lead to public humiliation. They knew that there was a movement, and that there was even legislation, that would back them up in saying they had a right to live as lesbians. They had a right to live with one woman or a number of other women, to raise children alone or collectively. They could not be discriminated against in their places of work or in their attempt to find housing because these were their choices and because they had followed their hearts.

Some women simply stopped dressing to please men, or stopped wearing makeup, or stopped always tilting their heads to the side when they addressed a male, or stopped using many of the other signs of acquiescence and fear that women are trained to use from childhood on. All of these things took guts, and gave us more strength. The message of feminism was a liberating one. It said to women, "You count. Your needs matter. You can make it. Take the risk. You'll have support, and you'll come through."

To me, the great crime of today is that all of the cultural messages are now negating the risks we took in the 1970s. I think there is no greater poverty than having to live in an atmosphere in which there is a lack of support for risk taking. It is the new economic insecurity that has set off a new form of cultural security. It makes women believe a different message, and the message is: "You can't make it without a man."

Even worse, for many women, is that the permissiveness of the 1970s did more to liberate men than it did to liberate women. After all, when a relationship breaks up, we know who usually winds up with the children. In many ways, therefore, the whole atmosphere of self-affirmation had an unequal effect, because of the unequal economic relationship between the sexes. Men, too, felt that they could make these moves and could do things differently. They learned that there was little social stigma placed on a man who walked out on a relationship when the babies were still in diapers. The man who once would have had to marry a woman he made pregnant, now considered himself chivalrous if he split the cost of an abortion.

On the surface, the romantic ideal has been dusted off and shined up and it

132

is again being presented to women as an inducement to get them back to their old business. Not back to their homes, mind you. The economy needs women in the work force. The economy is dependent on that burgeoning sector. Women are not being told to go home again; we should not think that is what we are hearing. We are being told to go back to doing double duty, to go back to working and taking care of the housework. Let us not disrupt the situation in which the average working woman spends thirty hours a week on housework, and the average working man spends an hour and a half. That is the situation now, and that is the situation the new Right wants women to embrace, and to embrace with love.

I want to tell you a story that a young male employee of an airline told me recently. He said that he had been talking to a passenger about the airline. The passenger confided to him that he had some good advice about how the airline should handle its female personnel. The passenger said, "The trick is to make sure always that the women are reporting to a man. All the women employees must always have a male superior. The reason is that women get a deep inner pleasure from serving men." The point is very clear!

The reason for reviving the old idea of "home" is not for the purpose of our returning to it, but it is for the purpose of stretching the ideal of romantic subservience to include the workplace. Behind that romantic ideal is a very sadistic idea: it is a idea that wants to manipulate the pleasure many women get from being warm and decent people into a way to hold them down; it is an idea that wants to manipulate women's traditional function of being maternal and giving and loving into a way to pay them less. It is really a vindictive and punitive attitude, and it is in accord with the new conservatism.

This attitude towards women is also in accord with the fear of the right wing that someone might get something for free. That is their big fear.

"There's no free lunch" is their favourite phrase, even if you are a hungry child in a school cafeteria, even if you are a welfare mother. People must pay for what they get. In marriage, men have to pay for sex with financial obligations. In marriage, women should have to pay for being kept by being subservient. Sometimes I think this is at the root of the right wing's obsession with homo-sexuality. I think what really bothers them is the thought that some people are getting away with having sex without having to suffer for it. Is this really love? Is Phyllis Schlafly really a loving person when she opposes abortion, but also opposes illegitimacy, and also opposes welfare? Is it really love to dangle the illusion of safety and security in front of women's eyes and then abandon them to the unpleasant consequences? It is not. It is the protection of a privileged lifestyle for a few at the cost of manipulating and lying to the rest.

So, let us get back to the idea of love itself, with a little more confidence and a little more understanding that we are, as feminists, not the negative movement. We are not the "anti-life, anti-family, anti-people movement," as we have been characterized. We are not confronting a loving and generous mentality; we are confronting a vindictive and punitive mind. Perhaps we have not talked enough about love in the women's movement, but we have learned a great deal about it through the risks that we took in the 1970s. We have gained a fundamental feminist insight, and it is this: there is very little love between unequals. Love between an oppressed person and an oppressor is as compromised an idea as love between a master and a slave.

Any concept of love that is not based on equality completely confuses me. I cannot grasp it. I have no idea what people could be talking about when they talk about love, except when it is on a basis of complete human respect and equality. If a woman is struggling for equal pay or for respect at work, or for her right to be free of the fear of rape when she walks down the street, or for her basic ability to control her own biological functions, and the man with whom she is involved does not support her in that right – if he does not support her fully and whole-heartedly and take concrete actions to show that he supports her – does he really love her?

It may be true that love, today, is an emotion primarily notable by its absence, and yet I think that we hold an image of love. I think it is an image that comes to us through the cause of the feminist movement. It is an image that comes to us when we understand what relationships could be like if we lived in a world of equality. There is an English author named Jill Tweedy who wrote a book called *In the Name of Love*. In this book, she said that love is like the light coming to us from a star that has not yet been born, coming to us backwards in time.[7] I think that makes sense because, if you share my idea of love – the idea that love can only be based on equality – and you look at human history, you know that love is an ideal which remains to be realized for the vast majority of people.

Yet we do have a tradition of thinking about love this way and we ought to remember it more often. Victoria Woodhall was the first woman to run for president in the United States, and this was at a time when women did not have the vote. She was also the first woman to publish *The Communist Manifesto* in America. From the lectern, when she declared her candidacy for President of the United States, she declared that she was a free lover – not only a feminist but a free lover.[8] Free love had a feminist connotation then. It was not like the sexual liberation of the 1960s. The free lovers were men and women who believed that women should have the same right to sexual autonomy as men did. The concept of free love had two parts. The first was very similar to our own demand for the right to control our own bodies. The first demand of the free lovers was the right to say no. It was the right of every married woman to refuse sex if she did not love her husband, or if she did not love him that night. Second, the free lovers said that, when a woman did love, she had a God-given right to give herself in love. She did not have to uphold the Victorian standards of repression.

We do have our own tradition of romantic love, therefore, as exemplified by women like Victoria Woodhall and Emma Goldman. We have a vision – a Utopian vision, admittedly – of a feminist romanticism, and I think we ought to be more proud of it and more confident of its value. It calls up an image of a world where people commit themselves fully to the equality of one another. It calls up an image of a world where women are truly respected by men, not loved for their docility or their subservience. It calls up an image of a world in which women can love women if they choose; men can love men if they choose; and women can love men if they choose, not out of dependency, not out of gratitude, and certainly not out of fear, but out of a freely-taken choice. Here I could almost be quoting the free lovers of the 1840s.

We hope for a world where people need not fear that pleasure will be despised and punished, a world where children are born wanted, not only by their parents but by a loving community. Yes, it is a Utopia. But no, I do not believe it is an impossible dream. I think it is an image that is far more realistic than the nostalgic and hypocritical romanticism of the members of the New Right who have actually been able to mobilize people to fight for their version of love. So I say that if they are able to motivate people to fight for a nostalgic return to tradition and a world which no longer exists, we also can fight for a world that does not exist now, but could exist in the future. We ought to be able to fight for our feminist Utopian dream.

135

11

Strategies for the Eighties

Margrit Eichler

Deirdre English

Judy Erola

Judith Gregory

JUDITH GREGORY As the research director for 9 to 5, The National Association of Working Women, I want to point to the strategic importance of clerical and service work, an area which is dominated by women. This area of employment is the fastest growing in the economies of both Canada and the United States. Eighty percent of clerical workers are women.[1] In Canada, 81 percent of women who work are employed as clerical or service workers.[2] This is one of the least organized segments of the work force. In the United States, less than 10 percent of women clerical workers are unionized in the private sector, less than 20 percent in the public sector.[3] Clerical and service work is characterized by sex, race, and age discrimination, by discriminatory practices both on the job and in retirement for older women. And the nature of the work is changing rapidly with the introduction of computer technology.

I think it is very important to recognize that women are strongly represented in growth areas in the economy. In the United States and Canada we are plagued by high levels of unemployment and it is easy to forget that there are areas that are expanding. These are the areas that have been absorbing women who have been moving into the work force in the United States at a rate of more than one million a year for the last decade.[4] In Canada, there are about 4.6 million women in the work force at present. There are estimates that two-thirds of all women of working age in Canada will be working by the year 2000, and it is into these service industries that women are going for employment.[5]

Fifty years ago in the United States, half of the work force was employed in manufacturing; now service work accounts for two-thirds of all employment.[6] Almost one in five of all American workers is a clerical worker.[7] In Canada, the shift towards a service-based economy has been even more dramatic. In the 1970s alone, the percentage of the work force employed in the service industries

136

has risen from 30 to 60 percent, according to a study by Heather Menzies for the Institute for Research on Public Policy.[8]

Sometimes we are told that our work in clerical jobs or in service jobs is not "real" work. It is "non-productive," and that is the problem with it - that is why it is worth so little. We know that is not true. It is not that our work is unproductive; it is not that it lacks social value; it is not that our employers could keep industry running without us. It is the characteristics of labour in this section, defined by management practices, that pose the problems. These problems are perpetuated by job segregration - the crowding of women into limited occupations and industries. One of the characteristics of service-sector work is low pay: the average United States clerical salary hovers around $11,000 a year. In 1979, one-third of women clerical workers in the United States earned less than $8,000 a year for full-time work. Today, about one in seven women clerical workers who head households has an income at or below the official poverty line (which is $8,450 for a family of four in the United States).[9]

The service industries are also characterized by increasing numbers of part-time and temporary workers. In Canada, from 1968 to 1978, the number of part-time jobs created was double that of full-time jobs created.[10] These jobs are overwhelmingly held by women, many of whom need permanent part-time jobs in order to handle family responsibilities. As we know, however, part-time workers are rarely granted fair wages and fair benefits in accord with their full-time counterparts. Some observers estimate that fully 15 percent of the work force in the United States will hold temporary jobs during the next decade. In manufacturing, in contrast, almost one in ten workers is part time. In the finance industry, 25 percent of the work force consists of part-time workers, who are mostly women. In the health industry and retail industries, as much as 55 to 75 percent of the work force in some regions of the United States is part time.[11]

Another related characteristic of service work is the high turnover among its employees. When high turnover is a deliberate policy, employers do not have to pay pensions for workers, because they do not stay in the job long enough to qualify; the work force remains unstable, making organizing more difficult. Workers are interchangeable, so that temporary work and part-time work can be extended more easily. All of these problems are vastly increased by the introduction of computer technology.

These features of service-sector work need to be challenged for the sake of women workers, and for the sake of the overall work force and the protection of our living standards. In this regard, both affirmative action policies and the strategy of comparable worth for work of equal value are especially important.

137

The effect of the conditions of work in service industries is a downward pull on the overall standard of living. The buying power or earning power of women clerical workers has declined by 7.4 percent in the last two years; whereas, for the average worker in the United States, that decline was 5.5 percent.[12] If you look at the industry sectors and real wages in the United States, you will see that, up to 1980, manufacturing wages stayed barely at the same level in value of wages twelve years ago; whereas, in the finance industry - the banks and insurance companies - workers are typically earning 67 to 75 percent in value of what they were earning in 1967.[13] Now, with the three record-high years of inflation that we have had in the United States, the manufacturing wages have also been pulled down below parity with 1967 wages in real buying power.

What we now see is an overall effort by corporations to transform what have been the high-paying and unionized sectors of the work force - to pull those jobs down towards the wages and working conditions in service work by an assault on unions, and by an assault on the wage levels in those jobs. Our demands for higher wages, better benefits and better working conditions in the service industry, therefore, are very important in fighting the degradation of the entire work force in our two countries.

Automation is being introduced in ways that make these conditions in service jobs even worse. This is in contrast to the glowing images that we have of the new technology. Last fall, I was on a panel in Toronto, at a major conference called "Quality of Work Life," where a management consultant on the panel with me described "the three new freedoms" that we get with computer technology - free time, free thinking and free movement. As he said, he has already entered into Alvin Toffler's "third wave"; he walks from his own electronic cottage into the New England woods. That is very nice for him, but it hardly represents new freedoms for us. Although there are potential benefits from computer technology, we, as women and as workers, are not receiving them. Our skills are being taken away. New skills are not being recognized or rewarded. We are doing more work at a faster pace for more people at once, at less pay or at pay levels that are not fair compensation. And we are excluded from the new job opportunities that are created. There is also increased stress related to office computerization. This takes a toll on our health on the job, and also on our lives at home.

Although automation is described in futuristic terms, it is based on old management ideas and goals. There is nothing new about piece rates; there is nothing new about shift work to get the most out of machines. There is nothing new about speedups carried out through production quotas and constant counts of keystrokes by computer. What is new about "the electronic sweatshop" is that these kinds of things, which managers have been doing for a very long time, are now being extended to many more jobs and carried to extremes in severe treatment of workers.

I believe it is a crucial strategy, in taking on this whole range of issues affecting our lives and our work, for women to build institutionalized bases of power. We must transform the movements that we have built and that have sunk deep roots in the 1970s, in order to change the balance of power politically, economically and electorally for women. In the 1970s, 9 to 5, The National Association of Working Women, began a national movement to create a common identity among the twenty million women office workers in the United States. We believe that we have succeeded in building that movement; we see it growing. We believe that in the 1980s, we shall see a major wave of unionization among clerical workers. All of those conditions I mentioned will bring us to the realization that we cannot keep changing jobs in order to look for a better situation. We need to change the working conditions on the jobs we now have.

DEIRDRE ENGLISH Just to mention technology in the workplace, I recently read somewhere that when men are taught to use the new computer technology, their wages go up. It is said that they have learned a new skill. When women learn to use the new technology, their wages do not go up. It is said that the new technology made their work easier.

I want to say that I see three priorities in the early 1980s for the women's movement. The first two are the fundamental pillars of women's liberation. Without them, women cannot even fight. The third is the goal itself, which we always have to keep in mind.

The first two priorities fundamental to women's liberation are: one, an independent means of income; and two, reproductive rights. Without both of these, women are victims. Without both of these, women are dependent, completely dependent. They can be made pregnant and there is nothing they can do about it; they can be told what to do and they do not have the resources to support themselves. If we do not have those, women cannot even fight. We cannot even begin to achieve women's liberation. We have to continue to struggle to secure these basic rights for women. (I think that Judith Gregory's organization, 9 to 5, is the most inspiring movement I know of in the United States, because of its concern for job rights.)

Our third priority is that we have to keep fighting for the goal of feminism. I shall give you my definition of feminism; it is very simple. Feminism is a movement for the total equality of the sexes, and "total" is the key word. Its meaning includes legislation, includes job rights, includes the bedroom, and includes casual conversation (to deal with the problems that Barbara Ehrenreich

139

has called "conversus interruptus").

This goal – total equality of the sexes – is a revolutionary one and we should make no mistake about it. It is an all-encompassing goal that would completely change both public and private life. It would change the very nature of the sexes themselves, and it would change all our traditional concepts of gender. Women would be very different and men would be very different. Our goal as feminists is not just that women should change – it is not just that we should become more like men as we move into the work world – it is also that men should become more like women. There are many, many things that we have to teach men. We need to be aware that we are fighting for the first two priorities, an independent means of income and reproductive rights, so that we can have a movement that will be able to fight for total equality of the sexes, so that we can transform all of social life. Unless we remember that this is always our goal, that we are really fighting for an ideal, for what I called before a Utopian feminist romanticism or perhaps just a feminist Utopia, we will not be inspired and we will not remember why we are fighting or what we are fighting for.

I just want to end my remarks by saying that, as important as wages are, and as important as legislation is, and as important as contraceptive technology and abortion clinics are, these are not the things that people really fight for. These are not the things that make women pour out their hearts or that really motivate us to care and to come together to fight in a revolutionary struggle. What we fight for are the same things that motivated all revolutionaries. We are fighting for our ideals. We are fighting for justice. We are fighting for fairness and dignity. I think it is a noble cause, and by remembering that, we will be inspired every day.

MARGRIT EICHLER What Deirdre just said summarized my own approach to feminism. I can wholeheartedly underwrite every word she said. Given that an independent means of income and reproductive rights are basic requirements in our fight for total equality, what else would I want to advocate for in the 1980s? Because, of course, we are talking about a total revolution, we are talking about a great array of goals for which we are striving.

If women are to have an independent means of income, they will be in the labour force irrespective of whether or not they are married, whether or not they have children. Reproductive rights means the right to choose to have children, as well as the right to choose not to have children. For me, then, one of the primary policy issues that confronts us in the 1980s is care for the children.

Looking at what is likely to happen in the 1980s, we can assume that divorce is going to increase. We are, I think, going to see a further increase in the number of one-parent households. At the present time, one-parent households are largely headed by women. And most of these families live in poverty. We have had an increase in the number of children born out of marriage; we have had an increase in the number of children born in marriage who now live with divorced mothers. Basically, I think we have to recognize that, if we want a full employment policy for women, we also must have a social policy which gives support to raising the children in the 1980s.

There are various ways in which this could be accomplished. At the present time, limited support is given to day-care centres. In Ontario, support is given by subsidizing day-care places. One of the consequences, therefore, is that you have a "ghetto-ization" of certain children in these day-care centres. It is my personal opinion that day-care centres are probably, for the majority of children, the best way to handle the issue of quality care, if the centres are of a good quality, of course. Many of them are not. We are seeing the growth of commercial centres that may give poor care.

There are situations, however, where day care centres are not the answer. What do you do if you live in an outlying area where there are not enough children to justify a centre? Or if your local centre may already have too many children enrolled? Or what do you do if your child is sick? It seems to me that we must work towards a more universal approach to the care of children.

My own preferred way of ensuring the care of children would be to create a child-care tax credit that would be available to all mothers, whether they are in or out of the labour force. If the mothers decide that they would like to spend time out of the labour force looking after their own children, or if the fathers want to do so, they would take the child tax credit as a wage replacement for themselves. If they decide that they wish to be in the labour force, they would take that same amount, whatever it is, and pay it either to a day-care centre or to somebody, including a relative, who would care for the child. (One of the problems in Ontario is that people are disentitled from benefits if the care giver is related by blood or by marriage.)

To summarize, then, since care of the children is a primary issue which we must address if we wish to have full employment for women, it seems to me the most equitable way to do this would be through a child tax credit. This is the one strategy for the 1980s that I should like to recommend for your consideration.

JUDY EROLA Last night when I was meeting with (as usual) an all-male audience, I was introduced in my first portfolio - or the one I was given first - as the Minister of Mines, and then as the "minister responsible for one of our most important natural resources." It was left at that. When I spoke, I said, "I'd like to straighten this out. Yes, I am the Minister of Mines and responsible for one of our most important natural resources, but it is the other natural resource that I consider more important."

That brings me to the first point I want to make. It concerns women in politics. The fact that I have a dual portfolio is an advantage, because it opens doors that would not otherwise be open to me and brings me into boardrooms in which I would not be welcome as the Minister Responsible for the Status of Women. As a matter of fact, when the latter portfolio was given to me, I said to the Prime Minister that I would take it only on the condition that I did not lose the portfolio in mines. I happen to like the mines portfolio, but I said that because, as Minister of Mines, I was able to be at meetings and in situations where women are not normally present and where the views of women are not normally heard. I think that is extremely important for women looking at the 1980s.

I participate as much as I can in feminist seminars and in all the areas in which I think we must work very hard. But at every feminist seminar or conference I say, "Please do not confine yourself only to this area." Women are also going to have to be a political force everywhere in the country, and in every field of endeavour, if we are going to make our cause and our purpose known. Often I find as I go into those fields where there are no women, that things happen to us women – as a result of omission rather than commission – simply because the women are not there. Nobody says, "Just a minute, what are you doing to women? How does this affect women?" And if we are not there, it just isn't going to happen.

So I urge you to consider the whole political arena and where we are going in politics. We can attend seminars, we can make recommendations, we can make use of every feminist strategy in the book, but unless we see that women are in positions of power, we are not going to be heard. I say this first because it is elementary and basic to the success of the feminist cause.

As for the strategies for the 1980s and the position of women in the labour market, the panelists are absolutely right. I was delighted, Deirdre and Margrit, to discover that you agreed with me on a very important point: that without economic security, women have no independence. We have no equality; we have what I call "paper rights." Economic security is not going to come about until we equalize the opportunities for women in the work force through maternity benefits, and through day care.

One of the areas that my colleague, Monique Begin, and I also feel very strongly about is the whole business of pensions. If women are not participating in pension plans, and if we cannot look forward to a life of security down the line, then we are still nowhere in terms of equality. One of our major priorities is to establish, once and for all in this country, a pension scheme that is fair to

142

women. That, I think, is our primary objective at the moment. When such a pension scheme is in place, we can then concentrate on the other areas that we believe to be important.

Day care is one such area. In Canada, of course, day care falls within provincial jurisdiction, and we at the federal level match funds through our Capital Assistance Program. I do not think that is enough. I think the federal government must take far more initiative in this area, and we are examining ways right now through the Status of Women. My coordinator, Maureen O'Neill, is the head of a committee that is looking at possible federal contributions to day care as well as the role that the federal government should be playing as an initiator. I might say, about federal government itself, that we now have day-care programs in four federal departments. And I am proud to say that I just found a Treasury Board application on my desk yesterday for a day-care centre for my own department.

I believe it is absolutely essential for day care to be close to where women work or live, so that we are not having to bundle up children and take them across town, and then go to another part of the town to work. And, for the child who is sick, there should be some sort of isolation facility in the day-care centre. The mother should be able to check in on her child to ease her mind while she is working.

Something else I consider a priority is the issue of violence against women. I shall be appearing before the Health and Welfare Committee, which is dealing with the subject of wife battering and other kinds of violence, including pornography. There is going to have to be an attitudinal change in this country. I got into a discussion just recently with someone who said, "I am more concerned about child abuse than I am about wife abuse." And I said that, of course, I was concerned about child abuse, but child abuse is something that is being taken care of in this country. Attitudinally, we all reject child abuse automatically. We all know that child abuse is the abuse of the innocent and is wrong. I hate to say it, but I do believe that wife abuse is still accepted in this country. It is accepted by many, in many parts of the country, as sort of a natural occurrence. You know: they only get what they deserve. Until we deal with the problem head on, until we deal with it in the courts, until we deal with it through our legislation (C53 is the bill concerning this that is coming forward), we are not going to achieve those attitudinal changes.[14]

I therefore appeal to all of you to examine what is happening in this country. I find that our legislators are often very quick to respond to the needs of the people in their own areas. So often, however, women do not go directly to our Members of Parliament to express our views. We go to Ottawa and preach to the converted (like me) when we should be preaching to our local

143

members. Our members vote for bills in the house, they come to standing committees, and they will often say to me, "Gosh, I haven't heard from anybody in my area who's concerned about that. There's no support for that. Nobody is really interested." And then I reply, "But they are interested. I talk to these women." I urge you to use the political system, to contact your members, to make your views known, to support those bills that are coming forward - or perhaps to find fault with those bills. (I do not, for example, find C53 perfect, but unless some of the women and some of the members are alerted to the possible deficiencies, changes are not going to be made.)

I also ask you to be politically realistic. I, as a practising politician, have to recognize, no matter how quickly I want things to happen and changes to occur, that the democratic process allows for the other side to be heard, and that, sometimes, the voices on the other side are not in agreement with our goals. We have to face those obstacles as politicians, and we have to try to marshall the forces within our country. But often those forces are marshalled very strongly by the other side.

So, although we feel we are right, we must recognize that politicians get a great deal of flak from the other side, in the House, in committees, and in the press as well. You may look at politicians and say, "What are they doing? They're waffling on this." It is not often a matter of waffling; it is a recognition of the political realities. We hope that, through a reasonable and pragmatic approach, we will move, if not to the level we would like to see, at least a notch forward. I say this in the context of a very recent experience. Just this week, Monique Begin and I were at an afternoon session in which we were looking at the changes in the pension scheme as they relate to women. We discovered that we have come a long way in twenty years. The pension changes that took place in 1967-68 were considered revolutionary at the time. We find them rather quaint now because we feel that they really did not deal with the concerns of women. But at least they recognized the fact that women existed and that something had to be done for them. We have come a long way since then in that even the bureaucracy now recognizes that women have been treated very badly in the pension scheme and that there is a fair amount of catching up to be done.

I must say, in conclusion, that our political system and Parliament reflect generally the state of society in our country, and they will move forward only at a pace that our society will accept.

JUDITH GREGORY In many ways, what you have heard from this panel is what I think of as the multi-level approach to organizing that we, as women, need. My particular concern is that of organizing at the workplace level, both through unions and through organizations that are not yet unions, because most clerical workers do not, at present, want to be part of a formal union.

Nine to 5, the organization for which I work, is not a union. (It has been called a pre-union by some writers.) We believe that our organization is helping to create the conditions that will allow women to see unions differently: to see them as institutions that can be our own, that can represent us in ways that unions have not historically represented the concerns of women. So at the workplace level, using both non-union kinds of organizing and union kinds of organizing, it is possible to transform workers' institutions into entities that can fight for public policies, going all the way up to the public policy issues that you have heard raised.

I think that when we talk about economic issues, to underscore what Deirdre and Margrit said, we are not simply talking about the dignity and rights of women as workers and as full participants in the political life of our society. Looking at the issues created by automation, as an example, we need to raise these issues as social and moral issues, not just as an economic issue tied to productivity or efficiency. When we think of the effect that automation has, it is clear to us that we are faced with the question of how many jobs will be available and of what types. Will office automation humanize jobs or de-humanize jobs? What effect will it have, not only in the workplace, but also in our lives at home and in our perceptions of ourselves?

I want to comment finally on the importance of upgrading the value that society and employers place on women workers. It is very important to have affirmative action and equal opportunity strategies so that women can move up to higher positions and can be represented in the boardrooms where women rarely appear. But we believe it is equally important to value and recognize the large numbers of women who are concentrated in the clerical and service industries, and in assembly-line manufacturing jobs. Both efforts require our attention, and both must be worked on in the 1980s.

DEIRDRE ENGLISH I agree with what Judith Gregory just said about how this panel, in many ways, give us an opportunity to see and practise what we have said so often in the women's movement: that we need to have multi-level strategies of organizing. It is undoubtedly true, certainly in the United States and I am sure here in Canada, too, that women in the women's movement have tended to neglect legislation and have tended to neglect the whole political process of lobbying politicians, electing politicians, getting women into public office, and then pressuring both women and men in public office to vote favourably on legislation that affects women. In the United States we have suffered from our desire to stay out of the mainstream, from our desire not to

145

work within the system. We have seen the Right sweep the system and now we are paying the price. One of the major questions of the women's movement, and especially of the left-oriented women's movement that I represent, is what kind of working relationship are we going to have with the legislators? And how are we going to communicate with each other in an effective way so that we enable someone like you, Judy, to help us? You have a difficult role because you are in the middle, and therefore, everyone will be unhappy with you.

And so I think it is all the more important for us that you continue to do what you have done in requesting to come here to visit a feminist audience. It is important that you go into male environments where you are the only woman; it is equally important that you come back and talk to your constituents and talk to the people from whom your ideas really come. It does not take much insight to see that almost every issue that you mentioned in your talk is an issue that arose in the grass roots. It did not arise in Parliament or Congress. These are issues that were first raised in the women's movement. We are the ones – the activists, the students, the teachers in women's studies, and many others – who form a rape crisis centre. We are the women who come together, without any government support, and start to take care of each other's children. These are the people who come up with the ideas and from whom you get your ideas. And that is not to take anything away from you – but that is how it works.

There is a movement, the movement is militant, the movement has ideas, the movement takes the risks, the movement is out there on its own. But the movement can be heard by those in power. We are fortunate if we have some politicians who will listen to those ideas. Sometimes, and understandably, we are offended when that happens. We say, "Well, she thinks it is *her* idea!" Or, "These people are treating our idea as if it is something new, and we have been doing it for ten years." That is the moment when communication may break down, and when it may become difficult for the movement to communicate with the mainstream.

I should like to suggest, therefore, that I think one of the most valuable strategies we can develop is to find a sisterly way of keeping communications open. I really do believe that women in the movement must have an appreciation of the problems of women in power. I am sure it is not fun to go to that boardroom and talk to those mining executives or whatever. I am sure that when you are in there fighting for something (even if it is something that women have been fighting for for ten years), you are talking to people who may think it is an absurd and outrageous scheme of your own devising.

We have to begin, I think, with an acceptance of the idea that there will be disagreements and conflicts among us and that we will honour the feminist

146

principles of struggle and criticism, that is, criticism within a context of the knowledge that we are all, basically, going in the same direction. I have some problems with certain positions that you have taken, Judy, but I do not know a great deal about them. I would not want to express any of my reservations or criticisms to you without also expressing my feeling that what you are doing on behalf of women is important. I might wish you were more militant, but I appreciate, and I think many people here will appreciate, how difficult that is for you in your role.

MARGRIT EICHLER I was delighted, Judy, with the issues that you mentioned. There is only one comment that I would specifically disagree with: I do not think that child abuse is totally rejected in Canada. Rather, I think it is accepted: we still have policies that allow the strapping of children in schools, and we still regard what is happening within families as a private affair.

I was delighted, as I said, with the issues you considered to be important, and I should like to comment further on two of them: maternity benefits and day care. As far as maternity benefits are concerned, it seems to me that if our ultimate goal is total equality, then not only should women have total equality in the labour market, but men should have exactly the same responsibility for child care as do women. And I would argue, therefore, that we should think about parental benefits, not maternity benefits. We recognize that childbearing itself needs special benefits attached to it, but there are social aspects to raising children that should also be available for fathers. Incidentally, I think the only way in which we can avoid employers discriminating against women is to leave open the option of taking parental leave to both the fathers and mothers.

It seems to me it is important to make day care available to everybody, irrespective of income. At the present time, with the way the levels are set, if day-care places were available, they would be prohibitively expensive for many people. This means that we would have to provide subsidies to people at a much higher income level than we do now. I wonder what your feelings are, Judy, on both the issues of parental benefits and on raising day-care subsidies significantly?

JUDY EROLA You are absolutely right, Deirdre, we need a multi-level approach, as I thought I had indicated in my opening remarks. And yes, you are right, I am in a very difficult position, because I am caught in the middle and I must always balance the practical and the possible with what you termed Utopia, or perfection. You know that you are never going to get there, but you keep on trying. I might add that I have been thirty years in the work force; there were times when I despaired completely but I do feel we have come a long way. It is marvellous to see the changes that have taken place in thirty years, to see the attitudinal changes and the actual physical changes such as child-care tax credits, which did not exist when my children were young. However, I must say it is still certainly not enough, as far as I am concerned.

It might be interesting for you to know that a study of the child-care tax credit program has been conducted, and preliminary indications are that, although we thought the upper income women would benefit the most, it is not so. In fact, the tax credits are being used, by and large, by those from the lower socio-economic bracket. The program is, therefore, effective, and I am very glad to see that. It means we have something on which to base any request for an increase in the child-care tax credits. I was also relieved to find that the study has borne out our theory that the program is not being abused (as some thought it would be), but it should be enlarged to take in the concerns that you were mentioning, Margrit.

You mentioned parental benefits as well, Margrit. I agree with you completely. How much of what you suggested will be practical and how much will be accepted at this moment, I do not know. But I do know that amendments to the Canada Labour Code include parental benefits, with the option to share maternity-or paternity-leave as a family unit, which I think is a step forward. My main concern, however, is that *women* get treated fairly in this package, and that is the approach I am taking. I would hope to make the changes part of a larger package but I do not think the country can afford paid paternity leave at the moment. It will come. I am more concerned that we get maternity leave and that we include, as an option, unpaid parental leave to be shared by both parents. I think that is something that we, as a government, can sensitize the public to through a first-step measure. And that is one of the ways, I believe, in which government can assist us women in reaching the goals we have for the 1980s.

12

Change, Hope and Celebration

Joan Turner

"What we see, we see, and seeing is changing."
Adrienne Rich[1]

The Distinguished Visitors Conference, "Perspectives On Women in the 1980s," reflected in the preceding chapters, was an exciting consciousness-raising experience. It affected our personal lives, our dreams and our nightmares. It altered our perceptions of reality. We felt strongly connected to other women across differences of religion, class, sexual preference, culture, status and geography. News of the conference travelled far and wide in Canada, partly because women from distant places such as Moncton, Ottawa, and Eskimo Point attended, and partly because of dynamic reporting both locally and nationally. Our video documentary of the conference has enabled us to continue sharing our excitement in living colour.[2]

Time has passed. It is now November, 1983. I take one last opportunity to reflect on my perceptions of events and changes (or lack of them) which have occurred since January, 1982. It is tempting to claim dramatic outcomes such as "feminism has taken root in the Manitoba School of Social Work in significant ways!" However, the wheels of change move very slowly. What has not been accomplished is all too clear.

The conference originated with women's concerns about the lack of female representation and perspective in the Manitoba School of Social Work's graduate (MSW) program. We are still concerned, in spite of the hiring in 1982 of two well-qualified female faculty members. Perhaps in time our outsider status as female faculty, and therefore, our experience with alienation and marginality, will culminate in greater knowledge and more precise understanding of women's issues. We hope so. In the meantime, women employees of the School go about their work teaching primarily practices and field to undergraduates, in administrative support positions and as secretaries. The philosopher Janet Radcliffe Richards has commented: "Society tends to take an unreasonably dim view of makers of fusses and upsetters of apple carts. Feminists who do get trapped into ungracious behavior can, with a great deal of justice, argue that the women who manage to remain 'nice' are nearly always giving in and putting up with what ought to be resisted. . ."[3] Perhaps her statement explains in part the defeat of the Equal Rights Amendment in the United States.

Unless we are well represented in places of power and decision making, we are vulnerable. We are not well represented in governments, nor in universities. We have learned that when we raise the questions from our places as outsiders, we "ruffle feathers." We are seen as petty, "into that women's lib stuff," interfering with the completion of important male-defined tasks.[4] The consequence is that what is defined as policy in graduate social work studies, for example, and as knowledge, is defined by men, infused with male assumptions about life, the world and its problems, and excludes female perspectives. Joan E. Cummings says that ". . . the dominant theoretical system and conceptual categories employed within and beyond social work to inform inquiry and to explain the human condition, have in the main been developed under male control, and from male experience. They have thus systematically incorporated a male perspective, and have filtered out a female one."[5]

Thanks to the women's movement, I believe that policies and programs will change in time. After all, change is a probability. I will continue to hope, and I will encourage women, including female faculty and students, to speak out and to act when it is opportune. I do not believe in pots of gold at the end of rainbows, but I do believe in rainbows.

I would like to comment on some of the highlights, events and changes which have occurred since the conference in January, 1982. Each of these highlights provides us with a sense of progress and a cause for celebration. I intend also to talk about language, power and expression, concepts which derive from the content of this book, and from related women's literature. I choose these concepts for their importance to me, personally, and to women collectively, as we move on into the 1980s. I will conclude with a song of celebration for women's lives, for endings and for new beginnings.

Can it be that Manitoba policy makers actually heard Gloria Steinem say, "The power of naming is a very political act"? Amendments made to the Manitoba Vital Statistics Act in August, 1983, provide parents with the choices of registering their children in the surname of either the mother or the father, or in a hyphenated combination of both names. Children can now legally bear their mothers' names! The distinction between legitimate and illegitimate children has been abolished. Children's legal rights will no longer be dependent upon legal marriage of parents.[6]

Legislative change comes about only through the painstaking work of a number of caring individuals and organizations. I have come to know and respect the work of the newly reconstituted Manitoba Advisory Council on the Status of Women. The Council's primary objective is "to bring about the equality of opportunity in treatment for men and women in the province."[7] Their role is to advise the government on matters relating to the status of Manitoba women. Since the spring of 1983, the Council has addressed the issues of family law and pensions, the controversial issue of reproductive health and most recently the issue of pornography. I am fortunate to be connected to the Council as field instructor for two BSW students. The School places students in other women-focused settings as well.

There is evidence in Manitoba of an emerging health and special service system dedicated to the provision of services specifically for women by women. The Manitoba Committee on Wife Abuse, the Fort Garry Women's Resource Centre, and the Elizabeth Fry Society have all come into being since the conference in January, 1982. All organizations struggle with limited short-term funding. All are dependent upon the active participation of female volunteers as board members and as counsellors. Native women, immigrant and refugee women, domestics, and women on welfare have organized themselves into self-help groups.

The Winnipeg Women's Counselling Group is also new. This group evolved through the initiative of women from the Manitoba Action Committee on the Status of Women and the Women's Health Clinic. It is an informal group with rotating leadership, which is open to women who work in the human services. It meets monthly and functions as a resource, support and discussion group for those who wish to be involved. A list of alternate services, including feminist counsellors, has been provided to members.

My own experience with these organizations is that women are working cooperatively together. Women are determined to help other women, energetically pursuing the feminist goals of justice and equality, sharing and caring. It is an exciting time. The needs are great and the problems distressing, but resources are developing. So many women in Winnipeg are now involved in women's organizations that it no longer seems very radical to participate in them. Over and over I hear women of all ages declaring themselves to be feminists. Like Helen Levine and me, women usually become feminists through painful life experience, and through a political and educational process.

As the women's movement grows in Manitoba and in Canada, the power of women to change the system becomes stronger and more threatening.

Fifty-three percent of Canadian married women are in the paid labour force.[8] Working women challenge old assumptions about women's place, and about the nature of women's and men's work.[9] Feminists are everywhere, in government cabinets, in the churches, in unions, in universities and in schools. We have the ability to connect with each other and the potential to work together in very powerful ways.

Those who wish to hold to history and tradition have become anxious. The conservative New Right gathers money, much of it from the rich and powerful, rallies churches to their cause on the basis of preservation of the nuclear family, calls for law and order, and urges political opposition to change.[10]

The focus of the conservative backlash in Winnipeg in 1983 has been abortion. In January, our campus was the setting for a debate on the subject. All of the actors were men, of course. During the winter and spring, newspaper advertisements, billboards which referred to murder of the fetus for convenience, ads on television, and letters to the editor daily reminded us of the seriousness of the issue and of the threat that reproductive freedom poses in a patriarchal society. Dr. Henry Morgentaler's therapeutic abortion clinic opened amidst much controversy and publicity. Police raided the clinic twice. The staff, most of whom were female, were jailed and charged under the criminal code. Meanwhile, many women and some men have joined efforts to organize the Coalition for Reproductive Choice.

I believe that, as women, we must have control over our bodies and we must have the right to choose from alternatives. As a social worker, I know too well the price that unplanned, unwanted children pay in our society. Rhetoric does not feed nor love children, nor does it provide for their basic needs.

Abortion is a moral dilemma which confronts individual women with decisions about conflicting responsibilities to self and to others. Carol Gilligan's research indicates that women make their decisions from an ethic of responsibility and care. She says: "In the different voice of women lies the truth of an ethic of care, the tie between relationships and responsibility.... The failure to see the different reality of women's lives and to hear the difference in their voice stems from the assumption that there is a single mode of social experience and interpretation. By positing instead two different modes, we arrive at a more complex rendition of human experience which sees the truth of separation and attachment in the lives of women and men, and recognizes how these truths are carried by different modes of language and thought."[11]

Carol Gilligan confirms what we know from experience. I am excited by her contribution to our understanding, for her work increases our ability to articulate the different voice of women. We want to be taken seriously, to have our creativity acknowledged, to be included and supported in research endeavours, to have our views represented in education for the helping professions.

We want to be heard too when we exclaim that texts and their contents do not reflect our experience. Mary Daly says it well: "Symbol systems and conceptual apparatuses have been male creations. They do not reflect the experience of woman but rather serve to falsify our own self-images and experiences."[12]

We must struggle with language, with words like *chairman, chairperson, chair,* because words carry assumptions about what will be. We will insist that the female as well as the male pronoun be used in course materials and forms used in our places of work, and in our churches. We must do so at the risk of seeming petty. I know that "you wouldn't hear a man hollering about being called 'Mrs.' or 'she' or 'her' or 'chairwoman' or 'Dear Madam.' A man knows who she is."[13] We need to experiment and to create new words to say what we mean.

We write and speak in the personal-political way of women, interweaving feelings and facts, the subjective with the objective, the heart with the mind. We use descriptive words of feeling and passion, words such as *love* and *sex, pain* and *joy, war* and *peace, helping* and *healing, birth* and *death, body* and *spirit,* words that are powerfully relevant to the lives of women. We talk about reproduction, about motherwork and child care, and about witches and crones. We know that at some time in our adult lives as women most of us will experience poverty. I can hear and see Dorothy O'Connell telling us to say "poor." Yes, let us tell it as it is.

If we are Canadian and female and single, there is a 50 percent chance that we will be poor.[14] If we are head of a female single-parent family with children under eighteen, there is a two-thirds chance that we will be poor.[15] Since the likelihood of being poor increases with age we face the prospect of being old and poor.[16] Even when we are employed full time there is a strong likelihood that we will experience poverty or marginal living. The average income of women in 1980 was $8,414 per year, and for men it was $16,918 per year.[17] Women throughout the world are poor. A United Nations study shows that women do between 66 and 75 percent of the work of the world, earn less than 10 percent of the world's income, and own less than 1 percent of the property.[18] When we contemplate the fact that women usually bear the burden of responsibility for child care, we know that the words *women* and *poor* go together. The situation is distressing the world over.

A University education is no guarantee against poverty. Pat and Hugh Armstrong tell us that "more than twice as many university-educated women as men have only part-time work...it must be assumed that a large number of women experience underemployment."[19]

153

While the proposed unionization of part-time faculty at the University of Manitoba may not immediately increase salaries, unionization is expected to provide part-time faculty (many of whom are women) with rights and benefits that at present only full-time employees enjoy. From time to time, over a period of twelve years, some of the women of the School of Social Work have tried to improve the situation for ourselves and for other part-time workers. For years we had little success. Now, at long last, real change is in sight. Yes, there will be a rainbow in our sky, and we will celebrate!

Many of the women who work at the University are secretaries and are members of the support staff union (AESES). They play a very important part in keeping the University humming. In February, 1982, for the first time ever, secretaries as well as administrative support staff secured the right to be full voting members in the School of Social Work Council. (School Council is the governing body for the School. It includes all faculty, including part-time faculty, and student representatives.) The decision to extend the vote would not likely have happened without the consciousness raising which occurred as part of the process of hosting the conference. Today we question why the support staff (all women) have no representation on the University's Search Committee to find a new director for the School. Once again women have no say in the critical decisions which affect them.

The culture of our workplace changes slowly. A word processor is purchased for the general office and the office staff assertively declare that they will control its use. And they do. Women make decisions to paint walls and replace carpets and to place plants in offices and classrooms. Women are expressing their caring.

Notices about events of interest to women are posted on bulletin boards. Films like, "Not a Love Story," about pornography, and another on incest, are shown in the student lounge and are open to everyone.[20] Women sit in heavy silence, watching, feeling, thinking. Few men attend.

The "culture" in some of the classes is changing too. Feminist writing is listed on bibliographies and referred to in class. Feminist counselling is demonstrated and discussed by female faculty members. Field instructors encourage analysis from a feminist perspective. Students write papers, do presentations and register for reading courses on women's issues. Writing by women about women finds its way onto the shelves of the School's Helen Mann Library.

The School's Continuing Education Program Committee pays attention to representation by gender on committees. Courses and teachers are chosen to reflect both male and female perspectives. Specific courses such as Feminist Counselling and Working With Women are included as electives within certificate programs for professionals and para-professionals. In spite of the fact that other women and I have primary leadership roles, constant vigilance seems to be necessary to ensure the presence of female perspectives throughout the program.

The Women of the School meet occasionally to share ideas and experiences, to monitor female representation on important School committees, to share good food, and to laugh. Women on Campus, a group led by the President's Advisory Committee on Women, invites women of the University community to meet for dinner and to hear female speakers on such topics as pornography and women and history. The Women's Centre on campus sponsored a conference on sexual harassment and sexist teaching in November, 1983.

And last, but not least, significant changes to the School's BSW curriculum are before a sub-committee of University Senate. The School has proposed, among other things, that all students be required to take at least one course about women. Two new courses, one called Social Welfare Policy and Women, and one called Social Work Practice and Women's Issues, similar to those taught during the past two years under other course titles as electives, have been designed.

On one hand, it seems that we have reasons to celebrate for consciousness raising, for changes in the culture of our workplace, and for the structural changes noted. On the other hand, it seems that the common experience of women in academia both on our campus and in general in North America is one of isolation and aloneness and of ongoing struggle. Women in academia have little power. In fact it is estimated that women hold only 1 percent of the positions of power.[21]

Before I close, I wish to speak about power and about expression. We cannot afford to feel, or to be, powerless. I believe that our power comes from valuing ourselves and our experiences. It grows with our emotional and political identification with others across the similarities and differences of age, culture, class, sexual preference, religion, status, profession and abilities. In the 1980s there are many opportunities for us to learn about power and to empower ourselves. Feminist authors Hilary Lips, Nina Colwill, Jean Baker Miller, Yolande Cohen, Dorothy Dinnerstein and Anne Wilson Schaef have written about women and power.[22] We can empower ourselves by attending conferences which stimulate and energize and enhance our connections with each other. There are workshops such as the one recently facilitated by social worker Therese Chatelain in which women experienced the trust and freedom to break through personal barriers and experiment with creative forms of expression. At this workshop, we danced and sang, screamed and cried, intensely feeling the pains and joys of women's lives. We experienced the kind of female power that Anne Wilson Schaef describes in *Women's Reality:* "In the Female

System, power is viewed in much the same way as love. It is limitless, and when it is shared it regenerates and expands. There is no need to hoard it because it only increases when it is given away....In the Female System, power is conceived of as personal power which has nothing to do with power or control over another."[23] We experienced a shared sense of leadership, of responsibility and of equality. We learned too, about our power to help and to heal, and about our spirituality. For more than three years I have been meeting with a group of friends who help and heal each other. And just recently, I became a member of a new small group of women who intend to meet to explore our spirituality.

Everywhere women are meeting in small groups and large to share ideas and experiences, to develop their bodies, spirits and minds, to nurture and console each other, and to develop strategies for political action. Yes, women are on the move!

And, it is time we recognized the wisdom of our elders. Let us value the experience of older women, insist that they be treated with respect. We cannot allow them to be warehoused, or to wander city streets as bag ladies for lack of alternate choices. It seems to me that rural communities have much to teach us about providing for our elders.

As we learn to care for and to respect each other across differences, as we learn about our power to love and to heal, our sense of responsibility for the peace and security of this world looms large. There are some who say that peace depends on us. (But surely, it depends on men too.) Women group together in places throughout the world (like the Moonstones have done in Winnipeg) to work for world peace. It is apparent that we must not allow our fears to inhibit us from personal-political expression of our power. We must find the courage to break through our silences. Mary Daly says: "Overcoming the silencing of women is an extreme act, a sequence of extreme acts....Breaking our silence means discovering our inner resources. It means finding our native resiliency, springing into life, speech, action."[24]

We may express ourselves in speech or in writing, through poetry, prose, music, art and film. We may choose to love and care for others in the best ways that we know how. We may march for the safety of the night, speak out for peace, propose legislative change. We may work as volunteers, as friends or as professionals to provide a helping hand to those who bear the scars of war, assault, incest, rape - power turned destructively, hatefully against women.

There are times when I touch a woman with massaging hands and I know that the blackness and the wounds and scars are deep - pushed into the darkness of the soul, buried deep in body tissue. As I touch, I know, I hear. I cry for her, for them, for us. My anger, too, runs deep. When we scream and yell, talk and

156

share, the pain is not quite so hard to bear.

From our deep source, like spring water from the new-found well, comes hope – hope for a better, peaceful, less violent tomorrow, for us, our sisters, our children, and for men too. With hope, there is celebration, joy, a song in our hearts, dance in our footsteps, warmth and tenderness, love and strength.

Now, on with the celebration: for endings, and for new beginnings.

Woman, your feet were made for dancing
Woman, your voice was meant to carry song
And your heart it was made for long, strong loving,
Your soul, to carry you along.
So kick your heels up fine lady
Let me see your fancy footprints
In the valley let your melody echo, unrestrained
Open your heart to the loving that waits in grassy meadows
And ride your spirit like a wild horse untamed.

Well, you know it wasn't long ago
Your dancing feet were bound and sold
It wasn't long away, your heart was owned, love locked away
Like young children you were seen and not heard.
Your spirit in cathedrals cried like the sound of a captive bird
So woman, you have a right to dance, you have a right to sing
This troubled world's in need of a little laughter that you bring
You spent a long time playing second fiddle,
It's time to play first violin
You've come a long, long way; you've got a right to play
Let the Celebration begin!

                    Karen Howe[25]

Selected Readings and Resources

We hope that readers will be stimulated to continue reading and learning about women. We suggest the following resource materials, beginning with those written by our distinguished speakers. In Part B we list Canadian resource catalogues and books. We also list the names and addresses of journals, newspapers and newsletters which focus on women. Since our conference included artists and musicians, we conclude this section with resources about women artists and their art, and women musicians and their music.

PART A: PUBLICATIONS BY CONFERENCE SPEAKERS

English, Deirdre, and Barbara Ehrenreich *Witches, Midwives, and Nurses: A History of Women Healers.* New York: Feminist Press, 1972.
———. *Complaints and Disorders: The Sexual Politics of Sickness.* New York: Feminist Press, 1974.
———. *For Her Own Good: 150 Years of Expert's Advice to Women.* New York: Doubleday, 1979.
Eichler, Margrit. "Women as Personal Dependents." In, *Women in Canada.* 2nd ed. Edited by Marylee Stephenson. Don Mills: General Publishing Co. Ltd., 1977.
———. "Social Policy Concerning Women." In, *Canadian Social Policy.* ed. Shankar Yelaja. Waterloo: Wilfred Laurier University Press, 1978.
———. "Women's Unpaid Labour," *Atlantis,* 3, no. 2, pt. 11, Spring, 1978, pp. 52-62.
———. "Family Income: A Critical Look at the Concept." *Status of Women,* 19, no. 4, Spring, 1980.
———. *The Double Standard: A Feminist Critique of Feminist Social Science.* Toronto: University of Toronto Press, 1980.
———. *Families in Canada Today: Recent Changes and their Policy Consequences.* Toronto: Gage, 1983.

Levine, Helen. "On Women and on One Woman as Provider and Consumer of Social and Health Services." In, *Women, Their Use of Alcohol and Other Legal Drugs.* Ed. Anne MacLennan. Addiction Research Foundation of Ontario, 1976, pp. 21-43.

———. "Feminist Counselling – A Look at New Possibilities," *'76 and Beyond,* special issue of *The Social Worker,* Canadian Association of Social Workers, Summer, 1976, pp. 12-15.

———. "Feminist Counselling." In, *Canadian Dimension.* May, 1979, vol. 13, no. 7, pp. 32-26.

———. "New Directions for Girls and Women: A Look at the Condition of Women in Society and Feminist Counselling." In, *Counselling: Challenge of the 80's,* vol. 2. Ed. Thomas H. Brown. Selected proceedings from the 1979 National Conference of the Canadian Guidance and Counselling Association, St. Johns, Newfoundland, 1980, pp. 383-408.

———. "The Power Politics of Motherhood: A Feminist Critique of Theory and Practice." With Alma Estable. Occasional Paper, Centre for Social Welfare Studies, Carleton University, 1981.

———. "The Personal is Political: Feminism and the Helping Professions." In, *Feminism in Canada: From Pressure to Politics.* Ed. Angela Miles and Geraldine Finn. Montreal: Black Rose Books, 1982, pp. 175-209.

O'Connell, Dorothy. *Chiclet Gomez.* Deneau Publishers and Company Ltd., 1977.

———. *Cockeyed Optimists.* Deneau Publishers and Company Ltd., 1980.

Steinem, Gloria. *Wonder Woman.* Holt, Rinehart and Winston Inc., 1974.

———. *Outrageous Acts and Everyday Rebellions.* New York: Holt, Rinehart and Winston Inc., August, 1983.

Ms. Magazine. Ms. Foundation for Education and Communication, Inc., 119 West 40 Street New York, N.Y., 10018, U.S.A., 1972-1983. Numerous articles and editorials.

Note: Readers who wish to borrow the one-hour video documentory, "Perspectives on Women in the 1980s," which includes excerpts from the concert and the art exhibit and was produced by Shirley Kitchen and Joan Turner, may do so by calling or writing the School of Social Work, University of Manitoba, Winnipeg, Manitoba, R3T 2N2, Canada, phone (204) 474-9877 or 474-9550.

PART B: CANADIAN REFERENCES

Initially we hoped to provide the "complete guide" to Canadian material. We quickly became overwhelmed by the vast possibilities of topics and the realization that the Canadian literature on women's issues has grown phenomenally in the past ten years. We also discovered that the Secretary of State, Women's Program Branch, has already taken on this mammoth task and is currently producing the *Women's Resource Catalogue*, an absolute "gold mine" of information. First produced in 1978 and most recently in January, 1982, the *Women's Resource Catalogue* provides reference to printed and audio-visual materials by, for, and about Canadian women. Topics highlighted include:

arts, birth planning, careers and life planning, credit, pensions, day care, female offenders, health, history, immigrant women, labour, law, low income women, single women, older women, native women, rural and isolated women, media, politics, sex role stereotyping, sexuality, violence, volunteerism, women's movement, women's studies, magazines, newspapers, newsletters, filmographies and women's bookstores and presses.

The material referred to in the catalogue includes only material produced after 1975 and excludes references to large publishers. The full reference is: *Women's Resource Catalogue*, Secretary of State, Women's Program, Copyright Minister of Supply and Services, Canada, January, 1983.

The Secretary of State, Women's Program, also produced an annual *Listing of Women's Groups*. This resource manual is also designed to contribute to the sharing of information among women and women's groups. The groups/activities listed in this annual are concerned with improving the status of women or are active on status of women's issues. A wide range of women's groups are listed, as are women's centres, rape crisis centres, transition houses, government programs for women, women's periodicals, and women's advisory councils. The complete reference for this annual is: Listing of Women's Groups, Secretary of State, Women's Program, Copyright Minister of Supply and Services, Canada, (1983).

We suggest the following references to books in print and current newspapers and journals to supplement the offerings in the *Women's Resource Catalogue*.

Books and Articles

Allan, Gladys L. *Dew Upon the Grass*. Saskatoon: Prairie Books, 1963.

Andersen, Margaret. *Mother was Not a Person*. Montreal: Content Publishing Limited and Black Rose Books, 1972.

Armstrong, Pat. *Women and Jobs: The Canadian Case*. Ottawa: Canadian Centre for Policy Alternatives, 1981.

Armstrong, Pat and Hugh Armstrong. *The Double Ghetto: Canadian Women and Segregated Work*. Toronto: McClelland and Stewart, 1978.

Armstrong, Pat and Hugh Armstrong. *A Working Majority: What Women Must Do For Pay*. Canadian Advisory Council on the Status of Women, Ottawa: Canadian Government Publishing Centre, Supply and Services, Canada, 1983.

Banfill, B.J. *Pioneer Nurse*. Toronto: Ryerson Press, 1967.

Bannerman, Jean. *Leading Ladies: Canada, 1639-1967*. Galt, Ontario: 1967.

Bassett, Isabel. *The Parlour Rebellion, Profiles in the Struggle for Women's Rights*. Toronto: McClelland and Stewart, 1975.

Canada's Mental Health. 26 March 1978. See: "The Effect of non-traditional families on Children's Mental Health" by B. McConnville; "The Impact of the Women's Movement – Implications for a Child Development Mental Health and Family Policy." by S. Stephenson; "Female Gender Identity" by E.P. Lester; Also, 28, no. 2, June, 1980, a special issue on Women and Mental Health.

Canadian Research Institute for the Advancement of Women. *Women and Work: An Inventory of Research/La Femme et le travail: un inventaire de recherche*. Ottawa: Canadian Research Institute for the Advancment of Women, 1978.

The Canadian Advisory Council on the Status of Women. *Women and the Constitution*. Ed. A. Doerr and M. Carrier. Ottawa, Ontario: 1981.

The Canadian Association of Social Workers. *Symposium on Inter-Spousal Violence,* 1981.

Canadian Council on Social Development. *Women in Need: A Source Book*. Ottawa: 1976.

Canadian Journal of Social Work Education. Special issue on "The Social Welfare of Women, vol. 6, nos. 2 and 3. Ottawa: Canadian Association of Schools of Social Work, 1980.

Caplan, Paula J. *Between Women: Lowering The Barriers*. Toronto: Personal Library, 1981.

Clark, Hart D. *Background Paper on Features of Interest and Concern to Women in the Canadian Retirement Income System*. Ottawa: Canadian Advisory Council on the Status of Women, 1980.

Clark, Lorinne and Debra Lewis. *Rape: The Price of Coercive Sexuality*. Toronto: The Women's Press, 1977.

Clarke, M. G. and Linda Lange. *The Sexism of Social and Political Theory*. Toronto: University of Toronto Press, 1979.

Cleverdon, Catherine L. *The Woman Suffrage Movement in Canada*. Toronto: University of Toronto Press, 1950, 1974.

Coffey, Mary Anne. *Inequality at Work*. Toronto: The Social Planning Council of Metro Toronto, and, Women's Studies and Affirmative Action Department, Board of Education, City of Toronto, 1982.

Collins, Kevin. *Women and Pensions*. Ottawa: Canadian Council on Social Development, 1978.

Colwill, Nina L. *The New Partnership: Women and Men in Organizations*. Palo Alto: Mayfield Publishing Co., 1982.

Connelly, Patricia. *Last Hired, First Fired: Women and the Canadian Work Force*. Toronto: The Women's Press, 1978.

Cook, Gail, ed. *Opportunity for Choice: A Goal for Women in Canada,* Statistics Canada and the C.D. Howe Research Institute, 1976.

Corrective Collective. *Never Done: Three Centuries of Women's Work in Canada*. Toronto: Canadian Women's Educational Press, 1974.

————. *She Named it Canada Because That's What it Was Called*. Toronto: Canadian Women's Educational Press (4th edition), 1975.

Crawford, Mary Elizabeth. *Legal Status of Women in Manitoba as Shown by Extracts from Dominion and Provincial Laws*. Manitoba Political Equality League, 1913.

Culleton, Beatrice. *In Search of April Raintree*. Winnipeg: Pemmican Publications, 1983.

Dulude, Louise. *Women and Aging: A Report on the Rest of Our Lives*. Ottawa: Advisory Council on the Status of Women, April, 1978.

————. *Pension Reform With Women in Mind.* Ottawa: Canadian Advisory Council.

Diamond, Sara. *Women's Labour History in British Columbia: A Bibliography, 1930-1948.* Vancouver: Press Gang, 1980.

Duncan, Joy. *Red Serge Wives.* Edmonton: Centennial Book Committee, 1974.

Economic Council of Canada. *One in Three: Pensions for Canadians to 2030.* Ottawa, 1979.

Equal Employment Policy for Women: Strategies for Implementation in the United States, Canada and Western Europe. Edited by Ronnie Steinberg Ratner. Philadelphia: Temple University Press, 1980.

Elhins, Valmi Howe. *The Rights of the Pregnant Parent.* Toronto: Waxwing Productions, 1980.

Evans, Gwynneth. *Women in Federal Politics: A Bio-bibliography/Les femmes au federal: une bio-bibliographie.* Ottawa: 1975.

Everywoman's Almanac. Toronto: The Women's Press. Annual publication.

Fitzgerald, Maureen, Connie Guberman and Margie Wolfe. *Still Ain't Satisfied! Canadian Feminism Today.* Toronto: The Women's Press, 1982.

Fowler, Marian. *The Embroidered Tent: Fine Gentlewomen in Early Canada (Elizabeth Simcoe, Catharine Parr Traill, Susanna Moodie, Anne Jameson, Lady Dufferin).* Toronto: House of Anansi, 1982.

Fraser, Janet and Eileen Hendry. *Women's Networks in Canada.* Based on the Proceedings of the First National Women's Network Conference, June, 1981. Vancouver: Centre for Continuing Education, U.B.C., 1983.

Gibbon, John M. and Mary Mathewson. *Three Centuries of Canadian Nursing.* Toronto: Macmillan, 1947.

Government of Ontario, Standing Committee on Social Development. *First Report on Family Violence: Wife Battering.* November, 1982.

Hacker, Carlotta. *The Indomitable Lady Doctors.* Toronto: Clarke Irwin, 1974.

Hall, M. Ann and Dorothy A. Richardson. *Fair Ball: Toward Sex Equality in Canadian Sport.* Ottawa, Canadian Advisory Council on the Status of Women, 1982.

Hauck, Philomena. *Sourcebook on Canadian Women.* Ottawa: Canadian Library Association, 1979.

Healey, W.J. *Women of Red River.* Winnipeg: Pequis Publishers, 1923.

Herson, Naomi and Dorothy E. Smith. *Women and the Canadian Labour Force.* Ottawa: Social Sciences and Humanities Research Council of Canada, 1982.

In Search of the Feminist Perspective: The Changing Potency of Women, March 4-5, 1978, University of Waterloo. Proceedings edited by Mary Kathryn Shirley, Rachel Emma Vigier. Toronto: Department of Sociology, Ontario Institute for Studies in Education, 1979.

Innis, Mary Quayle. *The Clear Spirit: Twenty Canadian Women and Their Times.* Toronto: University of Toronto Press, 1967.

Johnston, Jean. *Wilderness Women.* Toronto: Peter Martin Associates, 1973.

Kealey, Linda, ed. *A Not Unreasonable Claim: Women and Reform in Canada 1880's to 1920's.* Linda Kealey. Toronto: The Women's Press, 1979.

Kinnear, Mary. *Daughters of Time: Women in the Western Tradition*. Ann Arbor: The University of Michigan Press, 1982.

King, Lynn. *What Every Woman Should Know About Marriage, Separation, and Divorce*. Toronto: James Lorimer and Company, 1980.

Kumar, Pradrep and Alister M.M. Smith. *Pension Reform in Canada: A Review of the Issues and Options*. Research and Current Issues Series no. 40. Kingston: Queen's University Industrial Relations Centre, 1981.

Latham, Barbara, ed. *In Her Own Right: Selected Essays on Women's History in B.C.* Victoria: Camosun College, 1980.

Lawton-Speert, Sarah and Andy Wachtel. *Child Sexual Abuse and Incest: An Annotated Bibliography*. Vancouver: United Way of the Lower Mainland, 1982.

Light, Beth. *True Daughters of the North: Canadian Women's History: An Annotated Bibliography*. Toronto: OISE Press, 1980.

Lips, Hilary M. and Nina L. Colwill. *The Psychology of Sex Differences*. Englewood Cliffs N.J.: Prentice-Hall, 1978.

Mackay, Margaret. *Women in the Labour Force with an Emphasis on the Clerical and Service Occupations: A Selected Bibliography*. Available from Social Sciences and Humanities Research Council of Canada, 1982.

Mackie, Marlene. *Exploring Gender Relations: A Canadian Perspective*. Toronto: Butterworths, 1983.

MacLeod, Flora. *Transition House: How to Establish a Refuge for Battered Women*. Vancouver: United Way of the Lower Mainland, 1982.

Mann Trofimenkoff, S. and A. Prentice, eds. *The Neglected Majority: Essays in Canadian Women's History*. Toronto: McClelland and Stewart Ltd., 1977.

Marvin, M. "Annotated Bibliography: Women and Drugs." *Canada's Mental Health*. 22, 1974, pp. 13-19.

Matheson, G., ed. *Women in the Canadian Mosaic*. Toronto: Peter Martin Assoc. Ltd., 1976.

Menzies, June. *The Canada Pension Plan and Women*. Ottawa: Canadian Advisory Council on the Status of Women, 1974.

Miles, A. and G. Finn, eds. *Feminism in Canada, Theory and Practice*. Toronto: Black Rose Books, 1983.

National Council of Women of Canada. *Women of Canada, Their Life and Work*. Prepared for distribution at the Glasgow International Exhibition, 1901.

O'Brien, Mary. *The Politics of Reproduction*. London: Routledge and Kegan Paul, 1981.

Ontario Status of Women Council. *Women and Aging*. Toronto: 1981.

Pioneer and Gentlewomen of British North America, 1713-1867. Edited by Beth Light and Alison Prentice. Toronto: New Hogtown Press, 1980.

Phillips, Paul and Erin Phillips. *Women and Work: Inequality in the Labour Market*, Toronto: James Lorimer and Co., 1983.

Proulx, Monique. *Five Million Women: A Study of the Canadian Housewife*. Ottawa: Advisory Council on the Status of Women, 1978.

Sachdev, Paul. *Abortion: Readings and Research*. Scarborough: Butterworths, 1981.

Saskatchewan Labour Women's Division. *Saskatchewan Women 1905-1980.*

Savage, Candace. *Foremothers: Personalities and Issues from the History of Women in Saskatchewan.* Available from the author at 350 Carleton Drive, Saskatoon, Saskatchewan.

Savage, Candace. *Our Nell: A Scrapbook Biography of Nellie McClung.* Saskatoon: Western Producer Prairie Books, 1979.

Secretary of State Women's Programme. *Listing of Women's Groups.* Ottawa: Minister of Supply and Services Canada, 1982. (Annual)

Secretary of State Women's Programme. *Women's Resource Catalogue.* Ottawa: Minister of Supply and Services Canada, 1982.

Service, Dorothy Jane. *Women and the Law: A Bibliography of Materials in the University of Toronto Law Library.* 2nd. ed. Toronto: 1978.

Shaw, Rosa. *Proud Heritage.* Toronto: Ryerson Press, 1957.

Smith, Dorothy and Sara David. *Women Look at Psychiatry.* Vancouver: Press Gang Publishers, 1975.

The Social Planning Council of Metropolitan Toronto. *Inequality At Work.* Toronto: Thistle Printing Limited, 1982.

Solicitor General Canada. *A Rape Bibliography.* Ottawa: Minister of Supply and Services Canada, 1979.

Status of Women Canada. *The Employment of Women in Canada: Review of Policies for Equality of Opportunity, National Report of Canada to Working Party No. 6 on the Role of Women in the Economy.* Prepared for the Organization for Economic Cooperation and Development, 1982.

Stephenson, M., ed. *Women in Canada.* Don Mills: General Publishing Co. Ltd., 1977.

Swan, Carole. *Women in the Canadian Labour Market.* Development Task Force, Ottawa: Department of Supply and Services, 1981.

Van Kirk, Sylvia. *Many Tender Ties: Women in Fur Trade Society in Western Canada, 1670-1870.* Winnipeg: Watson and Dwyer Pub., 1980.

Williamson, Jane. *New Feminist Scholarship: A Guide to Bibliographies.* Westbury, N.Y.: Feminist Press, 1979.

Wilson, Susannah Jane. *Women, the Family, and the Economy.* Toronto: McGraw-Hill Ryerson, 1982.

Women at work: Ontario, 1850-1930. [edited by Janice Acton, et al.] Toronto: Canadian Women's Education Press, 1974.

White, Julie. *Women and Unions.* Canadian Advisory Council on the Status of Women. Ottawa: Canadian Government Publishing Centre, Minister of Supply and Services, 1980.

Perspectives on Women in the 1980s

Magazines, Journals, Newspapers, Newsletters

A Woman's Place
1225 Barrington Street
Halifax, Nova Scotia
B3J 1Y2

Atlantis
Mt. St. Vincent University
166 Bedford Highway
Halifax, Nova Scotia
B3M 2J6

Branching Out
P.O. Box 4098
Edmonton, Alberta
T6E 4T1

Broadside
P.O. Box 494
Station P
Toronto, Ontario
M5S 2T1
(416) 598-3513

Bulletin
Federation des Femmes du Quebec
1600, rue Berri-piece 3115
Montreal, Quebec
H2P 1S9
(514) 844-6898

Business
Women's Conference Institute
43 Victoria Street, Suite 30
Toronto, Ontario
M5C 2A2

Calgary Women's Newspaper
320 5th Avenue, S.E.
Calgary, Alberta
T2G 0E5

Canadian Farm Woman News
P.O. Box 6558
Winnipeg, Manitoba
R3C 3A6

Canadian Women's Studies/
Les Cahiers de la Femme
651 Warden Avenue
Scarborough, Ontario
M1L 3Z6

CAR/FAC
Canadian Artists Representation
Newspaper

Chatelaine
P.O. Box 1600
Postal Station A
Toronto, Ontario
M5W 2B8

Communiqu'Elles
Les Editions Communiqu'Elles
3585 St-Urbain
Montreal, Quebec
H2X 2N6
(514) 844-1761

Emergency Librarian
Sherrill Cheda
39 Edith Drive
Toronto, Ontario
M4R 1Y9

Equal Times
Federal NDP
301 Metcalfe Street
Ottawa, Ontario
K2P 1R9

Fireweed
P.O. Box 279
Station B
Toronto, Ontario
M5T 2W2

Healthsharing
P.O. Box 230, Station M
Toronto, Ontario
M6S 4T3
(416) 968-1363
Quarterly

Homemaker's
Comac Communications Ltd.,
2300 Yonge Street
Toronto, Ontario
M4P 1E4

Images
Kootenay Women's Paper
Box 736
Nelson, British Columbia
V1L 5R4

Entrelles
C.P. 1398
Succ. B
Hull, Quebec
J8Y 3Y1

Femme du Quebec
543 St-Clement
Montreal, Quebec
H1V 3C8
French

La Gazette des Femmes
Conseil du statut de la femme
700 boul. St-Cyrille est, 16e etage
Quebec
G1R 5G9

HERizons
The Manitoba Women's Newspaper
125 Osborne Street South
Winnipeg, Manitoba
R3L 1Y4
(204) 477-1730

Hysteria
Box 2481
Station B
Kitchener, Ontario
N2H 6M3

Journal
Canadian Federation of University/
Women Federation Canadienne Des
Femmes Diplomes Des Universites
University of Montreal
6128, A, Montreal, Quebec
H3C 3J7
(514) 733-3142

Kinesis
Vancouver Status of Women
400 A West 5th Avenue
Vancouver, British Columbia
V5Y 1J8
(604) 873-1427

Des Luttes Et Des Rires De Femmes
C.P. 687
Succ. N.
Montreal, Quebec
H2X 3N4

Makara
10011 Commercial Drive
Vancouver, British Columbia
V5L 3X1

Match
Match International Centre
401-171 Nepean
Ottawa, Ontario
K2P 0B4
(613) 238-1312

Network
Saskatchewan Action Committee on the
Status of Women
6128, A
c/o Ruby Schuman
12 Simpson Crescent
Saskatoon, Saskatchewan

Newsletter
Newfoundland Status of Women Council
P.O. Box 6072
St. John's, Newfoundland
A1C 5X8

NewsNouvelles
Planned Parenthood Federation
of Canada
200-151 Slater Street
Ottawa, Ontario
K1P 5H3

North Shore Women
Newsletter of the North Shore
Women's Centre
205-3255 Edgemont Blvd.
North Vancouver, British Columbia
V7R 2P1
(604) 987-4822

Powerhouse
3738 St. Dominique
Montreal, Quebec
H2X 2X8

Prairie Woman
P.O. Box 4021
Saskatoon, Saskatchewan
S7K 3T1

Priorities
517 East Broadway
Vancouver, British Columbia
V5T 1X4

Room of One's Own:
A Feminist Journal of Literature and
Criticism
The Growing Room Collective
1818 Waterloo Street
Vancouver, British Columbia
V6R 3G6

Selected Readings and Resources

Spirale
Women's Art and Culture
359 Dundas Street
London, Ontario
N6B 1V6

Status of Women News
National Action Committee on the
Status of Women
40 St. Clair Avenue East #306
Toronto, Ontario
M4T 1M9
Quarterly

The Northern Woman
316 Bay Street
Thunder Bay, Ontario
P7B 1S1

The Optimist
302 Steele Street
Whitehorse, Yukon
Y1A 2C5
(403) 667-4637

Newsletter
The Ontario Committee on the
Status of Women
P.O. Box 188
Station Q
Toronto, Ontario
M4T 2M1

Tightwire
Presented by the inmates of
The Prison for Women
Box 515
Kingston, Ontario
K7L 4W7

Union Woman
Organized Working Women
15 Gervais Drive, Suite 301
Don Mills, Ontario
M3C 1Y8

La Vie en Rose
3963 St-Denis
Montreal, Quebec
H2W 9Z9
(514) 843-8366

Voice of Women
African National Congress
Box 302
Adelaide Postal Station
Toronto, Ontario
M5C 2J4

Voices
c/o I. Andrews
R.R. #2
Kenora, Ontario
P9N 3W8

Wages for Housework
Toronto Wages for Housework Committee
Box 38, Station E
Toronto, Ontario
(416) 921-9091

Women of the Whole World
Box 188
Station E
Toronto, Ontario

Perspectives on Women in the 1980s

Women's Bureau Newsletter
Women's Bureau
400 University Avenue
Toronto, Ontario
M7A 1T7

Women's Network
81 Prince Street
Charlottetown, P.E.I.
C1A 4R3

Women's Caucus/UAAC
Barbara Zeigler Sungur
Dept. of Fine Arts
The University of British Columbia
403-6333 Memorial Road
Vancouver, British Columbia

Primary Sources

Canadian Advisory Council on the
Status of Women
P.O. Box 1541, Station B
Ottawa, Ontario
K1P 5R5
(Publication lists available from local offices.)

National Action Committee on the
Status of Women
40 St. Clair Avenue East, Ste. 306
Toronto, Ontario
M4T 1M9

Resources for Feminist Research
Ontario Institute for Studies in Education
Dept. of Sociology
252 Bloor Street West
Toronto, Ontario
M5S 1V5

PART C: ART AND MUSIC

During the conference a women's culture evolved as presentations, art and music were integrated. We offer some suggestions of Canadian art and music reflecting a feminist perspective.

Women Artists and Their Art

Arbour, Rose-Marie. *Art et Feminisme. Montreal: Musee d'art contemporain,* March, 1982.

Clueck, Grace. "Making Cultural Institution More Responsive to Social Needs." *Arts in Society,* Special Issue: Women and The Arts, Spring/Summer, 1974, vol. 2, no. 1.

Corne, Sharon. *Women Artists in Manitoba.* The Provincial Council of Women of Manitoba, 1981.

Fuse Magazine. (Special Issue) (6) #2, September, 1982. Several articles pertaining to Canadian women and art.

Selected Readings and Resources

Gwyn, Sandra. *Studies of the Royal Commission on the Status of Women: Women in the Arts in Canada.* vol. 7, 1971, foreword and pp. 10-28.

Martin, Jane. "Who Judges Whom: A Study of Some Male/Female Percentages in the Art World," *Atlantis,* vol. 5, no. 1, Fall, 1979, p. 127.

Martin, Jane. "Women Visual Artists on Canada Council Juries Selection Committees, and Art Advisory Panel; and Among Grant Recipients from 1972-73 to 1979-80." CAR/FAC, 1980.

Miller-Chevrier, Nancy. *Women in Culture.* Prepared for The Canadian Advisory Council of the Status of Women, March, 1981.

Politique d'egalite des Chances. Quebec: Ministere des Affaires Culturelles, February, 1981.

Rosenberg, Avis Lang. "A Fact Sheet For and About Women in Art." Vancouver, February, 1980.

———. "Women Artists and the Canadian Art World: A Survey." *Criteria.* Vancouver, 1978.

Mirrorings: Women Artists of the Atlantic Provinces. Halifax: Art Gallery, Mt. St. Vincent University, September, 1982.

Spirale: A Women's Art
and Culture Quarterly
359 Dundas Street
London, Ontario
N6B 1V6

Newsletter
Saskatchewan Women Artists
Association
c/o Rosemont Art Gallery
5062-4th Avenue
Regina, Saskatchewan
S4T 0J6

Women's Art Galleries
Mt. St. Vincent Art Gallery
Mt. St. Vincent Universty
Halifax, Nova Scotia
R3M 2J6

Powerhouse Gallery
3738 St. Dominique St.
Montreal, Quebec

Womanspirit Gallery and
Art Resources Centre
359 Dundas Street
London, Ontario
N6B 1V5

Art Organizations

Nellie McClung Theatre Group
1100 Wolseley Avenue
Winnipeg, Manitoba
R3G 1G7

Saskatchewan Women Artists Association
(SWAA)
116 Angus Crescent
Regina, Saskatchewan
R3E 1H9

Perspectives on Women in the 1980s

University Art Association-Women's
Caucus
Dept. of Fine Arts
University of British Columbia
403-6333 Memorial Road
Vancouver, B.C.
V6T 1W5

University of Manitoba-Women's Art Caucus
School of Art
University of Manitoba
Winnipeg, Manitoba
R3T 2N2

How to Obtain Information on Women Artists in Canada

Artists in Canada, Files in the National Gallery Library, Ottawa, 1977 (with updates).
Colin S. MacDonald, *A Dictionary of Canadian Artists,* Ottawa, Canada, 1977.
   (Canadian Paperbacks Publishing Ltd., 370 Queen Mary Street, Ottawa, Canada,
   K1K 1W7)

Recordings

Bishop, Heather. *Grandmothers's Song.* Mother of Pearl Records, Inc., 1979.
———. *Belly Button. Mother of Pearl Records Inc., 1982.*
———. *I Love Women . . . Who Laugh.* Mother of Pearl Records Inc., 1982.
Ferron. *Testimony. Lucy Records Ltd., 1980.*
Kaldor, Connie. *One of These Days,* Coyote Records, 1981.
MacIsaac, Joan. *Wintersong.* Mad Mansion Music, 1982.
MacNeil, Rita. *Born a Woman.* Manta Sound, 1975.
———. *The Rise and Follies of Cape Breton.* College of Cape Breton, 1980.
———. *Cape Breton Night at the Cohn.* CBC and Atlantic Folk Festival Series, 1980.
———. *Part of the Mystery.* Audio Atlantic Studios, 1981.

Notes

CHAPTER 1

1 Connie Kaldor, "There Comes a Time," 1979, recorded by Heather Bishop, *I Love Women . . . Who Laugh,* Mother of Pearl Records, Woodmore, Manitoba, 1982.
2 Joan Turner and Shirley Kitchen, "Perspectives on Women in the 1980s," video documentary, University of Manitoba School of Social Work, 1982 (60 min., colour).
3 Sara David, "Working Effectively with Women," *Canada's Mental Health,* vol. 28, no. 2 (June, 1980), p. 6.
4 Robin Morgan, *Going Too Far* (New York: Vintage Books, 1978), p. 1.
5 Judy Chicago, *The Dinner Party: A Symbol of our Heritage* (New York: Anchor Press, 1979), pp. 159-61. Starhawk estimates that more than 7 million women were killed. Starhawk, "Witchcraft and Women's Culture," Carol P. Christ and Judith Plaskow, *Womanspirit Rising* (San Francisco: Harper and Row, 1979), p. 262.
6 Chicago, *The Dinner Party,* pp. 149-61.
7 Barbara Ehrenreich and Deirdre English, *For Her Own Good: 150 Years of the Experts Advice to Women* (New York: Anchor Press, 1979), pp. 41-44.
8 Susan T. Vandiver, "A Herstory of Women in Social Work," ed. Elaine Norman and Arlene Mancuso, *Women's Issues and Social Work Practice* (Itasca: F.E. Peacock, 1980), pp. 21-26.
9 Helen Mann, *Notes for a History* (Winnipeg: School of Social Work, University of Manitoba), 1968, pp. 1, 4 and 7.
10 Information obtained from University of Manitoba sources and through telephone conversations with Thelma Lussier, Director, Institutional Analysis, University of Manitoba, April, 1983.
11 In 1983, two women were appointed Associate Vice-Presidents (Academic) giving women a presence in University policy decisions.
12 Information provided on August 18, 1983, by Carol McQuarrie, Research Officer, Association of Employees Supporting Education Services, University of Manitoba, with permission of Executive Council of AESES. Data current as of June 24, 1983.
13 University of Manitoba, "Distribution of Full-Time Teaching Staff by Age and Sex," *IS Book* (Institutional Analysis Book), 1981-82, Office of Institutional Analysis.

14 "Statistics Canada releases latest report on University Teachers," *University Affairs*, March, 1983, p. 18.

15 University of Manitoba, "Selected Statistics," *IS book*, 1981-82.

16 Information prepared by Linda Block, Administrative Assistant, School of Social Work, for meeting of Women of the School, November 9, 1982.

17 Information provided by Linda Block from School of Social Work records, University of Manitoba, May 1983.

18 Gillian Walker, "The Status of Women in Social Work Education," CASSW Task Force on the Status of Women in Social Work Education (Ottawa, CASSW, May 1976), p. 1. For a recent analysis of American women and academia, see Margaret L. Andersen, *Thinking About Women* (New York: Macmillan Publishing Co., 1983), pp. 223-33.

19 Gillian Walker, "The Status of Women in Social Work Education" in Joan Cummings, "Sexism in Social Work: The Experience of Atlantic Social Work Women," *Atlantis*, vol. 6, no. 6 (Spring, 1981), p. 71.

20 Bonnie Jeffrey and Martha Wiebe, "Women, Work and Welfare: The Saskatchewan Perspective," *The Social Worker* (Ottawa: CASW, Autumn, 1982), vol. 50, no. 3, pp. 135-36.

21 Statistics Canada update from the 1981 census, vol. 1, no. 5, May, 1983.

22 Joan Cummings, "Sexism in Social Work: The Experience of Atlantic Social Work Women," *Atlantis*, vol. 6, no. 6 (Spring, 1981), p. 68.

23 University of Manitoba, "Female-Male Balance among Academic Administrators, Faculty Members and Students," September 23, 1980. Amended and approved by Senate October 14, 1980 and approved by the Board of Governors October 22, 1980.

24 The Women's Caucus of CASSW meets annually at the CASSW National Conference, held in conjunction with the Learned Societies.

25 Jean Baker Miller, *Toward a New Psychology of Women* (Boston: Beacon Press, 1976), p. 12.

26 Miller, *Toward a New Psychology of Women*, pp. 8, 9 and 12.

27 Turner and Kitchen, "Perspectives on Women in the 1980s," video documentary.

28 Mary Daly, *GynEcology: The Metaethics of Radical Feminism* (Boston, Beacon Press, 1978), p. xiv.

29 David Ross, *The Canadian Fact Book on Poverty--1983*, Canadian Council on Social Development (Toronto, James Lorimer and Co. Publishers, 1983), p. 71.

30 Margaret Mitchell, "Mitchell Wants Women's Committee Established," *Action* (Winnipeg: Manitoba Action Committee, Status of Women, April, 83), vol. 10, no. 4, p. 10.

31 Manitoba Action Committee on the Status of Women, *Action*, Winnipeg, January, 1983, p. 11.

32 Morgan, *Going Too Far*, p. 11.

33 Heather Bishop, "I Love Women," recorded on *I Love Women . . . Who Laugh*, Mother of Pearl Records, Woodmore, Manitoba, 1983.

CHAPTER 2

1 Gloria Steinem's statement caused us to examine the situation at the School of Social Work at the University of Manitoba, and for Canadian universities. We were surprised to realize that the average age of undergraduate (BSW) students at the School of Social Work, University of Manitoba, in 1983 is 28 years, and the median age is 30 years.

Notes

The age range is from 19 to 55 years. The average age of graduate students (Pre-MSW and MSW) is 34 and the median age is 32 years. In 1982-83, 80 percent of social work undergraduate students were female, and 20 percent were male. In 1981-82, 71 percent were female and 29 percent male. Analysis by gender shows no significant difference in ages between male and female students. (Information provided by Hilda Hildebrand-Raudsepp, Admissions and Advising Officer, School of Social Work, University of Manitoba, from 1983 admissions data.)

In 1982-83, the median age of University of Manitoba undergraduate students was age 21, and for graduate students age 29. (Statistics Canada preliminary data provided by Office of Institutional Analysis, University of Manitoba, September 1983).

The median age of Canadian undergraduate university students in 1980-81 was: male full-time students, age 21; female full-time students, age 21; male part-time students, age 29; female part-time students, age 31. (Data obtained from Statistics Canada, *University Enrollment and Degrees,* 1981 [publication #81-204]).

In conclusion, while the median ages of full-time university students appears to have remained a youthful age 21, the median age of School of Social Work BSW students, University of Manitoba, has risen in the last decade to age 30. The older women in social work may be radicalizing the younger students, as Gloria Steinem suggests.

CHAPTER 3

1 Helen Levine and Alma Estable, "The Power Politics of Motherhood: A Feminist Critique of Theory and Practice," Occasional Paper (Ottawa: Carleton University Centre for Social Welfare Studies, 1981).
2 Robert Benton, dir., *Kramer vs. Kramer* with Dustin Hoffman and Meryl Streep, Columbia Pictures, U.S.A., 1979 (104 min.).
3 Robert Redford, dir., *Ordinary People* with Mary Tyler Moore, Donald Sutherland and Tim Hutton, Paramount Pictures, U.S.A., 1980 (123 min.).
4 Lawrence O'Toole, *Maclean's Magazine,* date unknown.
5 Levine and Estable, "The Power Politics of Motherhood," pp. 5-15.
6 John Bowlby, "Maternal Care and Mental Health," WHO Monograph, 1951; M. H. Klaus et al., "Maternal Attachment: Importance of the First Post Partum Days," *New England Journal of Medicine,* 1972; Rene A. Spitz, "The Effect of Personality Disturbances in the Mother on the Well-Being of her Infant," in *Parenthood, its Psychology and Psychopathology,* ed. E. James Anthony and Therese Benedek (Boston: Little, Brown and Co., 1970); Michael Rutter, *Maternal Deprivation Reassessed* (Harmondsworth: Penguin Books, 1976).
7 Margaret Birch, "Families in the '70's," Ontario Status of Women Open Meeting, Sarnia, Ontario, 1977, p. 6.
8 Birch, "Families in the '70's," p. 6.
9 Judy Syfers, "I Want a Wife," *Ms. Magazine* reprinted in Gornick and Moran, eds., *Women in Sexist Society.*
10 Margaret Polatnick, "Why Men Don't Rear Children: A Power Analysis," *Berkeley Journal of Sociology,* 1, no. 8 (1973), p. 60.

12 Levine and Estable, "The Power Politics of Motherhood," p. 20.
13 Levine and Estable, "The Power Politics of Motherhood," p. 20.
14 Levine and Estable, "The Power Politics of Motherhood," p. 22.
15 Nathan Epstein et al., "Family Categories Schema," unpublished paper, Department of Psychiatry, Jewish General Hospital, Montreal, Quebec, 1962.
16 Joseph Rheingold, *The Mother, Anxiety, Death and the Catastrophic Death Complex,* (London: V. and A. Churchill, 1967).
17 Frances L. Ilg and Louise Bates Ames, *The Gessell Institute's Child Behavior From Birth to Ten* (New York: Barnes and Noble, 1972), p. 209.
18 Levine and Estable, "The Power Politics of Motherhood," p. 28.
19 Adrienne Rich, *Of Woman Born: Motherhood as Experience and Institution* (New York: Bantam Books, 1977), p. 21.
20 Jessie Bernard, *The Future of Motherhood* (Harmondsworth: Penguin Books, 1975), p. 79.
21 Helen Levine, "On Women and On One Woman," in *Women: Their Use of Alcohol and Other Legal Drugs,* ed. Anne MacLennan (Toronto: Addiction Research Foundation of Ontario, 1976), p. 35.
22 Jackie MacMillan and Lisa Hoogstron, "Introduction," *Quest, a Feminist Quarterly,* 5, no. 3 (1981), p. 3.
23 Levine and Estable, "The Power Politics of Motherhood," p. 41.
24 Adrienne Rich, "The Taste and Smell of Life," *Broadside,* 2, no. 8, June, 1981.
25 Rich, *Of Woman Born,* p. 280.

CHAPTER 4

1 Ian Adams, *The Poverty Wall* (Toronto: McClelland and Stewart Limited, 1970), pp. 61-62.
2 If the marriage breaks down spouses may apply for splitting of Canada and Quebec pension plans. The pension issue is one of the most critical issues facing Canadian women in the 1980s.
3 Adams, *The Poverty Wall,* pp. 61-62.
4 Laurence Peter, ed., *Peter's Quotations* (New York: William Morrow and Company, Inc.), p. 498.
5 At some time around the American civil war, "A Housewife's Lament" was written by a Mrs. Sara Price of Illinois. The song is reprinted in Edith Fowke and Joe Glazer, *Songs of Work and Protest* (New York: Dover Publications, 1973).
6 Peter, *Peter's Quotations,* p. 499.
7 Robert Heinlein, *The Door into Summer* (New York: Doubleday, 1957).
8 Feminist Action Collective, P.O. Box 4454, Station E, Ottawa, Ontario. The pamphlet is entitled, "Women's Work."
9 Adams, *The Poverty Wall,* pp. 72-73.
10 Dorothy Sangster, "Up From Welfare," *Chatelaine,* vol. 50, August, 1977, pp. 36, 76-77.
11 Dorothy O'Connell, *Chiclet Gomez* (Ottawa: Deneau and Greenberg Company, Ltd., 1977).
12 Arthur Milner and Brian Searson, "There Must be Something Easier," Great Canadian Theatre Company, *Red Tape, Running Shoes and Razzamatazz,* Ottawa, 1980.
13 Bertolt Brecht, Eyre Methuen Ltd., 11 New Fetter Lane, London, EC4P 4EE, England.
14 Brian Searson, "Thirty-two Goin' on Seventy-three," Great Canadian Theatre Company, *Red Tape, Running Shoes and Razzamatazz,* Ottawa, 1980.

15 "She Was Poor But She Was Honest," *The Faber Book of Common Verse,* Michael Roberts, ed., with supplement by Janet Adam Smith, 2nd ed. (1942; rpt. London: Faber and Faber, 1974) pp. 164-65.
16 For information about social assistance benefits and poverty lines see David P. Ross, *The Canadian Fact Book on Poverty* (Toronto: James Lorimer and Co., 1983), p. 49.
17 Editorial, *Globe and Mail,* November 2, 1979.
18 Richard Johnson, letter to the editor, *Globe and Mail,* January 8, 1982.
19 Pierre Berton, *The Smug Minority* (Toronto: McClelland and Stewart, 1968).
20 Michael Audain, "Housing as a Social Program," address to Canadian Council on Social Welfare, Toronto, June 16, 1970.
21 Berton, *The Smug Minority.*
22 Keith Norton, Ministry of Community and Social Services, 1980.
23 "Cul de Sac," OTC Media, Ottawa, 1982 (video).
24 Toronto Social Planning Council, 1982.
25 Herman Miller, *Rich Man, Poor Man* (New York: Thomas Y. Crowell Co., 1964).
26 *Maclean's Magazine,* May, 1981.
27 Senate Committee on Poverty.
28 Peter, *Peter's Quotations,* p. 499.
29 In 1912, twenty thousand workers in Lawrence, Massachusetts, went on strike. Inspired by their banners, James Oppenheimer wrote the lyrics, which Caroline Kohlsaat set to music. The song is reprinted in Edith Fowke and Joe Glazer, *Songs of Work and Protest* (New York: Dover Publications, 1973). "Bread and Roses" was among the songs sung by Lissa Donner and Barb Angel at the conference, "Perspectives on Women in the 1980s," January 22, 1982.

CHAPTER 5

1 Government of Canada, *Indian Act* R.S.C. (Ottawa: Queen's Printer for Canada, 1970), Section (1)(b).
2 Government of Canada, Indian Affairs and Northern Development, *Indian Conditions: A Survey,* Ottawa, 1980

CHAPTER 6

1 Dorothy Smith, "Women and Psychiatry," in *Women Look at Psychiatrty: I'm Not Mad, I'm Angry,* ed. Dorothy Smith and Sara David (Vancouver: Press Gang Publishers, 1975), p. 2.
2 Nathan K. Rickles, "The Angry Woman Syndrome," *Archives of General Psychiatry,* 24 (January, 1971), p. 91.
3 Erik Erikson, "Inner and Outer Space Reflections on Womanhood," *Daedalus,* 93 (1964).
4 Erik Erikson, *Childhood and Society,* 2nd ed. (New York: W.W. Norton and Company, Inc., 1963), pp. 306-24.
5 *Obstetrics and Gynecology,* 4th edition, 1971.
6 Phyllis Chesler, *Women and Madness* (New York: Doubleday and Company, Inc., 1972), pp. 50-51.
7 Jessie S. Bernard, *The Future of Marriage* (New York: World Publishing Co., 1972), p. 40.
8 Smith and David, ed., *Women Look at Psychiatry.*

CHAPTER 7

1 "Cul de Sac," OTC Media Enterprises Inc., P.O. Box 4936, Station "E", Ottawa, 1982 (video).
2 Helen Levine, "On Women and On One Woman," in Anne MacLennan, ed., *Women: Their Use of Alcohol and Other Legal Drugs* (Toronto: Addiction Research Foundation of Ontario, 1976).

3 Levine, "On Women and On One Woman."

CHAPTER 8

1 U.S. News and World Report, September 18, 1978.
2 *The MacNeil/Lehrer Report,* "The Automated Office," WNET/Thirteen (New York: N.Y., July 4, 1980).
3 "Working Women, Race Against Time: Automation of the Office" (Cleveland: April 1980) reprinted in *Office Technology and People,* vol. 1 (Amsterdam: Elsevier Scientific Publishing Company, 1982) pp. 197-236. Nine to 5, The Association of Working Women (formerly called Working Women – the National Association of Office Workers) is a national organization of American women office workers.
4 Working Women Education Fund, *Warning: Health Hazards for Office Workers* (Cleveland, Ohio: Working Women, April 1981.)
5 Barbara Garson, "The Electronic Sweatshop: Scanning the Office of the Future," *Mother Jones,* July 1981, pp. 32-41.
6 Bureau of Labor Statistics data, U.S. Department of Labor, Washington, D.C. (BLS/USDL)
7 Evelyn N. Glenn and Roslyn L. Feldberg, "Degraded and De-skilled: The Proletarianization of Clerical Work," *Social Problems,* 25 (October, 1977); Evelyn N. Glenn and Roslyn L. Feldberg, "Proletarianizing Clerical Work: Technology and Organizational Control in the Office," *Case Studies in the Labor Process,* ed. A. Zimbalist (New York: Monthly Review Press, 1979).
8 Mary Murphree, Department of Sociology, Columbia University, *Rationalization and Satisfaction in Clerical Work: A Case Study of Wall Street Legal Secretaries* (New York: 1981).
9 Heather Menzies, *Women and the Chip: Case Studies of the Effects of Informatics On Employment in Canada* (Montreal: Institute for Research on Public Policy, 1981); Heather Menzies, Workshop on Women and Microtechnology, Women's Programme, Department of the Secretary of State, Ottawa, March 1981.
10 Garson, "The Electronic Sweatshop."
11 Administrative Management Society, *Office Salaries Directory, 1979-1980,* Willow Grove, Pennsylvania.
12 R. P. Uhlig, et al., *The Office of the Future,* vol. 1 (North-Holland, Amsterdam: 1979); FIET Conference on Computers and Work, Vienna, Austria, November, 1978 (Geneva: 1979); M. Thoryn, "Office Equipment Electronics Empties the Typing Pool," *Nation's Business* (February, 1979).
13 The Siemens Report is reported in "The Job-killers of Germany," *New Scientist,* June 9, 1978, and FIET Conference on Computers and Work.
14 Reported in "The Future with Microelectronics," *New Scientist,* April 16, 1979.
15 Menzies, *Women and the Chip.*
16 BLS/USDL, Washington, D.C.
17 BLS/USDL, *Industry Wage Surveys: Banking and Insurance,* December, 1976 (Washington, D.C. 1978).
18 Menzies, *Women and the Chip.*
19 Menzies, *Women and the Chip.*
20 Suzanne G. Haynes and Feinleib Manning, Md. DrPH, "Women, Work and CHD: Prospective Findings from the Framingham Heart Study," *American Journal of Public Health,* vol. 70:2 (February, 1980).

178

21 Michael J. Smith, et al., NIOSH, Division of Biomedical and Behavioral Science, *Potential Health Hazards of Video Display Terminals* (Cincinnati: June, 1981).

22 Anne Machung, "The Clerical Worker and Her Job," Diss. University of California, Berkeley.

23 Garson, "The Electronic Sweatshop."

24 Garson, "The Electronic Sweatshop."

25 Margrethe Olson, CAIS Working Paper #25 (New York: N.Y.U., 1981).

26 S.L. Sauter, G.P. Harding, M.F. Gottlieb and J.J. Quackenboss, "VDT-Computer Automation of Work Practices as a Stressor in Information Processing Jobs: Some Methodological Considerations," in *Machine Pacing and Occupational Stress: Proceedings of the International Conference*, Purdue University and NIOSH, March 1981, ed. G. Salvendy and M.J. Smith (London: Taylor and Francis Ltd., 1981).

27 B. H. Beith, "Work Repetition and Pacing as a Source of Occupational Stress," presentation to the International Conference on Machine Pacing and Occupational Stress (NIOSH and Purdue University, March, 1981).

28 Shoshanah Zuboff, "Psychological and Organizational Implications of Computer-Mediated Work," CISR #71, Sloan Working Paper #1224-81 (Cambridge, Ma.: MIT, Sloan School of Management, June, 1981).

29 Bo Goranzon and Kalle Makila, *Electronic Data Processing in the Social Insurance Offices, Programme of Action for the Swedish Union of Insurance Employees* (Stockholm: 1981).

CHAPTER 9

1 In 1951, married women were 29.9 percent of the female labour force; by 1971 they were 59.1 percent of the female labour force, according to Statistics Canada, *Employment and Earnings of Married Females*, Ottawa, December, 1979. Statistics Canada, *The Labour Force: Recent Labour Force Developments* (Ottawa: June, 1983) provides recent data: 52.8 percent of Canadian married women are in the labour force (table 6, p. 28). Fifty-five percent of married women in Manitoba are in the labour force (p. 29).

2 For further information regarding divorce rates, 1951-1981, see Statistics Canada, *Vital Statistics, Vol. II, Marriages and Divorces* catalogue 84-205 (Ottawa: Minister of Supply and Services, 1983), pp. xi and xii.

3 Statistics Canada, *Divorce: Law and the Family in Canada* (Ottawa: Ministry of Supply and Services, February, 1983), p. 212.

4 Statistics Canada, *Vital Statistics, Vol. II, Marriages and Divorces*, pp. 8 and 9.

5 Quoted in Philip H. Hepworth, "Family Policy in Canada: Some Theoretical Considerations and a Practical Application," unpublished paper, 1979.

6 Canadian Intergovernmental Conference Secretariat, *The Income Security System in Canada* (Ottawa: CICS, 1980).

7 Dennis Guest, *The Emergence of Social Security in Canada* (Vancouver: University of British Columbia Press, 1980), p. 60.

8 Canada, Health and Welfare, *Canada Pension Plan, Statistical Bulletin*, vol. 12, no. 4, 1980.

9 Canada, Health and Welfare, *Canada Pension Plan*. In December, 1980, male beneficiaries of female deceased pensioners received $171.81 and female beneficiaries of deceased males received $109.03.

10 Pat McNenly, "Paraplegic and Wife Find Love Expensive," *Toronto Star*, February 21, 1981, p. A13.

11 "Wife to Go to Let Vet Get Pension," *Globe and Mail,* August 15, 1980, p. 3.
12 Jon Ferry, "Disabled Pair Say Ontario is Ruining Marriage Plans," *Globe and Mail,* July 6, 1979, p. 12.
13 "Welfare Fraud of $5500 Jails Husband, Wife," *Globe and Mail,* October 16, 1981, p. 9.
14 Organization for Economic Co-operation and Development, The Treatment of Family Units in OECD Member Countries Under Tax and Transfer Systems (Report by the Committee on Fiscal Affairs) (Paris: OECD, 1977).
15 Jonathan R. Kesselman, "Pitfalls of Selectivity in Income Security Programs," *Canadian Taxation,* vol. 2, no. 3, 1981, p. 156.

CHAPTER 10

1 According to Lindsay Neimann, "Equality and Compensation: The Secondary Economic Status of Women," *Sexual Equality in the Workplace,* Ottawa, Minister of Supply and Services, 1982, table 1, p. 48, in 1979 female income was 57.9 percent of male income; that is even lower than Deirdre English's source suggests.

Statistics Canada data based on the 1981 census, vol. 3, catalogue 95-941, series B, indicates that the figures are now even more distressing. The average total income of males in the labour force is $16,918 while females earn $8,414. The median total income for males is $14,993 and for females it is $6,310.
2 This point is supported by David P. Ross, *The Canadian Fact Book on Poverty--1983* (Toronto: James Lorimer and Co.), 1983. ". . . the relationship between poverty and women is very strong." Female-headed families have a 36 percent rate of poverty (most of these are single-parent families) (p. 17). Seventy-five percent of all single-parent poor families are headed by females (p. 27).
3 This point is supported by Pat and Hugh Armstrong in *A Working Majority: What Women Must Do For Pay,* Canadian Advisory Council, Status of Women, Ottawa: Minister of Supply, p. 23. Furthermore, state the Armstrongs, "The biggest gap between male and female unemployment rates is for those with degrees, and more than twice as many university-educated women as men have only part-time work...it must be assumed that a large number of [these] women experience underemployment" (p. 23).

In *Women and Work* (Toronto: James Lorimer, 1983) Paul and Erin Phillips state: "The Bulk of the evidence...is that women receive significantly lower wages than men for the same type of jobs when an adjustment is made for education and experience" (pp. 59-60).
4 Karen Nussbaum interviewed by *Mother Jones Magazine.* For further elaboration of the Canadian situation see Armstrong and Armstrong, *A Working Majority,* pp. 8-13. "In Canada service work is the fastest growing occupation in employment terms. Women are the majority of those in service work."
5 For information about Canadian women and unions, see Julie White, *Women and Unions,* Ottawa, Canadian Advisory Council on Status of Women, 1980.
6 Henry Schipper, "The Truth Will Out: An Interview with Phyllis Schlafly," *Ms. Magazine,* January, 1982, p. 90.
7 Jill Tweedy, *In the Name of Love* (New York: Pantheon Books, 1979).
8 Judy Chicago, *The Dinner Party: A Symbol of our Heritage* (New York: Anchor Books, Doubleday, 1979), p. 186.

Notes

CHAPTER 11

1 Bureau of Labor Statistics, U.S. Department of Labor (BLS/USDL). A useful summary of data on women in the labor force in the U.S. is: *Perspectives on Working Women: A Databook,* Bulletin 2080, October, 1980, BLS/USDL, Washington, D.C.

2 Heather Menzies, *Women and the Chip: Case Studies of the Effects of Informatics on Employment in Canada* (Montreal: Institute for Research on Public Policy, 1981), pp. 5-13.

3 BLS/USDL, *Earnings and Other Characteristics of Organized Workers,* May, 1980, Bulletin 2105, gives data for men and women clerical workers separately and combined, public and private sector combined only. For estimated levels of unionization in the private sector, and an excellent overview on clerical unionization, see "Clerical Workers: How 'Unorganizable' Are They?" by David Wagner, *Labor Center Review,* vol. 2, no. l, Spring/Summer, 1979, University of Massachusetts, Amherst, Ma. For information about Canadian women and unions, see Julie White, *Women and Unions,* Ottawa, Advisory Council on the Status of Women, 1980.

4 USDL, Women's Bureau, *20 Facts on Women Workers,* December 1980, and *The Subtle Revolution, Women at Work,* Ralph E. Smith, ed. (Washington, D.C.: the Urban Institute, 1979).

5 Menzies, *Women and the Chip.*

6 See, for example, Eli Ginsberg and George J. Vojta, "The Service Sector of the U.S. Economy," *Scientific American,* March, 1981; data from U.S. Department of Labor.

7 BLS/USDL.

8 Menzies, *Women and the Chip.*

9 U.S. Department of Commerce, Bureau of Census, *Money, Income and Poverty Status of Families and Persons in the U.S.: 1980,* Current Population Reports, Series P-60, no. 127, August 1981, and BLS/USDL, "Urban Family Budgets and Comparative Indexes for Selected Urban Areas," USDL -81-195, April, 1981.

10 Menzies, *Women and the Chip.*

11 Barry Bluestone, P. Hanna, S. Kuhn and L. Moore, *The Department Store Industry in New England: Transformation, Investment and Labor,* Monograph, December, 1979, New England Economy Project, Joint Center for Urban Studies of MIT and Harvard University, Cambridge, Ma.; Carol Leon and R. Bednarzik, "Profile of Women on Part-Time Schedules," *Monthly Labor Review,* June, 1978; Karen Nussbaum, "Capital Mobility and the Shift to the Service Economy," National Conference/Alternative State and Local Policies, Pittsburgh, Pa., July, 1980, reprinted in *Radical America,* Fall, 1981.

12 Nine to 5, The National Association of Working Women, *Office Work in America,* April 1982, Cleveland, Ohio. Data from BLS/USDO, and U.S. Department of Commerce.

13 BLS/USDL figures for real wages and for earnings of workers with families by occupation and industry, for 1979, 1981.

14 Bill C53 is an act to amend the Criminal Code in relation to sexual offences and the protection of young persons and to amend certain other acts in relation thereto and in consequence thereof. First reading, House of Commons, Ottawa, January 12, 1981.

CHAPTER 12

1 Adrienne Rich, "Planetarium," in *Modern Poems,* ed. Richard Ellmann and Robert O'Clair (New York: W.W. Norton, 1976), p.434.

2 Joan Turner and Shirley Kitchen, *Perspectives on Women in the 1980s,* video documentary, University of Manitoba School of Social Work, 1982 (60 min., colour).
3 Janet Radcliffe Richards, *The Sceptical Feminist: A Philisophical Enquiry* (Middlesex, England: Penguin Books, 1982), p. 340.
4 Margaret L. Andersen, *Thinking About Women* (New York: Macmillan Publishing Co., 1983), p. 226.
5 Joan E. Cummings, "Sexism in Social Work: Some Thoughts on Strategy for Structural Change," *Catalyst,* no. 8, 1980, p. 8.
6 Robert Moglove Diamond, "Recent Developments in Legislation Relating to Family Law." Attorney-General's Department, Government of Manitoba, 1983, pp. 18 and 35.
7 Government of Manitoba, Order in Council #739, Winnipeg, July 6, 1983.
8 Statistics Canada, *The Labour Force, Recent Labour Force Developments,* Ottawa, June, 1983, table 6, p. 28. Fifty-five percent of the women of Manitoba are in the labour force (p. 29).
9 Zillah Einstein, "The Sexual Politics of the New Right: Understanding the 'Crisis of Liberalism' for the 1980's"; N. Keohane, M.Z. Rosaldo and B. Gelpi, *Feminist Theory: A Critique of Ideology* (Chicago: University of Chicago Press, 1982), p. 78.
10 Einstein, in "The Sexual Politics of the New Right," and also in A. Miles and G. Finn, *Feminism in Canada,* p. 304, discuss the backlash we are experiencing.
11 Carol Gilligan, *In A Different Voice* (Cambridge, Mass.: Harvard University Press, 1982), pp. 173-74.
12 Mary Daly, *Beyond God the Father: Toward a Philisophy of Women's Liberation* (Boston: Beacon Press, 1973), p. 7.
13 Gloria Kaufman and Mary Ann Blakely, *Pulling Our Own Strings* (Bloomington: Indiana University, 1980), p. 178.
14 Margaret Mitchell, quoted in "Few Options for Older Women," *Communications,* vol. 7, no. 4., Sept, 1983, p. 8.
15 David Ross, *The Canadian Fact Book on Poverty-1983,* Canadian Council on Social Development (Toronto: James Lorimer and Co., 1983), p. 30.
16 Ross, *The Canadian Fact Book on Poverty-1983,* p. 33.
17 Statistics Canada, 1981 census data, catalogue 75-941, series B, vol. 3, table 1.
18 United Nations Commission on the Status of Women 1980: cited in L. Leghorn and K. Parker, *Women's Worth: Sexual Economies and the World of Women* (Boston: Rutledge and Kagan Paul, 1981), pp. 4-5. Referred to by Margaret L. Andersen in *Thinking About Women,* p. 8, and by Angela Miles in "Ideological Hegemony in Political Discourse: Women's Specificity and Equality," A. Miles and G. Finn, *Feminism in Canada* (Montreal: Black Rose Books, 1982), p. 226.
19 Pat and Hugh Armstrong, *A Working Majority: What Women Must Do for Pay,* (Ottawa: Canadian Advisory Council on the Status of Women, 1983), p. 23.
20 Bonnie Klein, dir., "Not A Love Story," with Linda Lee Tracey, National Film Board of Canada, 1981 (68 min. 40 sec., colour).
21 Sharon S. Mayes, "Women in Positions of Authority: A Class Study of Changing Sex Roles," *Signs, Journal of Women in Culture & Society,* vol. 4 no. 3, Spring, 1977, pp. 556-68.
22 Hilary M. Lips, *Women, Men and the Psychology of Power* (Englewood Cliffs, New Jersey: Prentice Hall, Inc., 1981; Nina L. Colwill, "Power," in *The New Partnership: Women and Men in Organization* (Palo Alto: Mayfield Publishing Co., 1982), pp. 92-109; Jean Baker Miller, *Toward a New Psychology of Women* (Boston: Beacon Press), 1976; Yolande Cohen,

"Thoughts on Women and Power," ed. A. Miles and G. Finn, *Feminism in Canada* (Montreal: Black Rose Books, 1982), pp. 229-50; Dorothy Dinnerstein, *The Mermaid and the Minotaur* (New York: Harper and Row, 1976), pp. 160-97.

23 Anne Wilson Schaef, *Women's Reality: An Emerging Female System in the White Male Society* (Minneapolis: Winston Press, 1981), p. 125.

24 Mary Daly, *GynEcology: The Metaethics of Radical Feminism* (Boston: Beacon Press, 1978; Toronto: Fitzhenry and Whiteside Ltd., 1978), p. 21.

25 Karen Howe, "Celebration," recorded by Heather Bishop on *Celebration,* Mother of Pearl Records, Woodmore, Manitoba, 1981.

Contributors

KIM CLARE is Assistant Professor, Winnipeg Education Centre, School of Social Work, University of Manitoba. She assisted in the coordination and direction of the Selected Readings and Resources and with critical feedback and proofreading.

MARGRIT EICHLER is a professor at the Ontario Institute for Studies in Education and has written and spoken extensively on many areas of feminist research. Her most recent publications include, *The Double Standard: A Feminist Critique on Feminist Social Science* (1980), *Women and Future Research* (1980), and *Families in Canada Today: Recent Changes and their Policy Consequences* (1983). She is past-president of the Canadian Research Institute for the Advancement of Women, and co-founder of *Resources for Feminist Research*.

LOIS EMERY, co-editor of this book, is a field instructor at the School of Social Work, University of Manitoba, instructing students in their practice of social work. In the past, she has been both an educator and a practitioner, primarily in child welfare and family services.

DEIRDRE ENGLISH is Executive Editor of *Mother Jones Magazine*. Her extensive writing includes: *For Her Own Good: 150 Years of the Experts' Advice to Women* (1978), *Witches, Midwives and Nurses: A History of Women Healers* (1972), and *Complaints and Disorders: The Sexual Politics of Sickness* (1973). She is a graduate in Social Welfare from the State University of New York at Stony Brook, and has taught in the Women's Studies Program at the College of Old Westbury, S.U.N.Y.

THE HONOURABLE JUDY EROLA (Liberal-Nickel Belt) joined the Liberal party when she was eighteen. Defeated in her first campaign for election in

185

1979, she was successful in 1980, and very soon afterwards became a member of the Cabinet as Minister of Mines. In 1981, she received a second portfolio, that of Minister responsible for the Status of Women. One of her primary interests is pension reform, with special attention to the situation of homemakers. In August, 1983, she became Minister of Consumer and Corporate Affairs.

SHEILA GORDON is a Master's student at the School of Social Work, Carleton University, and was a student and research assistant at the University of Manitoba. She collected and organized the material for the Selected Readings and Resources.

JUDITH GREGORY is research director of 9 to 5, The National Association of Working Women. She has also worked for national public radio, doing documentaries and news. Her publications include *Race Against Time* (1980), *Warning: Health Hazards for Office Workers* (1980), and *Organizational Implications of New Office Technology* (1980).

HELEN LEVINE teaches at the School of Social Work, Carleton University. She has been active in the development of women's services and of women's studies in social work. Her current work as a feminist counsellor stems from earlier involvement in children's, family and psychiatric settings as well as active participation in the women's liberation movement. She is the author of numerous articles (see Part A, Selected Readings). Her most recent works include: *The Personal is Political: Feminism and the Helping Professions,* chapter 8 in *Feminism in Canada,* edited by Angela Miles and Geraldine Finn (Montreal: Black Rose Books, 1982) pp. 175-209.

DOROTHY LIVESAY is a poet, journalist, editor and professor. A founding member of the League of Canadian Poets, she received the Governor General's Medal for Poetry in 1944 and 1947, and the Royal Society's Lorne Pierce medal for Literature in 1947. She was writer-in-residence at the University of New Brunswick in 1966-68, the University of Manitoba in 1975-76, the University of Ottawa in 1977, Simon Fraser University in 1979, and the University of Toronto in 1983. Among her many publications are: *Green Pitcher,* 1928; *Selected Poems, 1926-56,* 1957; *Beginnings: A Winnipeg Childhood,* 1976; *The Woman I Am* (a selection of feminist poems), 1977; and, most recently, *The Phases of Love: Poems by Dorothy Livesay.*

DOROTHY O'CONNELL is a long-time activist in welfare rights and public tenants' right organizations. She has worked as a film editor, teacher, organizer, journalist and mother of five children. She is the author of *Chiclet Gomez* (1977) and *Cockeyed Optimists* (1980).

MARLENE PIERRE-AGGAMAWAY, past-president of the Native Women's Association of Canada, has been an activist in the advancement of native people in general and native women in particular. She has taught at Lakehead University and spoken widely on issues concerning native women.

GLORIA STEINEM is a founding editor of *Ms. Magazine*. Her extensive writing, which is well known internationally, has been very important to the women's movement. She is active as a speaker and organizer throughout North America. She is the author of *Wonder Woman* (1974) and *Outrageous Acts and Everyday Rebellions* (August, 1983).

JOAN TURNER is Associate Professor, School of Social Work, University of Manitoba. She chaired, with Neil Tudiver, the committee that organized the conference, "Perspectives on Women in the 1980s." Together with Shirley Kitchen, she produced a video documentory of the conference and, with Lois Emery, edited this book. She is a social worker and a motherworker. Until June, 1983, she was board member and vice-president of the Canadian Association of Schools of Social Work. Her publications (under the name Joan Zeglinski) include *Social Work Education for Rural and Northern Practice* (CASSW, 1976).